Color

Color

Paul Zelanski and Mary Pat Fisher

FIFTH EDITION

Prentice Hall Inc, Upper Saddle River, N.J. 07458

*To Josef Albers
and his students
and the students of his students*

Library of Congress Cataloging-in-Publication Data

Zelanski, Paul.
    Color / Paul Zelanski and Mary Pat Fisher.—5th ed.
        p. cm.
    Includes index.
    ISBN 0–13–195864–X
    1. Color—Textbooks. 2. Color in art—Textbooks. I. Fisher, Mary Pat, 1943– II. Title.

    QC495.Z45 2006
    535.6—dc22

                                                                                                2005051339

Editor in Chief: Sarah Touborg
Acquisitions Editor: Amber Mackey
Editorial Assistant: Keri Molinari
Director of Marketing: Heather Shelstad
Manufacturing Buyer: Sherry Lewis

Credits and acknowledgments of material borrowed from other sources and reproduced, with permission, in this textbook appear on page 9.

Pearson Education Ltd.
Pearson Education Australia PTY, Ltd.
Pearson Education Singapore, Pte. Ltd.
Pearson Education North Asia Ltd.

Pearson Education, Canada, Ltd.
Pearson Educación de Mexico, S.A. de C.V
Pearson Education–Japan
Pearson Education Malaysia, Pte. Ltd.

This book was designed and produced by
Laurence King Publishing Ltd., London
www.laurenceking.co.uk

Every effort has been made to contact the copyright holders, but should there be any errors or omissions, Laurence King Publishing Ltd. would be pleased to insert the appropriate acknowledgment in any subsequent printing of this publication.

Editor: Rada Radojicic
Copy Editor: Krystyna Mayer
Picture Researcher: Emma Brown
Designer: Ian Price

Front Cover: Sonia Delaunay, *Tango-Magic-City*, 1913. Collection Kunsthalle, Bielefeld, Germany. Photo © L & M Services B.V. Amsterdam 20050904.
Back Cover: Dale Chihuly, *Macchia*, 2005. © Dale Chihuly.
Frontispiece: J. M. W. Turner, *Light and Colour (Goethe's Theory: The Morning After the Deluge, Moses Writing the Book of Genesis)*, exhibited 1843. © Tate, London 2005

10 9 8 7 6 5 4 3 2

ISBN 0–13–195864–X

Contents

Preface

I see color both as the most subjective element of design, and as a poignant metaphor for human interaction. As a transcendental expression of light, color can be used as a means to evoke a mood beyond the realm of line or form, mass or weight. I have always been struck by the mysterious ways in which two inanimate patches of color can, when placed judiciously side by side, resonate so as to suggest a third color in the eye of the beholder—to "sing" if you will, a phenomenon akin to the meeting of two souls. Color is magical.[1]

STEPHEN ALCORN

Color is a subject that can be studied for a lifetime and still maintain its magic. Its importance permeates almost everything—whether as an integral part of an artwork, or used to give separate identities to the gases in a Hubble space photograph, it is continually working to augment our lives. It can be the reason why a work of art succeeds, or an advertisement captures the right audience. It can help a corporate identity become a universal symbol, it can make us feel calm or agitated when we walk into a room, or give us serenity within a perfectly designed garden space. Color is a powerful tool. It can stimulate and heighten all of our senses, and a knowledge of how this happens can give us the ability to use it in ever more creative ways.

This book is addressed to artists and art students of all media, providing an informative but non-dogmatic introduction to the many different approaches, including historical and scientific, to understanding color. Illustrations in the book show examples from a wide range of media—works by women and men of many cultures—to show the reader how color is part of the global experience. We have used quotations from working artists throughout the book to give a glimpse of how they feel about color, and artists' quotations are also used to introduce each new chapter. Technical sections have been modified for greater clarity and ease of understanding. The first time that a technical term is used, it appears in boldface in the text, and is defined both in the text and in the glossary. There is an appendix of studio Color Problems which is a treasury of practical experiments based on the teachings of the great colorist Josef Albers. When using these color problems in a teaching situation, it is best to have the students read the first two chapters to develop a general orientation and basic vocabulary before beginning them, and then to continue with the following chapters. Professor Emeritus Paul Zelanski, a former student of Albers, developed and used these problems with great success during his four decades of teaching art at university level.

New to the Fifth Edition

In this fifth edition of *Color*, we have added 44 new images, from rock art of the ancient Bushmen of Namibia, to twenty-first-century computer-generated art. We have consolidated, rewritten, and shifted information within Chapters 7 and 8, so that technologies dealing with light mixtures, such as the RGB (red, green, blue) of color monitors, are together in the chapter on Color, Light, and Computers. The need for a browser-safe color palette is explained within a new section on website design, and new images of digital art have been added. This chapter also deals with CMYK (cyan, magenta, yellow, and black), the standard ink colors of printing. This allows for an exploration of computers and computer-generated art first, with the issues of printing following closely behind, even though it is sometimes hard to separate the two in the real world, as each depends on the other and their needs relating to color control can overlap. A new section addresses digital printing and explains differences between inkjet, laser, and dye sublimation printers, and defines IRIS/IXIA giclée prints. Color profiling of monitor, scanner, and printer is discussed.

We have also added a section on color management, which is an essential part in all stages of designing and printing. Noemi Kearns and Keith Edwards of How 2 Design discuss how color management impacts the work of a graphic designer and explain how essential it is to understand all of the color choices in producing a final printed piece, and how color is often the key element in creating the perfectly designed solution for a client.

There are new sections on landscape design and crafts, as well as an expanded selection of images in Chapter 10 (Color in Fine Art). Overall, we have aimed to add clear updates to this new edition, especially the computer and printing sections, which we hope you will find informative. Hopefully it will provide readers with a base camp in their further explorations with color, and will remain a text that they can return to again and again.

Acknowledgments

Many people gave of their time and expertise, shared their artwork, e-mailed us their thoughts, and have left their marks on this edition. For this team effort, we are most grateful.

Thank you to Sherran Deems of Savannah College of Art and Design and Jeff Schwartz of Ringling School of Art and Design for reviewing this fifth edition. To the professors who graciously reviewed the earlier editions of this book, thank you for suggestions that have benefited all editions. To Michael Ulsaker of Michael Ulsaker Studio, our thanks for taking the time to talk to us about the realities of printing, even though it took you away from the business at hand. To Pam Zagarenski, we appreciate your artistic enthusiasm and generosity of spirit, and for continuing to do great art while using the initials PZ. Thank you, Rob Sutherland, for the extra time you spent to send us information on the neodymium glaze, and to John and Mary Matt for clarifications on color in religious symbolism. To Keith Edwards, your proofreading skills are remarkable, and thanks for sending a quotation that was perfectly edited. Josh Comen and Jenny Herrick, thank you for adding your knowledge of computers to the conversations over lunch, and for listening to Munsell's theory of color relationships in exchange. To Noemi Kearns, thank you for letting us use How 2 Design as a sounding board for all things involving the current design and printing world. To Ruth Zelanski and Ron Lambert, special thanks for providing your artwork for this edition, and warmest thanks for always being an e-mail away when questions arose that needed a quick response. To Robert Silvers, we appreciate your prompt e-mail giving us specifics about "Dove," and thank you to Chihuly Studios for being helpful and responsive to our enquiries. Jennifer Doud at Dailey Ads went out of her way to help obtain permission for the TV ad "Artists Against Piracy," and it was very much appreciated. And because of serendipity, perfect timing, and a lovely afternoon visit, we were able to obtain a few of Stephen Alcorn's poetic thoughts on color.

At Laurence King Publishing, Anne Townley provided excellent editorial support and great patience during the writing process—done with a friendly touch that carried us through months of effort. Rada Radojicic completed the editing process, her straightforward and kind manner making the final production work a seamless effort, and Emma Brown was a most efficient photo acquisition editor, obtaining permissions as quickly as we could get the photo credits to her, uncomplaining when there were necessary changes to be made. We appreciate the copy editing that Krystyna Mayer completed so successfully, and the flawless proofreading of the galley proofs and layouts by Helen Kemp and Mary Gordon-Smith. Vicki Robinson has our thanks for working so efficiently on the indexing. We are indebted to all of these talented and skilled experts, who, working as a literary unit, have produced this edition. Our dear friend Laurence King has been steadfastly supportive, as has Norwell F. Therien at Prentice Hall. Both have firm convictions of the value of this book in helping students understand and make full use of the complexities of color.

Annette Zelanski has done a tremendous amount of research and writing for this new edition. It is thanks to her that this is the best edition yet, and we offer her our great congratulations and loving gratitude.

Paul Zelanski
Mary Pat Fisher
May 2005

Photo credits

The authors, the publishers, and Laurence King Publishing wish to thank the artists, museums, collectors, and other owners who have kindly allowed works to be reproduced. In general, museums have supplied their own photographs; other sources, photographers, and copyright holders are listed here. Every effort has been made to contact all the copyright holders; should there be any errors or omissions, the publishers would be happy to make the necessary corrections in any future editions of this book.

1 Why Study Color?

Color is an expressive force in itself—a language in itself.

HANS HOFFMAN

COLOR is perhaps the most powerful tool at the artist's disposal. It affects our emotions beyond thought and can convey any mood, from delight to despair. It can be subtle or dramatic, capture attention or stimulate desire. Used more boldly and freely today than ever before, color bathes our vision with an infinite variety of sensations, from clear, brilliant hues to subtle, elusive mixtures. Color is the province of all artists, from painters and potters to product designers and computer artists.

The skillful control of color in a work of art allows the artist to guide the response in the viewer. In Henri Matisse's painting *La Femme au Chapeau* (shown in Figure **1.1A** in black and white), we see the portrait of a woman wearing a large hat. Without knowing the medium used for it, we accept the shades of gray we see and the work still makes spatial sense as a black-and-white reproduction. Matisse's skillful use of values allows this to happen. However, we in the twenty-first century have become so sophisticated in our color awareness that we can readily accept Matisse's choice of colors as shown in Figure **1.1B**, where we see a green shadow on the right, and purple, white, and yellow shadows on the left. We are drawn into this work by the use of color,

◀ **1.1A Henri Matisse, *La Femme au Chapeau*, 1905**
31½ × 23½ ins (80 × 59.6 cm).
San Francisco Museum of Modern Art, United States, bequest of Elise S. Haas.
Matisse's perfect use of color values in this work allows us to see the face clearly, even when reproduced in black and white. The same image is reproduced in color on the right.

▲ **1.1B Henri Matisse, *La Femme au Chapeau***
Matisse started the wildly colorful Fauvist Movement with a group of French artists in around 1903. Although most Fauvists had changed their style by 1907, their work greatly influenced other art movements that followed.

our reaction is more intense because of it, and the color version holds our interest for a longer period of time than the black-and-white one. In fact, Matisse's use of color encourages us to respond both visually and intellectually, as we question how the contrasting bright colors might relate to the solemn woman.

Color is used in everyday life to help us grasp information. Signs in airports and supermarkets may be color-coded to help us find our way amidst a barrage of visual stimuli. Businesspeople at their computers now routinely add color to their charts and diagrams to emphasize the differences between the factors they are analyzing. Colors are assigned to the details in Magnetic Resonance Images to help doctors spot and track tumors, for we can see contrasts more clearly in color than in black and white. And in the astonishing views of the cosmos revealed by the Hubble telescope, colors are assigned to invisible gases so that scientists can better see and distinguish them. In the star-forming nebula shown in Figure **1.2**, which has been named "Eagle Nebula," sulfurous gases have been represented as red, hydrogen as green, and oxygen as blue, resulting in a coherent visual image of this

▲ **1.2 Gas Pillars in the Eagle Nebula**
Hubble telescope photograph.
Colors have been manipulated to help distinguish the gases.

otherwise "fuzzy" area of the cosmos which is 7,000 light-years away from our planet.

The photograph in Figure **1.3** was taken during a NASA space shuttle mission in 1993, and clearly shows Brandberg Mountain and the surrounding dry landscape. Without the assigned colors that the Hubble space photograph used, or the infrared capabilities of a NASA Landsat photo, we can still learn a great deal about the geological history and seasonal patterns of this dry area from a colored photo from space. However, from this view, we miss Brandberg's best-known feature: a collection of thousands of Stone Age Bushman paintings at hundreds of sites along its walls (Figure 10.1). Since the granite in the area is full of feldspar, the mountain and its eroded plains can turn a deep red during sunrise and sunset, creating one of the most beautiful and colorful places in all of Namibia. Our modern imaging methods can tell us many things, but we need to keep in mind that what we are seeing may not be all there is to know about a particular view, and with the ease of computer enhancement, we aren't even sure anymore that the color we see reproduced is an intrinsic part of the scene. Matisse's portrait of his wife (1.1B) created a sensation in 1905. It was not the subject or her pose, or the pensive quality of her expression, but the forceful choice of discordant colors that disturbed viewers. In a hundred years of viewing that painting, we are still inspired to break color boundaries as we interpret, manipulate, and evaluate the colors of our imaginations and of the real world.

In art, color is a vehicle for expressing emotions and concepts as well as information, and it is a very powerful element of design. Its possibilities are limitless. For an artist, color is like notes for a musician and words for a speaker. A single note, a single word, can have infinite shades of meaning and expression, depending on how it is used, what surrounds it, and who is its audience.

The art of using color well is an open-ended, complex discipline which incorporates many different points of view and poses many questions. Scientists have tried for centuries to understand what creates colors in our world, and how we see them; yet we still have no absolute answers to these questions. Theories put forth by those studying the physics of light and the anatomy and physiology of vision still lie in the realm of hypothesis. Color theorists have tried to condense the infinite number of visible color variations into a few basic colors and to form theories about their relationship. But no one color theory has been widely adopted to explain all color phenomena. Psychologists are studying the impact of various colors on our emotions and health, but they find that individuals tend to differ in their responses. Art historians analyze the different ways in which color has been created and used in different times and places. Those interested in design try to discern how colors affect compositional factors, such as unity, emphasis, balance, contrast, and spatial awareness. Other specialists offer suggestions and attempts at standardization in the realms of mixing colors with lights and pigments, for there is a special science of color creation for each discipline.

To tap into the tremendous potential of color, artists must explore all of these intellectual approaches. But beyond these very important perspectives lies direct experience with color. Interestingly, Leary and Alpert's studies of hallucinogens during the middle of the twentieth century revealed that most people's responses to color were accentuated by taking hallucinogens. However, artists on the whole were little affected—because artists are already high on color most of the time. A layperson has to be told to look for an afterimage effect, for instance, but artists are always alert to color experiences.

Actually working with color, exploring its characteristics and potentials, carefully observing how colors work together, will teach you in ways that no theory can. The theories are useful ways of narrowing the field of exploration. Intellectual information provides a general map so that you do not have to wander randomly through the myriad halls of color. Beyond the intellect, one works intuitively, experimentally, with all senses alert. Only in this way can you discover the realities of color—and the journey is endless.

▲ **1.3 NASA, Brandberg Mountain, Namib Desert**
Photograph.
The perfectly formed dark circle that you see in this photograph is Brandberg Mountain, in western Namibia, Africa. It is a different color from the surrounding area, and easily reveals to us its ancient geological history, its dark brown inner circle being the remaining core of the ancient volcano.

2 Color Basics

Color is the probity of art. … Color gives the appearance of life.

EUGÈNE DELACROIX

TO develop a vocabulary for talking about colors, we must delve briefly into the physical properties of what we see as colors. While this vocabulary is useful, it is not always precise, for much of it is based on theoretical or scientific observations that do not necessarily hold true in artistic practice. And although the same terms are often used for describing colored lights and colored pigments, such as paints, they are quite different phenomena. When talking about colors, it must be made quite clear to which of these one is referring.

The Physics of Light

Physicists explain color as a function of light. A current theory is that energy from the sun consists of a series of separate energy packets, or quanta, traveling as continuous electromagnetic waves. They stimulate color sensations in our visual perception when they strike objects.

In the seventeenth century, the great physicist and mathematician Sir Isaac Newton (see Chapter 6) conducted a series of experiments demonstrating, among other things, that sunlight contains all the colors of the rainbow. He admitted a ray of daylight into a darkened room through a hole in a window shade and placed a glass prism where the ray would pass through it. As it did so and then came out the other side, the ray of white light was bent, or **refracted**, breaking it down into its constituent colors, which could be seen on a white wall beyond, as shown in Figure **2.1**.

Newton identified seven basic colors in the breakdown: red, orange, yellow, green, blue, indigo, and violet. Each hue is now thought to correspond to a certain portion of the range of wavelengths of radiant energy that can be distinguished by the human eye, called the **visible spectrum.** A **wavelength** is the distance between crests in a wave of energy. Wavelengths in the visible spectrum are measured in **nanometers**, each of which is only one-billionth of a meter. Differences between colors involve tiny differences in wavelengths. Figure **2.2** shows the designation of **spectral hues**, or the colors that can be seen in a rainbow, in terms of the wavelengths indicated by each hue name. "Red," for instance, is the name given to everything from about 625 to 740 nanometers, although we can distinguish many differing reds within that range, some of them merging into the area we call "orange." Red has the longest wavelengths; violet has the shortest.

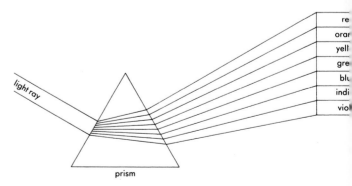

▲ **2.1** A modern rendition of Newton's experiment, breaking white light into the hues of the spectrum by passing it through a prism.

◀ **2.2** Colors of the visible spectrum are here identified as regions of certain wavelengths, measured in millimicrons (nanometers). The dark "Fraunhofer" lines represent some of the fine dark lines seen in a pure spectrum, revealing wavelengths that are missing in the light sample.

Beyond red and violet at each end of the visible spectrum lie wavelengths of radiant energy that humans cannot see, from infrared and ultraviolet outward. As illustrated in Figure **2.3**, the electromagnetic spectrum comprises radiations from the universe ranging from gamma rays to radio waves. The greatest portion of this spectrum is invisible to human sight.

Light Colors

Although red and violet are quite different in terms of wavelengths, they are visually similar at their outer extremes and can be mixed to produce purples that cannot be seen in the spectrum itself. Newton therefore proposed that the straight band of spectral hues could be bent into a circular model with the two ends joined (**2.4**). At its center was white—the result of mixing lights of all colors, as Newton had demonstrated by reconverging the colors of the spectrum through a second prism into a single ray of white light (**2.5**).

This was the first **color wheel**—an attempt to illustrate visual relationships among hues. Newton's color circle was adopted by many later aesthetic theorists as a way of explaining relationships between different colors.

Color theorists often speak of the colors in light as **additive**: the more they are mixed with other colors, the lighter

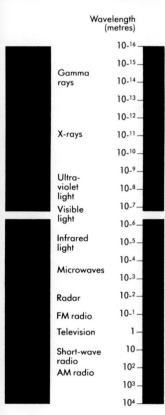

▲ **2.3** In the electromagnetic spectrum, only a very small portion of all radiant energy can be seen by humans.

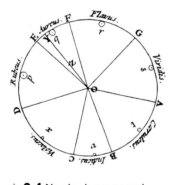

▲ **2.4** Newton's proposed color wheel, created by joining the two ends of the visible spectrum. Although this model does not correspond to the linear array of wavelengths, it is useful for analyzing relationships among colors.

▲ **2.5** Newton demonstrated that white light is the composite of all spectral hues by breaking it down into the visible spectrum, then converging these rays through a second prism back into white light.

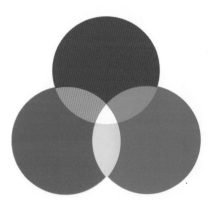

▲ **2.6 Light colors**
If colored lights in the light primaries red-orange, green, and blue-violet are projected in overlapping circles, they mix to form the light secondaries yellow, magenta, and cyan. In additive mixtures, the secondaries are paler than the primaries. Where all three primaries overlap, they produce white.

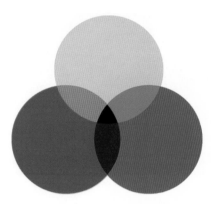

▲ **2.7 Pigment colors**
In subtractive, or pigment, mixtures, the primaries are traditionally said to be red, yellow, and blue. If two primaries are mixed, they theoretically produce the secondaries orange, green, and purple. If all three are mixed, they theoretically produce black. However, in paint mixing, it is not possible to mix all colors from any three primaries.

they become. White light can even be recreated by mixing only three carefully chosen colored lights: green, blue-violet, and orange-red. These same colors can be used to mix most of the colors that humans can distinguish, but cannot themselves be mixed from other colors. They are therefore known as **primary colors**. As illustrated in Figure **2.6**, where the primaries orange-red and green overlap, they create yellow; green and blue-violet can be mixed to form indigo (known as "cyan" in printing and photography); and blue-violet and orange-red overlap to form magenta. The yellow, cyan, and magenta formed by mixing two primaries are called **secondary colors**; in light mixtures, these are more luminous than primary colors. White, as we have seen, results from mixing all three primaries together at the proper intensities, and black is the absence of all light.

Light mixtures can be created by superimposing lights of different colors, by showing two different colors in rapid succession, or by presenting small points of different colors so close to each other that they are blended by our visual apparatus. In the past, experiments with light mixing had to be done by projecting and overlapping colored lights on a wall. However, the advent of computer graphics has opened a vast world of instantaneous and mechanically precise light mixing for aesthetic exploration. Cathode ray tubes used in video receivers and computer graphics monitors have three electron guns corresponding to the light primaries: red-

orange, green, and blue-violet. When the beams from these guns strike the light-sensitive **phosphors** on the surface of the screen in varying combinations and intensities, they can create a great array of luminous color sensations.

In the fractal computer image shown in Figure **2.8**—the beautiful visual expression of a mathematical formula—the lightest areas occur where the rays are most concentrated and the darkest areas where the rays are least concentrated. The stunning yellows are entirely mixed; there is no yellow gun in a cathode ray tube. If you examine a yellow image on a television or computer screen very closely, you can see that it is formed by the juxtaposition and overlapping of orange-red and green bits of light.

Pigment Colors

Colors seen on the surface of objects operate in a very different way from those seen in beams of light. When daylight or some other kind of incident light strikes a surface, certain wavelengths may be absorbed and others reflected by its **pigments**, or coloring matter. The **reflected** wavelengths blend to form the color "seen" by the viewer. To cite a

▶ **2.8 Heinz-Otto Peitgen and Peter H. Richter, Fractal image based on the process $x \longrightarrow x^2 + c$**

▲ **2.9** On the conventional 12-color wheel of pigment hues, the primaries are red, blue, and yellow; the secondaries are orange, green, and purple; and the tertiaries are mixtures of adjoining primaries and secondaries. If colors are mixed with their complement (the hue lying opposite on the wheel), a neutral gray should be created, as indicated in the center.

simple example, the surface of an apple absorbs all wavelengths except those which create the sensation of red; these are reflected into the eye of the viewer. An object that appears black absorbs almost all wavelengths (in the darkest of pigments, carbon black, 97 percent of the incident light is absorbed). In theory, a surface that appears white absorbs no wavelengths; all are reflected and mixed. This ideal is never met in practice; the closest one can come is absorption of only 2 percent of the incident light.

In traditional color theory, there are three pigment colors—red, blue, and yellow—that cannot be mixed from other colors and from which all other colors can be mixed (see **2.7**; more on this in Chapter 8). These characteristics would define them as primary colors.

Mixtures of the pigment primaries red, blue, and yellow theoretically yield the pigment secondaries orange, green, and purple (sometimes called violet). When these secon-

daries are mixed with their adjacent primaries, they yield **tertiary colors**: red-purple, red-orange, yellow-orange, yellow-green, blue-green, and blue-purple. If one starts with three primaries, one gets three secondaries and six tertiaries, giving a total of 12 colors, as shown in Figure **2.9**.

However, with pigments, the ability to mix all other colors from only three primaries is possible only in printers' inks and color photography. Transparent inks or photographic dyes in chrome yellow, magenta, and cyan, plus black, and the white of the paper can be used to approximate most colors that the eye can see. Even then, despite advances in printing technology and our efforts to render colors precisely, the colors in the figures in this book or any other book may still be slightly inaccurate.

In paint mixing, it is not possible to mix all colors from any three basic primaries. Some theories would therefore add green to the list of paint pigment primaries to make more mixtures possible. In 1905 the color standardist Albert Munsell (1858–1918) proposed five pigment primaries: green, blue, purple, red, and yellow (which he called **principal hues**). We recommend that new students use ten paint colors and mix all others from them. These pigment mixing

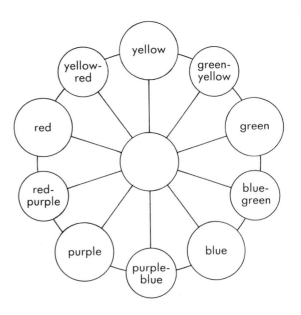

▲ **2.10** Color theorists have proposed other color models, including this one by Albert Munsell, which is based on five principal colors and the intermediate colors that can be obtained by mixing them. The result is a 10-point wheel, as opposed to the traditional 12-point wheel shown in Figure 2.9.

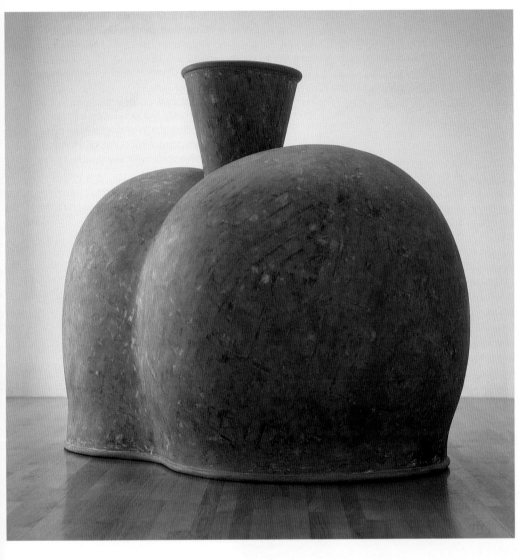

◄ **2.11 Peter Shelton,
Bluedress, 1990–2000**
Mixed media, 63½ × 70 × 50 ins
(161.2 × 177.8 × 127 cm).
Los Angeles Louver Gallery,
California, United States.
**This is a striking example of
the union of shape and hue in
a sculpture. We are free to
bring our own personal color
associations to the enjoyment
of the piece.**

issues are dealt with in detail in Chapter 8; the point here is that the concept that only three primaries exist is more true of light mixtures than of paint pigments.

Saturation, Hue, Value

Between each of the hues on a 12-point pigment wheel (2.9) are many more possible gradations as adjacent colors are mixed. It is also possible to mix colors that are not adjacent to each other. Mixing those that lie opposite each other on the color wheel, for example, tends to yield a chromatic gray. Two colors that are opposite each other on the color

wheel are called complementaries. By definition, complementaries are two hues which when mixed form a neutral gray. Another and opposite effect of complementaries, as we will see in Chapter 9, is that when placed side by side rather than mixed, they tend to intensify each other optically.

The degree to which colors are grayed by being mixed with their complementaries is called **saturation**, also known as "intensity." In their purest, most brilliant state, colors are at maximum saturation; as they become more and more neutral, they are said to be lower in saturation.

The matching of complementaries is not a precise science, however. The 12-point three-primary wheel shown in Figure 2.9 is only one of many suggested models for color relation-

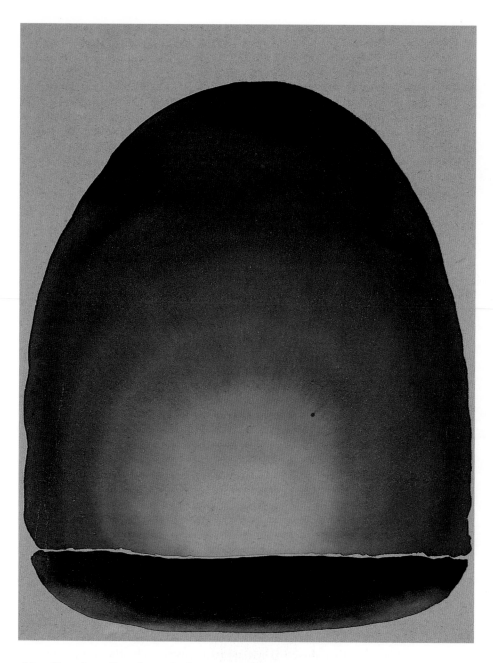

◀ **2.12 Georgia O'Keeffe, *Light Coming on the Plains II*, 1917**
Watercolor on paper, 11⅞ × 8⅞ ins
(30.2 × 22.5 cm).
Amon Carter Museum, Fort Worth, Texas
(1966.32).
The subtle color variations in this painting are based on value gradations in a single hue, plus transparent mixtures of the blue watercolor with the yellow of the groundsheet.

ships. Drawing a line through the center of this wheel shows yellow and purple, red and green, and orange and blue to be pairs of complementaries. But the 10-point color wheel that results from Albert Munsell's five primaries (**2.10**) yields slightly different results: Yellow is the complement of purple-blue, green of red-purple. Only the pairing of blue and yellow-red (orange) remains the same as on the 12-point wheel. The medium being used will also have a bearing on

complementary relationships; fabric dyes and ceramic glazes do not produce exactly the same mixtures as paint pigments. Because the mixtures and intensifying interactions between complementaries are of great importance in some approaches to color usage, artists must experiment and observe carefully to see which combinations best produce the effects they seek.

In describing the variations among colors, **hue** is the quality we identify by a color name, such as "red" or "purple."

It corresponds to the wavelength of a color. Saturation is a measure of the relative purity or intensity of a color. A third property of colors is **value**, sometimes known as "brightness" when light mixtures are being discussed. Value is the degree of lightness or darkness in a color.

The use of the same color blue makes the value changes in Peter Shelton's *Bluedress* (**2.11**) very evident. Even with minor color variations in the painted surface giving it a slight texture, our eyes still read it as a massive blue form, where the taut shapes interact with the surrounding light, creating optical color impressions ranging from light to very dark blues. The simplicity of the forms, the understated reference to the human body, and the juxtapositioning of organic shapes with the geometric "neck" give the sculpture a playful quality. How does the use of one overall color in this piece affect our impression of it? Would the use of additional colors change how we perceive the values?

In pigment mixtures, value can be adjusted by the addition of black or white or by thinning the mixture so that a lighter ground shows through. The potential gradations are infinite, though there is a finite limit to the number of differences in value humans can distinguish. In *Light Coming on the*

▲ **2.14** Sample representation of change in value and saturation for the hue yellow.

Plains II (**2.12**), Georgia O'Keeffe uses a dark blue watercolor, mixed with black for lower values and also thinned to create increasingly higher values as they reveal and mix with the high yellow of the groundsheet. The lightest values are referred to as "high," the darkest as "low."

When pigments of equal value are mixed, the resulting color is darker rather than lighter, since more wavelengths are absorbed. Because this process subtracts from the light reflected, pigment mixing is called **subtractive color mixing**. This darkening, which occurs during actual paint mixing, is not demonstrated in the traditional theoretical color wheel of pigment relationships shown in Figure 2.9.

One way of introducing variations in value into the diagram showing color relationships is to make a three-dimensional model. Albert Munsell's color "tree" represents value gradations along a vertical axis, with variations in hue indicated by changes around the perimeter, and variations in saturation presented as horizontal steps from the vertical axis (**2.13**). Any color along the vertical axis—from white at the top, through grays, to black at the bottom—is called a **neutral**. Colors close to this axis and thus of low saturation are also commonly called "neutral." Colors horizontally further outward from this axis can be called **chromatic hues**. A colored version of the model is shown in Figure **2.14**. Note that the model is not symmetrical. If saturation is measured in equal steps, each hue is found to have a different number of

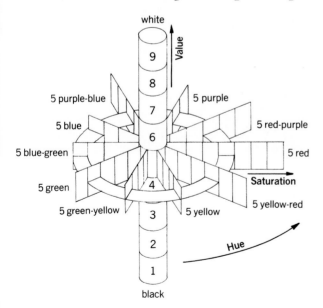

▲ **2.13** In Munsell's three-dimensional model of color relationships, hues are presented around a central axis that represents value changes. Saturation is measured outward from this axis, from the grays of the central pole to the highest saturation possible for each hue. The degree of saturation at the fifth step of value is shown here.

▲ 2.15 The Munsell Color Tree
Albert Munsell's model attempted to show gradations in
saturation horizontally without changing value, which was
represented along the vertical axis. Gradations in saturation
were presented as mixtures of hues with their complements,
based on the opposite hues in a 10-point color circle.

potential steps and to reach maximum saturation at a different
point along the value scale. Yellow, which is a light color in
its purest form, reaches its maximum saturation at the eighth
step of value (**2.15**). Blue, a darker hue in its pure form, reaches
maximum saturation at the fourth step of value. For purple, of
which the purest form is a dark color, maximum saturation
occurs even lower on the value scale, at the third step.

Although many terms commonly used in describing
colors are obviously subject to question—some theories even
find fault with the terms "additive" and "subtractive"—the
concepts of wavelengths, light mixtures, pigment mixtures,
primaries, secondaries, hue, value, saturation, and complementaries will be useful as we pursue our study of color.

3 Perceiving Colors

Color is the subjective perception in our brain of an objective feature of light's specific wavelengths.

LEONARD SHLAIN

THE colors we see are not simply a function of differing wavelengths; they are actually our response to visual stimuli via complex processes that occur in our perceptual apparatus. These involve the way our eyes register colors, classify the inputs, and transfer them to the brain, and the way the brain decodes the signals. At our present state of scientific knowledge, much of the process of color perception can be described only theoretically. We simply do not yet know how we see colors. Furthermore, the brain may override what the eyes tell it. The more research is done, the more reluctant scientists are to make generalizations about this complex subject. And some of us are able to perceive colors with senses other than our vision, such as hearing and feeling.

The Human Eye

Light, varying in wavelength and brightness, enters the human eye through its transparent outer covering, the cornea. The muscles of the iris contract and expand to admit less or more light through the pupil, depending on the amount of light available. The light which has been admitted is then focused on the back surface of the eye by three refracting media: the aqueous humor, the crystalline lens, and the vitreous humor (**3.1**).

The back of the eye is covered by the **retina**, which consists of many specialized cells arranged in layers. The layer most important to color vision consists of the photorecep-

tors called **rods** and **cones**. They are so named because of their differing shapes. Rods allow us to distinguish forms in dim light, but only with black and white vision; cones function under brighter lighting to allow us to perceive hues. Thus we cannot perceive hues well at night. It appears that rods function in light as well as darkness, for stimulation of the cones also excites the rods.

Before light reaches the rods and cones, it must also pass

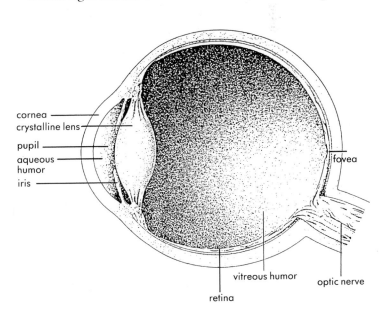

cornea
crystalline lens
pupil
aqueous humor
iris
fovea
vitreous humor
optic nerve
retina

▲ **3.1 The structure of the eye**
Discrimination of colors begins when light entering the pupil reaches the retina, which lines the inside of the eye.

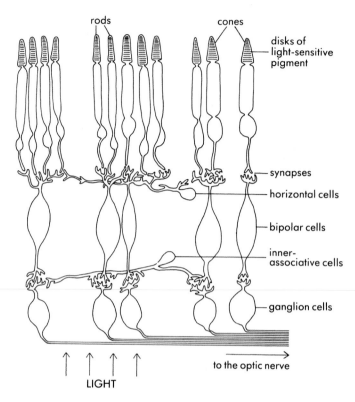

▲ **3.2 Rods and cones**
After light excites the light-sensitive pigments in the rods and cones, electrochemical messages are relayed to the visual cortex in the brain across a network of nerve cells

▲ **3.3** We see colors most clearly in the 2-degree area of the visual field that lies directly in front of our eyes.

through layers of nerve cells, as indicated in Figure **3.2**. Only about 20 percent of the light that reaches the retina actually registers in the photoreceptive rods and cones. The rest is simply unseen.

At the center of the back of the eye is an area about one millimeter in diameter known as the **fovea**. It contains only cones. Light falling on this small area gives the sharpest color definition. When we are examining details in an image, we automatically move our eyes until what we want to see is centered on the fovea.

We see colors most accurately in a very narrow field of view—only about 2 degrees directly in front of our eyes, out of the 360-degree field surrounding us (**3.3**).

The approximately 100 million rods and 6 million cones in each eye communicate with the brain via the optic nerve. The photoreceptors send their electrochemical messages to the optic nerve across synapses (gaps) in a complex network of optic nerve fibers. The bipolar and ganglion cells are thought to gather and pass on signals from the rods and cones; the horizontal and inner associative cells seem to integrate activities across the retina. In the fovea, each cone is connected to a single bipolar cell and a single ganglion cell, whereas signals from rods and cones on other parts of the retina are bundled together.

Information from the two eyes is transmitted to various areas on both sides of the brain, where it is somehow reintegrated to form a single image. Almost one-third of the gray matter of the cerebral cortex is involved in this complex process.

Seeing Colors

After centuries of analyzing the anatomy and physiology of color vision, scientists still have no definite proof of how the cones work. They do know that the rods contain disks of a light-sensitive pigment called visual purple, or **rhodopsin**. When light strikes this pigment, it bleaches, reducing the electrical signals for darkness otherwise transmitted by the rods. In the dark, our rods have large amounts of unbleached rhodopsin, allowing us to perceive forms with very little light present. The rods can function at light levels up to one thousand times weaker than the visual system based on the cones.

Like rods, cones also contain light-sensitive pigments, called **iodopsins**, but their nature and functions are still

◀ **3.4** Stare at the black dot in the center of the red turtle for 15 to 30 seconds. Then transfer your gaze to the black dot to the right. The luminous blue-green after-image "drawn out of" the white is a successive contrast phenomenon.

matters of conjecture. Of the many theories advanced, the one in current favor is that there are three general kinds of cone pigments: one for sensing the long (red range) wavelengths, one for the middle (green range) wavelengths, and one for the short (blue-violet range) wavelengths. These primary levels of response are thought to mix to form all color sensations, just as additive mixtures are made from colored lights. Yellow, for instance, is a sensation triggered by activation of the green- and red-sensitive cones. Red-sensitive and green-sensitive cones predominate in the retina, with relatively few blue-sensitive cones. The idea of three basic kinds of cones is called the **Trichromatic Theory**. It was first advanced in 1801 by the English physicist Thomas Young and developed in the mid-nineteenth century by the German physicist Hermann von Helmholtz.

This theory, however, only explains what happens in the photoreceptors under direct light stimulation. It is now thought that electrochemical signals transferred from these receptors to the brain are handled somewhat differently. In this second stage of a process that may actually have other unknown stages, colors may perhaps be discerned in pairs of opposing colors. According to the **Opponent Theory**, some response mechanism—perhaps specialized cells in the visual cortex—registers either red or green signals, or either blue-violet or yellow. In each pair (red/green, blue-violet/yellow) only one kind of signal can be carried at a time, while the other is inhibited. These pairs correspond roughly to the complementary colors on color wheels. Another set of cells responding to variations between white and black is thought to operate in a non-opponent fashion, yielding a range of values.

After-images

The Opponent Theory, which has been supported by electrical analysis of nerve cells in various animals, helps to explain why we do not perceive a reddish-green or a bluish-yellow. It can also be used to explain phenomena such as **after-images**, visual sensations that occur briefly after a color stimulus is gone. When we stare at a highly saturated color for some time and then at a neutrally colored area, we "see" an illusory image in the color complementary to the one at which we had been looking. It may be that when the signalling mechanism for one color is fatigued, its opponent color is no longer inhibited. You can verify this effect by first staring at the dot in the center of the red turtle in Figure **3.4** and then transferring your gaze to the dot on its right. What you will see is the "opponent" of red: a greenish light in the same shape. This after-image effect is also called **successive contrast**. After-images occur in our visual perception all the time, but most of us are not usually aware of this phenomenon. If you spend some time looking at a person with brightly colored cloth-

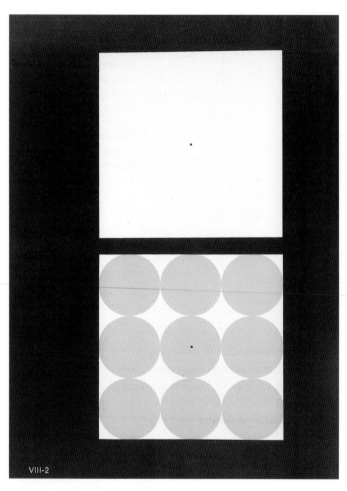

VIII-2

▲ **3.5 Josef Albers, *Color Diagram VIII–2***
Stare at the dot in the center of the yellow circles for 30 seconds.
Then quickly look at the dot in the white square above. Note
everything you see in each case.

ing and then look away, you can perceive an after-image of
the person in complementary colors.

After-images cannot be explained simplistically, however.
Consider Figure **3.5**, created by Josef Albers, whose work
centered on what happens visually in the interaction
between object, eye, and brain. If you stare at the black dot in
the center of the yellow circles for quite a while and then
suddenly transfer your gaze to the black dot on the white
square, you will see not only a luminous blue-violet after-
image of the circles but also, and even more conspicuously,
yellow diamonds corresponding to the spaces between the
circles. We can only guess at what is happening in our perceptual apparatus to create this effect. In fact, nobody yet

▲ **3.6 Ruth Zelanski, Old factory building
photographed in the early morning, at noon, and in
late-afternoon sunset, 2001**
Photographs reveal that changes in natural light throughout the
day bring a great shift in surface color, from blue-gray to almost
gold. But unless people consciously pay attention to such shifts—as
many artists do—they tend to interpret the colors as being
constantly the same as those in the noon photograph.

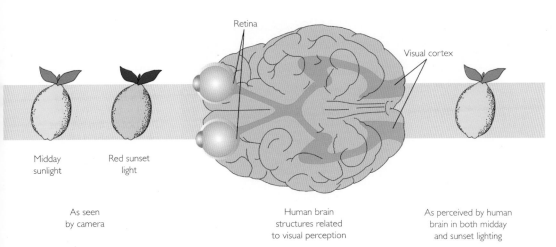

Retina

Visual cortex

Midday
sunlight

Red sunset
light

As seen
by camera

Human brain
structures related
to visual perception

As perceived by human
brain in both midday
and sunset lighting

◄ **3.7** Because of the human tendency to perceptual color constancy, studied by E. H. Land, a lemon which appears yellow in white midday sunlight but more reddish at sunset will still be perceived as a yellow lemon at that time of day because all its surroundings also shift equally toward red.

knows how we see the simplest of color phenomena, let alone the extremely complex array of colors that we perceive every waking moment.

Color Constancy

One unusual scientific discovery has cast doubt on attempts to discover structures in the eye and brain corresponding directly to wavelengths of light. It was described in 1959 and 1977 by E. H. Land, the developer of the Polaroid instant photograph process. In his original work, Land projected two black-and-white slides taken of the same scene from two projectors in such a way that they overlapped exactly. One slide was taken with a red filter and projected through a red filter; the other was taken with a green filter but projected with white light. When projected on top of each other, they nonetheless reproduced an approximation of the hues of the original scene, including blues, yellows, oranges, and greens. Land's discovery also worked when yellow and red lights were used in the projectors. Neither traditional wavelength theories nor trichromatic theories can explain this phenomenon, for Land's research subjects discerned colors with much less information than was ever thought possible. No blue wavelengths needed to be present for people to "see" blue, for instance.

One explanation for Land's results would be that higher structures in the brain were interpreting the colors of familiar objects rather than "seeing" them. But in Land's later experiments, people successfully perceived the hues in abstract patterns of colored squares. Land proposed that there is some mechanism in the human brain that makes it

work differently from a camera. A camera will reveal that a building looks bluish in the morning and reddish in late afternoon, because of different lighting effects. By contrast, humans tend to perceive the building as if its color were constantly that which is perceived in white midday sunlight (the middle image in Figure **3.6**). This strange but familiar phenomenon by which colors subjectively seem to remain the same under different kinds of illumination is called **color constancy**. Land suggested that it must be the result of some perceptual apparatus in the visual cortex of the human brain that works in conjunction with the color perceptors in the retina of the eye. His **retinex**—"retina" plus "**cortex**"—theory has been vindicated by neurobiological research that demonstrates the existence of a network of tiny peg-shaped "blobs" in the visual cortex at the back of the human skull. These seem to compare visual information from an object with what is seen immediately surrounding it. Colors in the immediate vicinity seem more important in these mental computations than colors at a distance. If a lemon is seen against a green leaf at sunset, the fruit will still look yellow relative to the leaf because the ratio of wavelengths coming from the fruit and the leaf remains the same. Even though the environment is totally bathed in reddish light, the leaf will still be perceived as green—rather than brownish—in comparison to the lemon (**3.7**).

There are times, however, when color changes in an object are very much in evidence to a viewer, having been incorporated by the artist specifically to give an added element of surprise. In the case of Rob Sutherland's porcelain pot (**3.8**), the underglaze color of the interior of the

◀ **3.8 Rob Sutherland, Pots with neodymium glaze under tungsten and fluorescent lighting**
Porcelain, oxidation fired, w: 4 × h: 3½ × d: 4 ins (10.1 × 8.8 × 10.1 cm). The pot on the left was photographed under tungsten lighting, the one on the right under fluorescent light. The images show the marked change that a neodymium glaze can give to a porcelain pot.

pot, as well as the round shapes recessed among the off-white textural surface, can change dramatically from a lavender blue to a yellow green, depending on whether they are seen under tungsten or fluorescent lighting. The change is so abruptly different that it is hard to carry over a memory of the color of one pot when looking at the other, so that the pots in the two images could easily be mistaken for two entirely different pots. This effect is caused by the neodymium in the underglaze, an abundant "rare earth" used in many industrial applications that is highly prized for its ability to give a purple coloring to glass; potters appreciate its secret ability to create a "two for one" color experience.

Variables in Color Perception

It seems safe to say that color sensations occur in the responses of our perceptual apparatus. They are not inherent properties of objects. In fact, few animals other than humans even seem to see the world through trichromatic color vision. And humans may differ in their color responses. Given our individual differences in all other physiological areas, it is highly likely that we also differ in color vision.

Genetic and Cultural Differences
Recent research in molecular biology reveals that a minimal genetic difference between two people in terms of a particular amino acid affects their cone cells and thus the way they

see colors. Two people looking at the same red object, for instance, may see its color differently. In fact, these studies indicate that there may be an almost infinite variety of ways that people see what is known as "red."

Major variations from the norm can be discovered as forms of color blindness. These are genetic defects found most often in men, some 7 percent of whom cannot distinguish red from green. But even those who are not color blind have no way of knowing whether they are seeing precisely the same red when looking at the same Coca-Cola label, even though the input to both sets of eyes will be of the same wavelength.

Cultural differences also come into play, to a certain extent. We have learned different ways of categorizing color, and these influence what we "see." The indigenous people of the Ituri Forest in Africa refer to dark values of all hues as "black" but have many different labels for white and brown, referring to subtle distinctions that those from cultures who simply say "white" or "brown" may not notice.

Emotions
It is likely that our emotional state influences our color perception. When people are depressed, they may perceive colors as being dimmer than when they are happy. As severe depression sets in, people often describe a visual sensation of darkness. Scientific research shows that our pupils open wider when we look at something we like, thus allowing more light to enter. They narrow when we look at something we do not like, thus decreasing the amount of light that enters. We speak

of "seeing red" when we are angry, and of "feeling blue" when we are sad. Perhaps these statements are also linked to empirical realities in our neurobiological processes.

Design Factors

Little is known of these individual emotional variations in color perception, but scientists and artists have identified some design variables which can be manipulated to influence color perception. Among them are the size of the colored area and its surroundings.

All other things being equal, a large expanse of color will generally appear brighter than a very small area of the same color. Zwelethu Mthethwa's huge C-print shown in Figure **3.9** presents a startlingly large field of highly saturated blue—a most unexpected color for an interior—in a nearly life-sized format that almost fills the viewer's field of vision if he or she is standing near it. If a color field is very small or far away, it will tend to dull and lose the sharpness of its edges. In Figure **3.10**, the same colors appear different, depending on the amounts used and what is next to them.

Thus in some cases, a small area of a color appears darker than a larger area. However, the effect will also depend heavily on the color of the background. The only hard and fast rule that can be applied is that *all colors are affected by the colors around them.* Consider the apparent shift in value of a

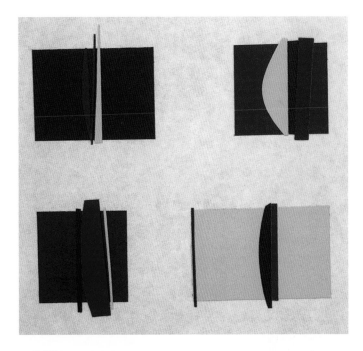

▲ **3.10** The same four colors have been used in these collages, but if you look closely at them, you will perceive differences in their hues and saturation depending on the size of each color's area and what is next to it.

uniform gray strip in Figure **3.11**. The strip is actually a uniform color, but as its surroundings become darker, it appears much lighter; as its surroundings become lighter, it appears much darker. The only way to convince yourself that the strip is of uniform color is to cover its surroundings with pieces of paper, so that you can see it in isolation.

Adjacent colors can also change each other's apparent hues. In *Splendor of Red* by Op Artist Richard Anuszkiewicz, a flat red square background has been overpainted with lines of green and blue, creating diamonds that appear to be of an entirely different red than the base color (**3.12**). Actually, the diamonds are the base coat itself, but when you superimpose colored lines on top of a color, with variations of spacing and length, new shapes can appear as well as new colors. If you still need to prove that there is only one shade of red in this painting, you would have to cover up the blue and green lines. This would, at the same time, prove that there are not really diamonds painted on the surface, either. Artists involved in the Op Art Movement were fascinated with these types of color interactions, where the nonexistent was made visible.

▲ **3.9 Zwelethu Mthethwa,** *Untitled,* **2000**
C-print, 70½ × 95 ins (179 × 214 cm). Jack Shainman Gallery, New York.
Size plays an important role in our perception of colors: a large color field will appear brighter than a small one.

▲ **3.11** The line through the center is actually a solid, uniform gray, but next to darker grays it appears light and next to lighter grays it appears dark.

Lighting

A third important variable in color perception is the light in which we see an object. Typical fluorescent light has a blue cast; incandescent light is reddish-yellow. The color of daylight continually varies as the sun's angle changes in relationship to the earth; clouds and particles in the atmosphere also cause variations in light diffraction. In general, with some particulate matter in the air, daylight will shift in color from blue in the early morning through white to red in the late afternoon. These changes in turn affect the colors reflected from objects.

We nonetheless tend to perceive colors as unchanging, because of our visual memory. A white card will still look white to us, whether we see it under a yellow candlelight or "white" daylight. Because of this tendency, introduced earlier as color constancy, we might say that our house "is" the medium brown that it appears at midday under a slightly overcast sky, even though its color early in the morning is a dark blue-brown, and late in the afternoon a reddish brown, and even though the areas in shadow are much darker than those in direct sunlight. As indicated earlier, something in our brains compensates for the actual changes, allowing us to generalize our color perceptions and therefore recognize familiar objects so that we do not, for example, think we have come home in the evening to the wrong house. E. H. Land, in noting that we will compensate for the extra redness in tungsten filament lights without believing that the objects illuminated have changed in color, suggested that

the eye, in determining color, never perceives the extra red because it does not depend on the flux of radiant energy reaching it. The eye has evolved to see the world in unchanging colors, regardless of always unpredictable, shifting and uneven illumination.[1]

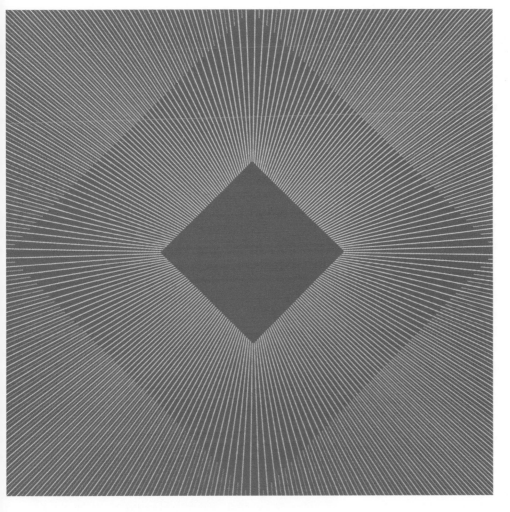

◀ **3.12 Richard Anuszkiewicz, *Splendor of Red*, 1995**
Acrylic on canvas, 6 × 6 ft (1.83 × 1.83 m).
Yale University Art Gallery, New Haven, Connecticut. Gift of Seymour H. Knox.
Richard Anuszkiewicz was a pupil of Joseph Albers (see Figure 9.21), with whom he shared a strong interest in color perception. He went on to become one of the leaders of the Op Art Movement.

Although this mental process is automatic, protecting us from visual chaos, those who choose to be more observant can override it. In search of visual truth, the French Impressionist Claude Monet (1840–1926) observed and painted the exact same scenes—haystacks, poplars along a canal, the face of a cathedral—under many different lighting conditions, documenting the great changes that actually occurred. Discarding the idea that objects possess a certain color, Monet trained his eye to see each moment in its freshness. He stated:

> *This is what I was aiming at: first of all, I wanted to be true and accurate. For me, a landscape does not exist as landscape, since its appearance changes at every moment; but it lives according to its surroundings, by the air and light, which constantly change.*[2]

To observe the effects of light on Rouen Cathedral, Monet rented a room opposite the cathedral and spent months there working at paintings on different easels corresponding to the different times of day. Of the twenty canvases in the completed series, the two shown in Figures **3.13** and **3.14** illustrate the great differences he observed even in the color of stone. In full midday sunlight, the façade is awash with gold, with slight blue shadows, and some surfaces are bleached almost white by the brightness of the sun. At sunset, by contrast, Monet saw the surface as a pale bluish pink, with rich oranges and reds in the building's recesses.

Lighting is important to artists not only in observing the world around them but also in creating and displaying their works. Paintings and frescoes created hundreds of years ago were painted by natural light or artificial light from candles or oil lamps. Under stronger lighting in modern museums, their hues may look brighter than they did to their creators, if the surfaces have not faded. In the northern hemisphere, some artists seek natural northern lighting for their studios because this light changes the least during the day as the sun moves through the sky from east to west; in the southern hemisphere, a southern exposure is more unchanging. Artificial lighting is preferred by others because it does not change at all, assuming that no natural light comes in at the window, and because works are ultimately most likely to be seen under such lighting. These lights do affect color sensations, however. Familiar incandescent tungsten lights are typically redder than midday daylight. The light given by fluorescent tubes usually depends on the fluorescent chemicals that coat the tubes. Figure **3.15** shows the great differences in the same collage photographed with daylight film under daylight, incandescent tungsten light, and ordinary fluorescent light. Since regular fluorescent lighting is bluish, a warm pink fluorescent tube may be paired with a bluish one to give a more even white light. More expensive "full-spectrum" fluorescent tubes are color-corrected to approximate sunlight. Colors created under yellow incandescent lighting may appear more brilliant when taken outside under natural light.

The desire to view works of art in natural lighting is strikingly apparent in the new designs and renovation projects of art museums. Walls are being opened up to let the outside in, to give the viewing public a chance to see the works of art in a combination of natural and artificial light, as well as to create a sense of openness, to "unbox" the rooms. Now that technology offers a variety of ways to screen out the ultraviolet light that is so harmful to colors in artwork, the use of large expanses of glass is no longer considered a restrictive element for art museum designers.

In New York City, the design efforts of Japanese architect Yoshio Taniguchi and Kohn Pedersen Fox (KPF) have combined to create the expanded Museum of Modern Art (**3.16**), a supremely confident and refined space that both astounds and welcomes viewers. Its sheer size, spanning the block from 53rd to 54th Street, with its vertical six-story stack of galleries arranged around a 110-foot- (33-meter-) tall atrium, offers a continual glimpse of what is still to be explored. Natural light filters throughout to balance the artificial illumination, culminating with the skylit sixth floor. In the renovation of the older Goodwin-Stone building, new Thermolux panels that had been part of the original 1939 building but had been lost during previous renovations were

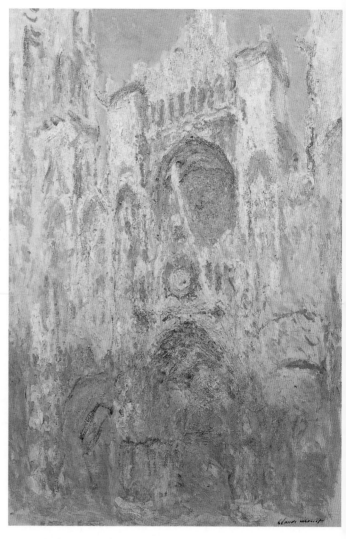

▲ **3.13 Claude Monet, *Rouen Cathedral, Effect of Sun, End of Day*, 1894**
Oil on canvas, 39⅜ × 25⅜ ins (100 × 64.3 cm).
Musée Marmottan, Paris.
Monet overruled the human optical tendency to color constancy, recognizing and portraying the actual color shifts that occur with changing lighting.

▶ **3.14 Claude Monet, *Rouen Cathedral, the Portal and the Albane Tower. Full Sunlight. Harmony in Blue and Gold*, 1894**
Oil on canvas, 42⅒ × 28½ ins (106.9 × 72.3 cm).
Musée d'Orsay, Paris.

◀ **3.15** The same collage photographed (a) with daylight film in daylight, (b) with daylight film under incandescent tungsten light, (c) with daylight film under fluorescent light. Daylight film in daylight is a fairly accurate reproduction of the actual colors. Incandescent tungsten light gives a reddish cast to the colors; ordinary fluorescent light gives a blue-green cast.

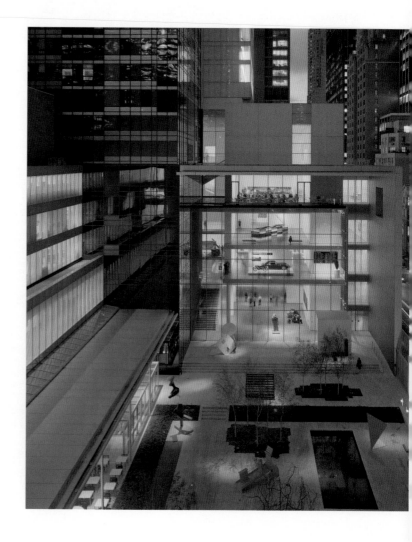

▶ **3.16 Museum of Modern Art, New York, photographed by Tim Hursley**
In 1997 the architect Yoshio Taniguchi won the competition to renovate and enlarge the Museum of Modern Art. New galleries now define the western edge of the sculpture garden, creating a showplace of light and openness.

▲ **3.17 Davide Mercatali and Paolo Pedrizzetti, *Hi-Fi Tap/Mixer***
The shiny chrome of this faucet is so reflective that its own color is difficult to distinguish from those of reflected surrounding colors.

installed, creating a luminosity of diffused light that extends from the second- to the third-floor galleries.

Surface Qualities

In addition to size, surroundings, and lighting, the color we perceive depends, in the case of pigments, on the characteristics of the surface from which it is reflected. A three-dimensional surface will not reflect light uniformly. As in Figure 2.11, many optical color variations will seem to play across its surface, even if the object is actually of a uniform color. Reflection of light from its outermost contours will be strongest, making them appear optically very light, even if the material is actually of dark color. A rough or porous matte surface will reflect light in a more diffuse manner. It will appear lighter or darker as it curves away from the light source, but without the extreme highlights characteristic of a glossy surface.

Materials have different reflective qualities. The same hue will appear different if it is on wood, metal, canvas, paper, ceramics, or cloth. A shiny surface will also reflect the colors around it. The chrome finish of Davide Mercatali and Paolo Pedrizzetti's water tap (**3.17**) carries a complex array of reflections, including a variety of yellow values that develop as it picks up the solid yellow of its surroundings, reflected to

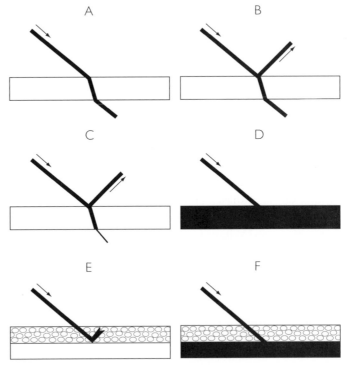

▲ **3.18 Reflective qualities of surfaces**
a) Refraction—a ray of light passing through a transparent surface is refracted (bent) and then transmitted onward.
b) Reflection and transmission—some light may also be reflected from a transparent surface, depending on its surroundings and the angle from which it is seen. If the surface is shiny but non-transparent, light is reflected from the surface but not transmitted through it.
c) Translucence—a translucent or semi-opaque surface transmits only a little light. Some light is reflected, and some absorbed.
d) Absorption—the least reflection occurs when light strikes a dark matte surface. The light is instead absorbed. In opaque materials, a bright white surface reflects the most light and absorbs the least.
e) White ground—in painting, if a translucent layer of pigment and medium is spread over a white ground, some light is reflected back upward through the paint, giving brilliance and luminosity to its colors. The more opaque the paint, the less this effect occurs.
f) Dark ground—a dark ground beneath a layer of translucent paint absorbs rather than reflects light rays, so there is no appearance of brilliance or luminosity.

various degrees as it curves through space, plus the black of its own fittings, and even its own highlights, re-reflected. Figure **3.18** indicates ways that light will be reflected, refracted, or absorbed by differing surfaces.

Nonvisual Color Perception

Some of us may perceive colors through senses other than our vision. The ability to feel colors with our hands is not uncommon among blind people. Try it yourself: Take several sheets of silkscreen colored papers in different hues, close your eyes, and run your hands over them. Can you feel any differences? Yellow, for instance, may feel much clearer and "faster" than red.

Also, some people perceive colors when hearing sounds. Associations between colors and musical keys, notes, or instruments are so common that a body of research exists surrounding this kind of **synesthesia** (the combining of two forms of perception). The composer Scriabin, for instance, associated musical keys with colors. He experienced the key of C as red, G as orange, D as yellow, A as green, E as light blue, B as whitish blue, and so on. Scriabin even composed a special symphony, *Prometheus*, with a part for projected colored lights as "a powerful psychological resonator for the listener."[3] Scriabin's vision was to use

> *a great white hall with a bare interior dome having no architectural decorations. From this dome the shimmering colors would rush downwards in torrents of light.*[4]

People with synesthetic perception tend to experience rising pitch or quickening tempo as lighter colors; somber passages are readily perceived as dark colors. As the painter and art theorist Wassily Kandinsky asserted: "The sound of colors is so definite that it would be hard to find anyone who would try to express bright yellow in the bass notes, or dark lake [a red-purple] in the treble."[5]

The association of colors with certain sounds is, on the

▲ **3.19** Carol Steen using light to display the colors she perceives while hearing music. Photograph by Kay Chernush.

whole, a subjective matter. Rimsky-Korsakov "saw" the key of A as "rosy," rather than Scriabin's green. Contemporary synesthetic composer Michael Torke wrote "Bright Blue Music" in D major, and "Green Music" in E major.

Females are far more likely to experience synesthesia than are men. When New York artist Carol Steen (Figure **3.19**) was a child learning to read, she was quite surprised to discover that her friends did not experience "A" as pink, as she did. Tastes trigger color sensations for her as well: "I see the most brilliant blue after I eat a salty pretzel." And for her, pain is definitely orange. Acupuncture also evokes such clear sensations of colors and shapes that she paints them. This heightened world of color experience was previously viewed as a kind of mental illness. But scientists now have extensive documentation that what synesthetes experience are real perceptual phenomena, although they still are not certain how they occur. Carol Steen says:

> *It's the only way I know of perceiving. If someone said they were going to take it away, it would be like saying they were going to cut off my leg.*[6]

4 Psychological Effects of Color

● ● ● ●

By trial and error, color can be used to evoke a visceral reaction antecedent to words.

PAUL GAUGUIN

T is universally accepted that colors affect us emotionally. Bright reds, oranges, and yellows tend to stimulate us, while blues and greens often make us feel more peaceful. Colors can therefore be used to express emotions and even to evoke them. Here again, however, we must beware of simplistic assumptions, for very slight differences in colors can produce quite different effects. Even the same color green can have the opposite effect on two people, pleasant for one but annoying to the other.

Warm and Cool Colors

We associate the colors of fire—reds, yellows, oranges—with warmth. This is not just an abstract notion, for physiological research indicates that under red lighting our bodies secrete more adrenalin, increasing our blood pressure and our rate of breathing, and actually raising our temperature slightly. Imagine how warm you would feel in the sitting room designed by David Hicks shown in Figure **4.1**. Yellows and

◀ **4.1 David Hicks, Sitting room of a house in Oxfordshire, England, 1970s**
Red is usually experienced as a warming color.

▲ **4.2 Luis Ortega, House and pool designed for Duke Comegys, Los Angeles**
Blues and greens are considered cooling.

oranges have a similar effect, though they are not as warming as strong reds.

By contrast, feel the coolness of the greens and blues in the poolside area of a Los Angeles house designed by Luis Ortega (**4.2**). We associate blues and greens with the cooling qualities of water and trees, and physiological research shows that green or blue lights will slow our heartbeat, decrease our temperature, and relax our muscles.

Hues in the red area of the color wheel are therefore often referred to as "warm," while those in the blue and green range are called "cool." These terms are relative rather than absolute. Notice how the intensity of the red walls and floor

in Figure 4.1 makes the oranges, yellows, and pinks of the painting over the sofa seem cool by contrast; the "hot" pinks in the easel painting on the left seem positively icy.

W Seoul's Away Spa (**4.3**) uses a combination of warm and cool hues in this pool area, with the added bonus of having the pool's colors coded for hot, warm, and cool water. The intensity of the blue and green hues seems to maintain the intensity of the red rather than detract from it, which gives an overall feeling of vibrancy and warmth to this commercial space.

In addition to the influence of surroundings, it is possible to discern warmer and cooler variations on a single hue. As the value of a hue becomes lighter, it generally appears cooler. And the addition of a small amount of a cooler hue to a red or a warmer hue to a green will create what could be called a "cool red" or a "warm green." In Figure **4.4**, which compares colors mixed by printers' ink formulas numbered according to the Pantone Mixing System (PMS), a single unit of yellow has been substituted for one of the eight units of Rubine Red in PMS 219 to create PMS 205. Does PMS 219 feel warmer or cooler to you than PMS 205? Surely PMS 217, which has only one part of Rubine Red to 31 parts of white, is cooler than either of the darker reds.

Physiological Effects

Mystics have long held that we emanate a colored glow, or aura. Some feel that its presence has been verified by Kirlian photography, a special process for capturing the usually invisible energies that radiate from plants and animals. The color of the aura, as seen by clairvoyants, is thought to reflect the state of a person's health and spirituality. According to

◄ 4.4 PMS 217, 205, 219
Do you experience any subjective difference in warmth between these colors?

the mystic Corinne Heline, gold is the auric color of spiritual illumination, clear blue or lavender indicates a high spiritual development, orange a predominantly intellectual nature, clear green a sympathetic nature, and pure carmine or rose-red an unselfish, affectionate quality. Duller colors are associated with materialistic, fearful, or selfish qualities. A dark gray aura with brown and red in it accompanies depression.

According to physiological research with the effects of colored lights, red wavelengths stimulate the heart, the circulation, and the adrenal glands, increasing strength and stamina. Pink has a more gently stimulating quality and helps muscles to relax. Orange wavelengths stimulate the solar plexus, the immune system, the lungs, and the pancreas, and benefit the digestive system. Yellow light is stimulating for the brain and nervous system, bringing mental alertness and activating the nerves in the muscles. Green lights affect the heart, balance the circulation, and promote relaxation and healing of disorders such as colds, hay fever, and liver problems. Blue wavelengths affect the throat and thyroid gland, bring cooling and soothing effects, and lower blood pressure. Deep blue lessens pain. Blue-green light helps to decrease infections, soothe jangled nerves, and correct weakness in the immune system. Indigo light helps to counteract skin problems and fevers. Violet light affects the brain, has purifying, antiseptic, and cooling effects, balances the metabolism, and seems to suppress hunger.

Given these apparent physiological effects of colored lights, there is a science of healing with colors, or **chromotherapy**. People are bathed with colored lights, placed in colored environments, or asked to meditate on specific colors thought to stimulate particular glands. This form of treatment dates back thousands of years to the "color halls" of the ancient Egyptians, Chinese, and Indians.

Although color healing has remained largely an occult science, chromotherapy is being taught in some nursing schools and alternative medical centers, and the medical profession as a whole makes use of color in certain treatments. For example, premature babies with jaundice are cured by exposure to blue light.

▲ 4.3 W Seoul, Away Spa
This is W Hotels' first Asian property, of which the Away Spa is a great attraction. The use of bold color combinations gives the impression of good health and youthful exuberance. Built in the Walkerhill district of Seoul, it is a collaboration between New York's Studio Gaia, who designed the public spaces and rooms, Tony Chi, who was responsible for the restaurants, and Hong Kong architects RAD.

A more prominent use of color therapy occurs in interior design. Psychological literature is full of attempts to determine how specific colors affect human health and behavior and how best to put the results into effect. Bright colors, particularly warm hues, seem conducive to activity and mental alertness and are therefore increasingly being used in schools. Cooler, duller hues, on the other hand, tend to sedate. Henner Ertel studied the effects of environmental color among schoolchildren in Munich. The interior design colors with the most positive intellectual effects in Ertel's study were yellow, yellow-green, orange, and light blue. Surrounded by these colors, children's IQ scores rose by up to 12 points. In white, brown, and black environments, IQ scores fell. In addition, Ertel found that an orange environment made the children more cheerful and sociable and less irritable and hostile.

In some institutional situations, a calming environment is beneficial. In a study conducted by Harry Wohlfarth and Catharine Sam of the University of Alberta, the color environment of 14 severely handicapped and behaviorally disordered eight-year-olds was radically altered. The classroom was changed from a white fluorescent-lit one with bright orange carpeting and orange, yellow, and white colored walls and shelves to one with full-spectrum fluorescent lighting and brown and blue walls and shelves. The children's aggressive behavior diminished and their blood pressure dropped. As one nurse reported:

> I found the children and myself considerably more relaxed in the new room. The afternoons seemed less hectic and instead of running out of time for our activity, we ran out of activities.

> I also found at lunch I was more relaxed and was able to eat something without feeling sick.... The noise level really went down in the Phase II room, which seemed to keep everyone from getting upset as the day went on. [1]

When the environment was then experimentally changed back to the way it had been before, aggressive behavior and blood pressure returned to their previous levels.

Interestingly, the same effects were found in both blind and sighted children in Wohlfarth and Sam's study, suggesting that we are affected by color energies in ways that transcend seeing. One hypothesis is that neurotransmitters in the eye transmit information about light to the brain even in the absence of sight, and that this information releases a hormone in the hypothalamus that has numerous effects on our moods,

mental clarity, and energy level. In what Wohlfarth calls the science of "color-psychodynamics," colors that seem to increase blood pressure and pulse and respiration rates are, in order of increasing effect, red, orange, and yellow. Those decreasing these physiological measures are green (minimal effect), blue (medium effect), and black (maximum effect).

The legendary Notre Dame football coach Knute Rockne attempted to use awareness of the physiological effects of colors competitively. To stir up his own players, he painted their locker room red. He had the visiting team's locker room painted in blue-greens, thus sedating them both before the game and when they returned to relax at half-time. Similarly, the influence of environmental color was demonstrated in one factory where workers were complaining about feeling cold. Rather than raise the thermostat, management decided to paint the blue-green walls coral. The complaints stopped.

Lest we hasten to repaint everything in attempts at behavior modification, we should note that physiological color responses are complex. The precise variation of a hue has a major impact, but one that is rarely addressed by psychological research. One shade of pink may be calming, while another may be stimulating. Although mystics find certain blue-violets conducive to a very high spiritual state, a group of college students said that a blue-violet they were shown tended to make them feel sad and tired. These same students found that a color described by the researchers as "cool green" made them feel angry and confused.

Furthermore, initial responses to a color environment may be reversed over time as our body adjusts to the new stimulus. It is known that some time after blood pressure is raised by red light it drops below the normal level; after blood pressure is lowered by blue light, it eventually rises to a higher than normal level.

Color Symbolism

Our responses to colors are not just biological. They are also influenced by color associations from our culture. In societies where most adults drive cars and are familiar with stop lights, there is an automatic association of red with "stop" and green with "go." In cultures where cars are rare this clear-cut association does not exist.

In Western industrial cultures, black is associated with death; mourners wear dark clothes and the body is trans-

▲ **4.5 Rogier van der Weyden, *The Deposition*, c. 1435**
Tempera and oil on wood, approximately 7 ft 3 ins × 8 ft
(2.2 × 2.4 m).
Museo del Prado, Madrid, Spain.
The symbolic use of color was one way to give medieval viewers a better understanding of this altarpiece at a time when most of the population was illiterate.

ported in a black limousine. In ancient Egypt, however, statues of Osiris were painted black to indicate the period of gestation when seeds are sprouting beneath the earth; black was associated with preparation for rebirth rather than with an ending of earthly life. People in the West Indies use bright colors to commemorate deaths, in celebration of the soul's departure for a happier existence. In China and India the color used for mourning is white—because of the humility of wearing undyed cloth and the association of white with peace and coolness. In some Native American tribes, black is associated with introspection; white is seen as the color of winter, of purification and renewal.

Despite regional differences, red is associated with vigorous life in many cultures, easily associated with the color of blood, as well as with fire, warmth, brightness, and stimulation. The earliest humans were buried with red ocher pigments, perhaps with the hope that the deceased would live on in another plane of existence. In Rogier van der Weyden's *The Deposition* (**4.5**) color was used not only to tie the composition together, but also as a nonverbal language to help viewers in the 1400s to understand and clarify the layers of meaning within this altarpiece. Red, the symbol of birth and

exuberant life, was a fitting choice for John the Evangelist's robe on the far left, as he played an essential part in the growth of the new Christian religion.

Until the invention of aniline dyes, blue was a precious color, expensive and rare. In late-medieval works of religious art, blue was often chosen to depict the Virgin Mary, linking her to the color of the sky, and therefore to the heavens. Her robes were often a lighter blue when she was painted with a young Christ, but as this altarpiece shows, changed to a somber blue-black at the time of her son's death. In Catholic art even to this day, blue is still the color most associated with Mary.

In Victorian times, flowers were used in an elaborate color-coded language. Very specific phrases could be sent to a friend or lover by including several flower types, and even different hues of the same blossom, in a bouquet. We still use a red rose to symbolize love, and a yellow one for friendship.

If there is any doubt about whether we are still tied to color symbolism in the twenty-first century, take a moment

▲ **4.6 Andy Warhol, *Mint Marilyn Monroe*, 1962**
Oil and silkscreen enamel on canvas, 20½ × 16½ ins (52 × 42 cm).
Jasper Johns Collection 2000, Andy Warhol Foundation for the Visual Arts, New York.
Andy Warhol used colors in an exaggerated way to represent Marilyn Monroe's image as a Hollywood sex symbol.

to think about pale pink and pale blue. In spite of the sexual revolution, proud new parents still want their offspring to be properly recognized. If they wrap the baby in a mint green, light yellow, or white blanket (these colors are known as "neutral" baby colors), strangers still ask "Is your baby a boy or a girl?" The sexual color coding of light pink (for girls) and blue (for boys) has worked so well for generations that these pastel shades can be referred to as "baby pink" and "baby blue" and we all seem to know exactly what is meant. In today's Western society, even the most liberal-minded parents are still reluctant to wrap their newborn baby boy in a pink blanket. Children's clothing and greetings card designers, as well as color consultants for yarn manufacturers, have been dealing with these particular color restrictions for years.

As a milder version of red, without red's saturated intensities, pink is often associated with affection and sweetness. However, when Andy Warhol used pink for the flesh tones in *Mint Marilyn Monroe* (**4.6**), he controlled its lighthearted quality by graying it down, by presenting it as a flat, mask-like shape, and surrounding it with a harsh, brassy yellow that does not seem to get along with any of the other colors. In fact, every color in this piece seems to be uncomfortable in its surroundings, as if the lighting is too harsh. Even when using a large area of pink, Warhol created the overall image of a bold sexual icon, leaving only the haunting expression in her half-closed eyes to hint at the real person within.

Personal Color Preferences

Not only have we inherited cultural associations, but we also respond to colors in individual ways. Imagine that you are viewing Sharon Booma's large red painting, *No Standing* (**4.7**), or standing in Larry Bell's neon-lit installation piece, *Leaning Room II* (**4.8**). In each case, color is used to unify the work, and to give meaning to space and shapes. Although each work uses a different medium, we still have our own personal reaction to the colors, whether we are viewing a painting or walking inside a room full of color. What if you were inside Bell's installation on a cold day. Would it seem to be a cooler blue? Would you enjoy the sensation of that blue more if it surrounded you on a hot summer's day? Would Sharon Booma's painting seem warmer on a cold or hot day? Even when an artist has a color well integrated into the

▲ **4.7 Sharon Booma, *No Standing*, 2004**
Oil and acrylic, 75 × 75 × 3 ins (190.5 × 190.5 × 7.6 cm).
Sharon Booma's painting saturates our vision with color. With skillful manipulation of both the surface texture and the underlayment of paint, her large, broad areas of color are filled with visual interest.

work, two people can see it and react differently, depending on variables too numerous to control.

Psychological research has revealed some variables that help explain individual differences in color responses. To wit: We are most responsive to the pleasure of sheer color as children. From early infancy, babies respond to brightly colored objects. Among adolescents, the sensation-seeking prefer red, while the more reserved prefer blue. Elderly people have a significant preference for light over dark colors. People with certain mental illnesses—particularly schizophrenia—show a preference for nonchromatic, neutral colors (white, black, brown, gray) while manic depressives generally prefer chromatic hues. Extroverts tend to prefer warm hues; introverts like cool hues. However, people may be drawn toward colors representing qualities they lack, for balance. Red, for instance, is usually the preference of vibrant, outgoing, impulsive people, but timid people may also be drawn to it.

▶ **4.8 Larry Bell, *Leaning Room II*, 1970**
Sheet rock, paint, and fluorescent light installation based on leaning room, artist's studio, Venice. Collection of the artist.

▲ 4.9 Photograph of female model painted green, blue, and red, and wearing necklaces of black leather and feathers
Colors, used creatively, can help attract the perfect buyers to a product.

Those who are feeling frustrated or angry may be repelled by red.

Individual color preferences are so distinctive that they have been used for purposes such as personnel selection, treatment of the elderly, medical diagnosis, and therapy since the middle of the twentieth century, when the Swiss psychologist Dr. Max Luscher developed his Luscher Color Test. He proposed that a person's selections and rejections of specific colors reveal information about his or her psychological characteristics. In the Luscher Color Test, subjects are given colored cards to line up from most to least favorite. The full test involves 73 color cards; the most commonly used version has dark blue, blue-green, green, orange-red, yellow, brown, black, and gray as choices. A person who prefers blue, according to Luscher's conclusions, tends to be passive, sensitive, tender, and loving; a person who prefers orange-red tends to be active, aggressive, competitive, and lusty. Dr. Luscher also proposes that a proper inner balance of the four "psychological primaries," red, green, blue, and yellow yields a happy, well-adjusted person. In Figure **4.9**, the design team painted the model's face and hair blue, green, and red-orange, and the flesh tones add a yellowish tan. If one were to follow the Luscher guidelines for inner balance, the happy and well-adjusted avant-garde consumer should be quite attracted to this ad.

The samples used for Luscher testing are not always uniform in color, nor is there general agreement about the direct correlation of color preferences with personality traits, but color choices are nonetheless of interest to artists, particularly in applied design.

Not only personality but also geography may influence our color preferences. According to the work of the psychologist E. R. Jaensch, people from strongly sunlit countries tend to prefer warm, bright colors, while those from countries with less sunlight tend to prefer cooler, less intensely saturated colors. Jaensch speculated that in brighter environments, people's eyes have adapted to protect them from sunlight so there is a physiological bias toward these warm colors. In areas where the sun is not so bright, people's eyes are more accustomed to drawing ambient light from the sky and are thus biased toward cool colors. Scandinavians tested showed a preference for blue and green, while Mediterranean people preferred red.

Our own color preferences are important to us. A study of six- to eleven-year-olds wearing goggles with colored eyepieces while doing a pegboard test (imagine this situation!) showed that they completed the test much faster and more accurately when they were wearing goggles of their favorite color.

Unconscious color prejudices are also sometimes apparent in artists' works. However, to use a musical analogy, it is limiting to try to play everything on the violin when a whole orchestra of instruments is at one's disposal. Artists can explore the entire range of hues, at all levels of value and saturation, in order to create any effect they desire.

Emotional Effects

Given their physiological effects, different hues seem to create different emotional responses in those who see, wear, or live with them. Although there are no hard and fast rules about the effects of different colors, color therapist Suzy Chiazzari specifies these associations between emotions and particular hues:

Red: vitality, strength, warmth, sensuality, assertion, anger, impatience
Pink: calmness, nurturance, kindness, unselfish love

Orange/peach: joy, security, creativity, stimulation
Yellow: happiness, mental stimulation, optimism, fear
Green: harmony, relaxation, peace, calmness, sincerity, contentment, generosity
Turquoise: mental calmness, concentration, confidence, refreshment
Blue: peace, spaciousness, hope, faith, flexibility, acceptance
Indigo/violet: spirituality, intuition, inspiration, contemplation, purification
White: peace, purification, isolation, spaciousness
Black: femininity, protection, restriction
Gray: independence, separation, loneliness, self-criticism
Silver: change, balance, femininity, sensitivity
Gold: wisdom, abundance, idealism
Brown: nurturance, earthiness, retreat, narrow-mindedness[2]

Such associations are rather common, but on the other hand cannot be considered absolute. Consider the heated comments of color specialist Faber Birren about the seemingly innocuous color white:

A prominent decorator once told me that "white is the best thing for walls. It is neutral and it blends with everything!" This is preposterous. If you've read Moby Dick, you may remember the hair-raising description of white as the most portentous, desolate and heinous of all visual sensations.

White is terrible when you get too much of it. It hurts the eyes. Worse than this, it makes you feel sterile and naked and as vacant as shadow. Neutral? It puts restaurants out of business and hospitals out of patients.[3]

Although psychologists have conducted experiments to see how people respond to certain colors in isolation, in everyday life we see hundreds of thousands of colors in infinite combinations and unique contexts. The actual emotional effect of a specific color in an artwork depends partly on its surroundings and partly on the ideas expressed by the work as a whole. To be surrounded by blue, as in the Larry Bell installation (4.8), is quite different from seeing a small area of blue in a larger color context, such as the blue covers on the

◀ **4.10 Emil Nolde, *Autumn Sea XVI*, 1911**
Oil on canvas, 29 × 34½ ins (73 × 88 cm). © Nolde-Stiftung, Seebüll, Germany.
Yellow is commonly used to evoke a happy mood, but it may also be associated with fear.

◀ **4.11 Still from the film** ***Red's Dream*****, produced by Pixar on Pixar Image Computer, 1987**
"A Night in the Bike Store" is computer-rendered in local color, complete with shadow effects.

poolside chaises shown in Figure 4.2. And to illustrate the importance of thematic context, consider the use of yellow in Emil Nolde's *Autumn Sea XVI* (**4.10**). This highly saturated yellow is often associated with happy, uplifting emotional effects, but Nolde has used it in such a way that it evokes feelings of terror and turmoil. For one thing, he has used it to fill the sky, broken by streaks of red-purple and black. No sunset ever looked like this. Spatially, the black regions seem to be advancing over our heads, getting darker and darker as they approach us. Nolde has placed our point of view almost down in the roiling water itself, as if we are drowning in it, with the sky pressing down menacingly above. Nolde (1867–1956) was a leader in the German Expressionist movement, using colors to express inner psychological states rather than outer realities.

Local and Expressive Color

There are two opposite ways of using color in representational art. At one extreme is **local color**—the color that something appears from nearby when viewed under average lighting conditions. We think of the local color of a banana as

yellow, for example. Thinking in terms of local color can, however, be deceptive. Many colors can be perceived across the surface of a banana. In the realistic scene from the computer-generated film *Red's Dream* (**4.11**), the artists have programmed the computer to take into account the light from five different light sources; two of them cast shadows that affect both value and hue in accurate local color.

At the other extreme is the **expressionistic** use of color, whereby artists use color to express an emotional rather than a visual truth. Human skin comes in many colors, but never in green. Nonetheless, George Segal has expressively used green for the faces as well as figures of men standing silently waiting for the dole during the Depression (**4.12**). If they had pink faces, we might think them drunk, but the green cast creates a sickly, depressing impression of their solitude, social embarrassment, and unaccustomed poverty.

Expressive use of color may dispense altogether with repre-

▶ **4.12 George Segal,** ***Depression Bread Line*** **(detail), 1991**
Plaster, wood, metal, and acrylic paint, full work 108 × 108 × 36 ins (274.3 × 274.3 × 91.4 cm). FDR Memorial, Washington, D.C. Courtesy, Sidney Janis Gallery, New York.

◀ **4.13 George Chaplin, *Turner*, 2001**
Oil on canvas, 66 × 78 ins (168 × 198 cm).
When color is used without any figurative imagery, it may nonetheless evoke emotional responses. What do you feel when looking at these floating colors? Why has the artist compared this work with that of J. M. W. Turner (see 9.11)?

sentational imagery, as in George Chaplin's *Turner* (**4.13**). This is a painting which does not even look like a painting, for it is impossible to see how the colors were applied to the canvas, or which color was applied first and which last. The colors just float there, sometimes in the background, sometimes in the foreground, ephemeral, unbounded presences that shift during the day with changes in natural lighting. Chaplin explains:

Color is both the subject and object of my painting, and I celebrate it for its emotional and spiritual impact. Each work develops as an intuitive and sensory experience through subtle transitions of varying amounts of color. These combine to produce a kinetic illusion of light and space. I feel my way of working is directly aligned with the process of change in nature. A temporal analogy is the chromatic shifting of atmosphere apparent in the minutes of a sunrise.[4]

5 Compositional Effects of Color

Art is harmony. Harmony is the analogy of contrary and similar elements of tone, of color, and of line, conditioned by a dominant key, and under the influence of a particular light.

GEORGES SEURAT

ANALYZING color use from a strictly design-oriented point of view, we find that in addition to its emotional influence, color can strongly affect the composition of a work. Color choices may be based as much upon perceptions of space, unity, and emphasis as upon the artist's desire for realism or psychological suggestion. Shapes and textures are part of this organizational process, but color also plays a major compositional role. In this chapter, we analyze the effects of color irrespective of the ways artists have used shapes and textures; in reality, however, all elements of design are interrelated.

Spatial Effects

Colors can influence our spatial perceptions in many ways. For one thing, hues that are lighter at maximum saturation (yellows, oranges) appear larger than those that are darker at maximum saturation (blues, purples). According to the Munsell system of classifying colors, yellow reaches maximum saturation at step 8 of value, whereas blue does so at step 4, and purple at step 3. And highly saturated colors tend to appear larger than those that are less saturated.

In Donald Sultan's painting *Twenty-Eight Colored Flowers*

◀ **5.1 Donald Sultan, *Twenty-Eight Colored Flowers July 15, 2004***
Enamel, flock, tar, and spackle on linoleum tile over masonite, 96 × 144 ins (243.8 × 365.7 cm).
Courtesy of Ameringer & Yohe Fine Art, New York, NY.
Color choices, when controlled by the artist, can affect the movement and spatial quality of a work.

◀ **5.2 Photograph by Gordon Whitten of Hoodoos at Bryce Canyon, Bryce Canyon National Park, Utah, 1991**
Color contrasts appear greater the closer they are to the viewer, while colors in the far distance lose their sharp contrasts, often taking on a blue atmospheric haze. Landscape artists can use this effect to create depth in their works.

July 15, 2004 (**5.1**), we see identical flower shapes, their larger-than-life scale pushing them into abstraction. The use of many colors in values from light to dark makes it difficult to look at one flower alone; our eyes easily move from color to color, and as we keep looking, the paler flowers begin to expand, the darker ones to contract. The black centers seem to be the stabilizing force, holding the flowers apart. The longer one looks, the more the flowers want to move around.

When a color expands visually, it may also seem closer to the viewer than colors that seem to contract. Look again at the flowers in Figure 5.1. Do the white ones seem to pop forward optically? A related perceptual phenomenon makes warm colors appear to advance and cool colors to recede. Although that seems to be the case with these flowers, artists can bring any color forward or push it back, depending on what other spatial devices they use.

An awareness of these color effects is often useful. Interiors that are physically small can be made optically larger through avoidance of large areas of highly saturated warm colors, which tend to fill the space visually. In David Hicks's room (4.1), red seems to be advancing into the room from all sides—walls, floor, and furniture—creating a cozy atmosphere. A high ceiling can be made to appear lower by painting it in a color that advances optically. In landscape design or painting, spatial planes can be set up by using colors that advance visually and colors that recede visually.

Spatial advancing or receding also results from contrasts between colors. Through our experiences in the world, we have learned that hue and value contrasts are greatest in things close to us, and less apparent in things seen at a great distance. This effect is called **atmospheric perspective**. In areas where there is particulate matter in the air, distant forms also appear bluish because of the scattering of short blue wavelengths in sunlight.

In Gordon Whitten's photograph of the Hoodoos at Bryce Canyon National Park in southwestern Utah (**5.2**), the color contrast between the near columns (hoodoos, or goblins) and the farther ones can clearly be seen. The varying mineral deposits that color the layers of the limestone rock are brighter the closer they are to the viewer, and seem to be coated with a blue haze in the distance. Automatically our brain assigns different spatial planes due to these decreasing contrasts. Representational artists have long used atmospheric perspective as one means of creating the illusion of deep space on a two-dimensional surface. So well established is this convention—and the real-life experiences on which it is founded—that contemporary artists can evoke sensations of three-dimensional space through use of color alone.

The view in Russell Sharon's *Untitled Landscape* (**5.3**) appears to recede into very deep space with his skillful use of yellow. The strong presence of a horizon line is created where the lighter and darker yellow shapes meet, while the merest suggestion of a brownish yellow along that line creates an anchoring presence, perhaps of buildings or trees seen from miles away. Even without the clue in the title, it is easy to read this painting as a landscape, and if we were living in a flat, open land, where our daily point of reference was a strong horizon line, where the sky touched down in

▲ **5.3 Russell Sharon, *Untitled Landscape*, 2004**
Oil on canvas, 62 × 62 ins (157.4 × 157.4 cm).
Shown at Cheryl Hazan Gallery, New York, United States,
April 1–May 9, 2004.
Other clues besides diminishing contrasts can create an illusion of depth in landscape paintings, and one of the strongest is the presence of a horizon line.

▲ **5.4 Claude Monet, *Waterlilies, Sunset*, detail, 1914–26**
Whole painting 79 × 236 ins (200 × 600 cm).
Musée de l'Orangerie, Paris.
In the maze of color sensations which may come from below, on, or above the surface of the water, how do you interpret the spatial position of the more subdued colors at the top of the picture plane?

all directions, this painting might not seem abstract at all. Perhaps we have a stronger association with the horizon than we do for color associations, because in this work we see depth of space without the usual aid of colors fading into the distance.

Spatially, water presents a highly interesting surface, because it is both transparent and reflective. Thus the colors one sees while looking at water may lie on the surface, beneath the surface, or above, reflected from the surface. Claude Monet devoted many years to this mysterious subject, painting the water in his garden at Giverny again and again, in endless permutations. In paintings such as the detail from a sunset version of *Waterlilies* (**5.4**), we are at a loss to sort out the spatial mysteries of what we see. We are apparently looking down and across the surface, seeing grasses beneath, reflections of overhanging trees, reflections of a brilliant gold and pink sunset, and floating waterlilies all intermingling. The same greens and blues come forward here, recede slightly into the distance there. Poet Paul Claudel explains:

Claude Monet, at the end of his long life, after having studied all the different motifs that nature creates with color effects in reply to light, has addressed the most docile, the most penetrable element—water—which is at the same time transparent, iridescent, and reflective. Thanks to water, he has become the painter of what we cannot see. He addresses that invisible spiritual surface that separates light from reflection. Airy azure captive of liquid azure. … Color rises from the bottom of the water in clouds, in whirlpools.[1]

In nonobjective as well as representational art, we interpret contrasts in hue and value as having spatial meaning, making some areas appear to pop forward, while others seem to recede into the background. Gene Davis's *Diamond Jim* (**5.5**) is painted in stripes that continually vary in degrees of hue and value contrasts. At first glance it appears totally flat, but as you continue to stare at it without trying to hold it flat mentally, it will quickly develop a spatial

▲ **5.5 Gene Davis, *Diamond Jim*, 1972**
Acrylic on canvas, 6 × 8 ft (1.83 × 2.44 m).
Courtesy Gene Davis estate.
If you stare at Davis's painting, it will lose its flatness and become a complex series of intervals which seem to exist on different planes in space.

▶ **5.6 Milton Glaser, Fold-out poster of Aretha Franklin**
With the exception of Aretha's face, Glaser's flat shapes appear to be lying side-by-side across a two-dimensional plane. Economical use of highlights gives the face a three-dimensional appearance.

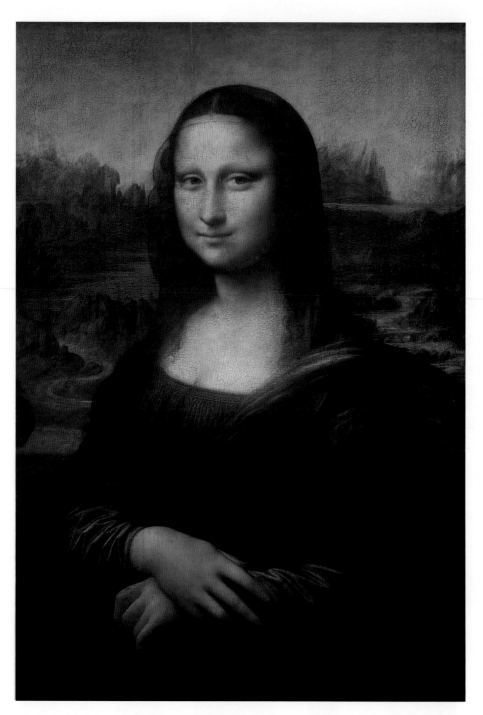

◀ **5.7 Leonardo da Vinci,**
***Mona Lisa*, 1503–6**
Oil on panel, 30¼ × 21 ins (76.8 × 53.3 cm).
Musée du Louvre, Paris.
Leonardo was a master at using
subtle gradations of color to create
softly rounded forms and the illusion of
deep space.

pattern that goes in and out. Analyzing how each area works is very instructive. But Davis warns that he himself has used no color theories in creating his stripe paintings. He says:

> My whole approach to color is intuitive. If a certain color seems called for, I tend to use the reverse. Actually, I'm interested in color to define intervals. … I'll put a red here on the right and, let us say, three feet away I will use another red. Now, that's going to define the interval between those two stripes in a way it would not do if I made this other stripe green, because then there would not be a dialogue established between those two stripes. … My work is mainly about intervals, that is, like in music. Music is essentially time interval, and I'm interested in space interval.[2]

When colors are held to a consistent value and saturation level, even highly contrasting hues will appear quite flat. Milton Glaser, in designing the Aretha Franklin poster (5.6), claimed that the flat shapes refer back to Art Deco and the work of Matisse. All except the yellow areas are consistently high in saturation; the yellows are lower in value than the high light of a highly saturated yellow, and thus correspond to values similar to those of the other hues. For the most part, the shapes lock together two-dimensionally like pieces of a jigsaw puzzle. They do not appear to overlap, a visual clue that would suggest three-dimensional space, because the uniformity of value and intensity holds them all on the same plane.

The only area of the Aretha Franklin poster that appears three-dimensional is the singer's face. By adding areas in a single lighter value, Glaser gives us the impression of a more rounded form in three-dimensional space.

When transitions between lighter and darker values are developed more gradually to depict three-dimensionality, the effect is called **chiaroscuro**. Developed to a high art by Renaissance painters, chiaroscuro (literally, "light and shade") is the portrayal of the effects of light and shadow across a three-dimensional form. Areas facing a light source are executed in lighter values, while those curving away from the light are depicted in darker values. The mind of the viewer immediately interprets this information as evidence of three-dimensionality. An example that is famous for its subtlety is Leonardo da Vinci's *Mona Lisa* (5.7).

Leonardo shared his observations about some subtleties of chiaroscuro effects in real life, such as the effects of deep shadows:

> Colors seen in shadow will display less variety in proportion as the shadows in which they lie are deeper. The evidence of this is to be had by looking from an open space into the doorways of dark and shadowy churches, where the pictures which are painted in various colors all look of uniform darkness. Hence at a considerable distance all the shadows of different colors will appear of the same darkness.[3]

Balance and Proportion

In addition to suggesting spatial concepts, colors also give a visual suggestion of a certain weightiness or lack thereof. Generally speaking, highly saturated or busily detailed areas will draw attention and therefore seem to carry more weight than less saturated or visually simpler areas.

In some cases, artists create a feeling of imbalance with the help of color, but they do so in intentional violation of the principle of balance. Russian Constructivist painter Kazimir Malevich insisted on working solely with relationships among colored geometrical forms. Naturalistic representation thus set aside, one can clearly see the sense of imbalance in his *Suprematist Painting* (5.8). He expected viewers to read their own feelings into such works. Here the red square at the base seems to belong to a different world from that of the tilted black rectangle that looms above it. The unsaturated red square seems quietly alive and stable, like an established peasant culture, whereas the tilted, skewed rectangles of more saturated colors above might be suggestive of an industrializing culture that is increasingly out of balance. The red square is complete; other color fragments are nearby but do not intrude on it. By contrast, the weighty but teetering black rectangle is cut across again and again by contrasting color shapes. It even seems to have "lost" some pieces of itself, black scraps which have become detached at the upper left.

The sense of balance or imbalance is usually achieved largely through intuitive manipulation of the elements and principles of design (such as symmetry, light-and-dark contrast, and emphasis). Colors affect each other so strongly that no absolute statements about relative visual weight can be made that would apply to all cases.

Artists may manipulate colors more for the sake of balance in a composition than to establish a certain mood or to give a true representation of the external world. In a graphically brilliant cartoon strip of "Krazy Kat" (5.9), the

▲ **5.8 Kazimir Malevich, *Suprematist Painting*, 1915**
Oil on canvas, 40 × 24½ ins (101.5 × 62 cm).
Stedelijk Museum, Amsterdam.
Malevich expected viewers to bring their own interpretation to his work, but surely the question of balance is involved in the content of this painting. Does the red square in the bottom seem visually weighty enough to serve as the fulcrum for the teetering black shape above, or does this composition seem intentionally out of balance? Do the colored shapes superimposed on the black rectangle seem to add to or subtract from its visual weight?

artist George Herriman begins with a black sky in which floats a red and green moon, a fittingly isolated and eerie backdrop to Krazy Kat's statement, "I are illone." The sky and earth then change hues throughout the remaining panels, setting up blocks of color that are satisfyingly varied but yet visually balanced. The large rectangle of black sky on the bottom anchors the whole work and repeats the visual theme stated in the first panel. This repetition invites the viewer to compare the two, reinforcing the discovery that Krazy Kat's assumption of solitude is not at all true.

In contrast to balancing lighter and heavier visual weights, another kind of color balancing is designed to satisfy the viewer's sense of aesthetic proportion. In every work of more than a single color, areas of light, dark, and medium values exist in a certain mathematical relationship to each other, as do more and less saturated colors and warm and cool colors. These relationships have been translated by some color theorists into rules for proper color use. Some theorists feel that warm and cool hues should cover approximately equal areas in a work, thus creating a satisfying symmetry of hues. There is an approximately equal ratio of reds and yellows to greens and blue-purples in Jacob van Hulsdonck's *Plums and Peaches* (**5.10**). The composition is apparently carefully worked out with reference to balancing of hues, despite the seemingly innocent informality of the scattered fruits. Other recommendations about color balancing are discussed in Chapter 6, where we examine color theories. It must be noted, however, that many successful works do not conform to any theory of color balance.

Joseph Raffael's watercolor *Spring* (**5.11**) exemplifies this nonconformist approach, where at first glance it seems that the large bright peony blossom is exploding from the left side of the paper. Were it not for the strong diagonal of the stem and the leaves bringing our eye back to the bottom right-hand corner, the addition of a darker pink blossom partially hidden on the right, and the deep shadows spreading across the bottom, we would be looking at whatever was to the left of the blossom rather than at the painting. As it is, with just the barest of balancing acts Raffael keeps us within his work.

◄ 5.9 George
Herriman,
"Krazy Kat"
strip, January
17, 1937
How has Herriman
used colors to
achieve visual
balance in this
cartoon strip?

▲ **5.10 Jacob van Hulsdonck (1582–1647), *Plums and Peaches*, early 17th century**
Oil on copper, 11¼ × 13¾ ins (28.5 × 35 cm).
Private collection.
Compare the total areas covered by "warm" and "cool" colors in this composition. Do you think they are intentionally balanced against each other?

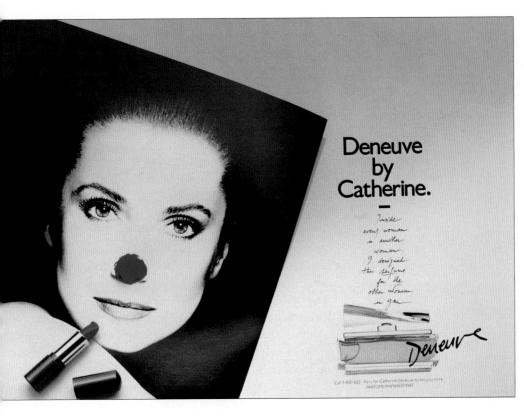

◀ **5.12 Advertisement for Deneuve perfume by Parfums Stern and Bloomingdale's**
The surprise and visual contrast of the red nose catches our attention; the yellow of the perfume is also accentuated by contrast.

Emphasis

A stronger consideration for many artists is the desire to emphasize certain areas of a work, drawing them immediately to the viewer's attention. This objective is particularly crucial in advertising art, for the viewer's attention must initially be seized and then guided in such a way that the product name and image will be noticed, despite all the visual distractions of modern life. One strategy involves visual understatement of everything surrounding the product so that it will stand out better, by contrast. In the two-page advertisement for Catherine Deneuve's perfume (**5.12**), everything on the right-hand page is neutral grays and black except for the elegantly sensual bottle of perfume. It is yellow and consequently appears extremely luscious and

desirable in contrast with the neutrality of its setting. The real attention grabber is on the left-hand page of the spread: the lipstick-colored red nose on Deneuve's beautiful but grayed face. The red captures our attention and immediately makes us wonder why. To find out, we must slow down enough to read the handwritten message on the right-hand page: "Inside every woman is another woman. I designed this perfume for the other woman in you." As we finish reading the message, we are back at the perfume bottle and the product name.

Sometimes a whole work calls attention to itself by contrast with its surroundings. Brightly colored sculptures stand out vigorously in dull-colored urban environments. When an artist uses an **open palette**—that is, choosing hues from all parts of the color wheel—at high saturation, as Milton Glaser did in his Aretha poster (5.6), we cannot help but notice the work. However, when an open palette is used with hues at very high or low values, rather than at maximum saturation, the effect will be much quieter, much subtler.

◀ **5.11 Joseph Raffael, *Spring*, 2003**
Watercolor on paper, 45 × 63 ins (114.3 × 160 cm).
Nancy Hoffman Gallery, New York, United States.
Joseph Raffael uses elements of imbalance to activate the space within this watercolor, creating a visual tension that keeps our eyes moving back and forth across the entire work.

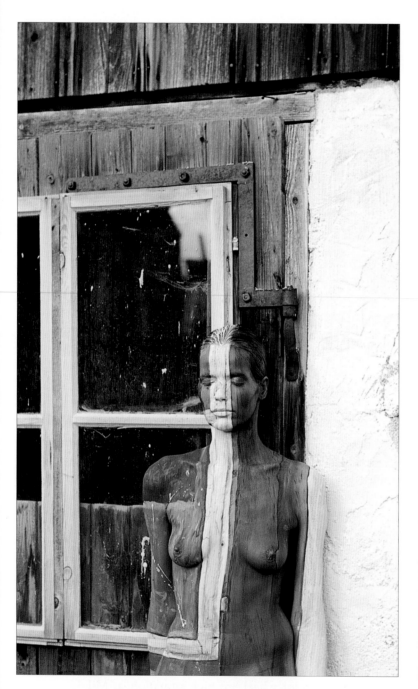

▲ **5.13 Vera Lehndorff and Holger Trulzsch,**
***Wooden Door with Window* (detail), 1975**
Cibachrome photograph, 19½ × 19½ ins (49.5 × 49.5 cm).
With a limited palette, there may be variations in value but
little variety in hue. Vera's natural coloring has been painted
to match the limited palette of her surroundings.

Unity

There are many principles of design that can subtly unify a
work of art. Use of color to unify a composition often
revolves around repetition of a certain color theme. One
possibility is a very **limited palette**. The artist chooses only
a few non-contrasting hues, perhaps combined with neutral
whites, browns, grays, or black. The result is usually coherent
because nothing pulls away from the central colors. A surprising use of a limited palette is *Wooden Door with Window*
by Vera Lehndorff and Holger Trulzsch (**5.13**). Vera has been
painted to look like a continuation of the door, in browns,
whites, and blues that largely eliminate her natural skin
tones. Where the transformation is successful, she almost
blends optically with the building. We can hardly distinguish
her arm against the white plaster, for there is very little contrast in value and hue between the two. Edges of shapes and
forms become soft and nebulous when there is little color
contrast between them, whereas edges of highly contrasting
hues, as in the Aretha poster (5.6), are "hard," or sharply
defined.

It is also possible to repeat colors throughout a composition when a more open palette is used. One way of doing so
is actual repetition of the same color note throughout the

▲ **5.14 Ben Vautier, *Ben's Store*, 1958–73**
Installation. Musée National d'Art Moderne, Paris.
In this mad collection of found objects, statements about art
and life, and references to the artist himself (e.g. "Ben is a
genius"), does the repetition of a few main colors help to bring
unity to the chaos?

composition. In the cacophony of Ben Vautier's installation, *Ben's Store* (**5.14**), red pops out again and again, with black as a persistent foil. Another approach is to mix a little of a single main color into everything else, giving that color a subtle prominence in the work, such as the yellow ocher light that plays across Salvador Dalí's *The Christ of St.-Jean-de-la-Croix* (**5.15**). Another painterly method is to allow the color of a single undertone to show through and thus influence all areas of the work.

Although unity is a traditional objective in art, many contemporary artists have departed from tradition to create works that do not look or feel unified. Even Gene Davis, whose paintings are clearly unified by the repetition of color stripes (5.5), muses:

> One of the things that really interests me a great deal is the idea of shattering the unity of a work of art. In other words, who says a work of art must have unity? Why not something that's fragmentary? … Fragments are often very interesting. … When is a work finished? … Oftentimes when a work is just a fragment, it's better than it is when it's finished.[4]

This iconoclastic, intuitive approach is a counterpoint to heavily theoretical, intellectual approaches to color theory, which are explored in some detail in the next chapter.

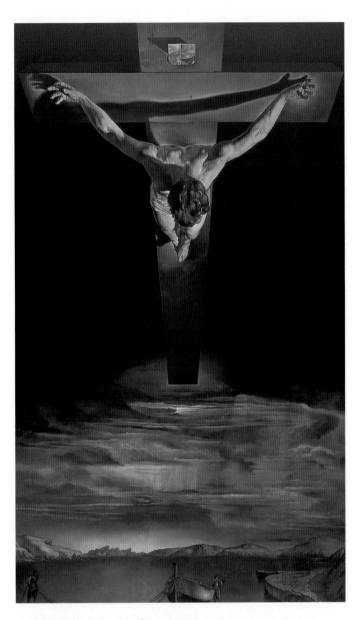

▲ **5.15 Salvador Dalí,** *The Christ of St.-Jean-de-la-Croix*, **1951**
Oil on canvas, 80 × 45½ ins (205 × 116 cm).
Glasgow Art Gallery and Museum.
Where does the light in this painting seem to come from, and with what color does it seem to bathe everything?

6 Theories of Color Relationships

Color is the final art, which is, and will always remain, a mystery.

PHILIPP OTTO RUNGE

IN order to work with colored lights and particularly with colored pigments, artists have long sought a framework for understanding the great variations among colors—how desired colors can be mixed from materials at hand and how these mixtures relate to each other visually. Specifics of color mixing are covered in the next two chapters. In this chapter we look at a number of attempts to devise a systematic framework for explaining the similarities and differences among colors.

Few artists have ever worked exclusively from a single color model. Each of the color theorists discussed in this chapter has contributed useful observations about optical color phenomena and relationships among colors. Color is such a mysterious phenomenon that even opposing theories may each be correct, to a certain extent.

Early Theories

The ancient Hindu *Upanishads*, the early Greek philosophers and physicians, and the Arab physicist Alhazen all developed theories about color vision—what colors are and how we see them—to help explain the world around them. Aristotle's ideas drew particular attention. He explained similarities among colors by "the common origin of nearly all colors in blends of different strengths of sunlight and firelight, and of air and water" and recognized that "darkness is due to privation of light." To Aristotle, all variations were the result of mixtures of darkness and light. Crimson, for example, was a combination of a certain amount of blackness with firelight or sunlight.

For many centuries after Aristotle, colors were explained according to his theories. The reds seen at sunrise and sunset were thought to result from the mixture of white sunlight with the darkness of night that was just departing or approaching; the red seen in fire was a mixture of the white light of the fire and the darkness of the smoke. Green was more shadow than light, and blue was more shadow still. These ideas followed Aristotle's procedure: "Verifications from experience and observation of similarities are necessary," he wrote in his *De Coloribus*, "if we are to arrive at clear conclusions about the origin of different colors."[1]

Leonardo da Vinci

Ever curious, always combining his dual passions for science and art, the great Renaissance artist Leonardo da Vinci (1452–1519) included color theorizing in his explorations. Although earlier philosophers had not treated white and black as colors, Leonardo included them among the "simple" colors that are the artist's basic tools: white, yellow, green, blue, red, and black. He observed the phenomenon later known as **simultaneous contrast**, which demonstrated that complementary hues intensify each other if juxtaposed:

> *Of different colors equally perfect, that will appear most excellent which is seen near its direct contrary: a pale color against red; a black upon white; ... blue near a yellow; green near red: because each color is more distinctly seen when opposed to its contrary, than to any other similar to it.*[2]

In his *Virgin and Child with St. Anne* (**6.1**) Leonardo used the yellow flesh tones of the figures to intensify the reds and blues of their clothing. He created a much-needed mid-distance between the figures and the mountains by the placement of the tree in the upper right-hand corner, its dark shape in complete contrast with the pale landscape beyond, which pushes the mountains even further into the distance.

In the compilation of Leonardo's notes, published posthumously in 1651 as the *Treatise on Painting*, he devoted considerable attention to his observations on blueness in the atmosphere. He concluded that we only see this blue by contrast with black:

> *I say that the blueness we see in the atmosphere is not intrinsic color, but is caused by warm vapour evaporated in minute insensible atoms on which the solar rays fall, rendering them luminous against the infinite darkness of the fiery sphere which lies beyond and includes it.... As an illustration of the color of the atmosphere I will mention the smoke of old and dry wood, which, as it comes out of a chimney, appears to turn very blue, when seen between the eye and the dark distance. But as it rises, and comes between the eye and the bright atmosphere, it at once shows of an ashy gray color; and this happens because it no longer has darkness beyond it, but this bright and luminous space. ... Colors will appear what they are not, according to the ground which surrounds them.[3]*

In addition to carefully noting the optical effects of color combinations, Leonardo also described atmospheric perspective and shadow effects in considerable detail. He used his observations of color to improve his own paintings, developing to a fine art the subtly graded values and hues of chiaroscuro modeling and the softly blended, smoky quality known as **sfumato**, hauntingly represented in the hands, face, and hazy background landscape of his famous *Mona Lisa* (5.7).

Newton

In contrast to Leonardo's careful observations of color phenomena in real-life situations, the British physicist Sir Isaac Newton (1642–1727) turned color theory into a laboratory study of the properties of light, in an attempt to derive some systematic, logical framework for understanding color. As we noted in Chapter 2, Newton demonstrated that all the spectral hues are present in white light. He made

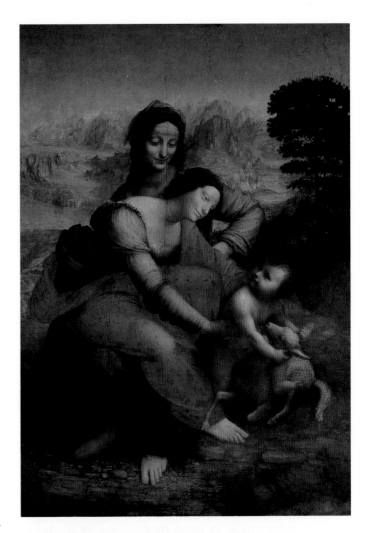

▲ **6.1 Leonardo da Vinci, *Virgin and Child with St. Anne*, 1508–10**
Panel, 5 ft 6⅛ ins × 4 ft 3¼ ins (1.68 × 1.3 m).
Musée du Louvre, Paris.
Leonardo's well-thought-out color theories of simultaneous contrast, chiaroscuro, sfumato, and aerial perspective are all evident in this painting.

from them the first color circle representing color relationships (2.4). The segments of his circle stood for the seven hues he distinguished in the spectrum (although the choice of seven seems to have been mystically based on the seven Musical Tones and the seven Heavenly Spheres). He called these "primary colors," and noted their "best" aspect falling on the circumference of the wheel midway between the lines dividing the hues. Newton did not present his model in color, but he envisioned that hues would be most "intense and florid" on the circumference, becoming gradually "diluted" with whiteness as they approached the center. The center of his color circle was white, the mixtures of all hues in light. Newton noted that if only two hues lying opposite each other on the wheel were mixed, the result would not be white but "some faint anonymous Color." He suggested the possibility of producing white by mixing three light primaries but was unsuccessful in his experiments:

> *I could never yet by mixing only two primary Colors produce a perfect white. Whether it may be compounded of a mixture of three taken at equal distances in the circumference I do not know, but of four or five I do not much question but it may. But these are Curiosities of little or no moment to the understanding of the Phaenomena of Nature.*[4]

Harris

Working with pigments rather than lights, an English entomologist and engraver named Moses Harris developed the first model of pigment primaries. Following the discovery by a French printer, J. C. Le Blon, in 1731, that all hues could be reduced to mixtures of red, yellow, and blue pigments, Harris created a beautiful illustration of the theory. In his *Natural System of Colors* (c. 1766), a highly influential though extremely rare volume, he offered a detailed color circle in hand-tinted color (**6.2**). In its center are the three pigment primaries, which he called "primitives"—red, blue, and yellow—from which all other colors could theoretically be mixed. From them he derived the secondary or "compound" hues: orange, purple, and green. Mixtures of primitives and compounds yielded two intermediate stages, in which the hue less represented in the mixture was named first ("orange-red," for instance, is more red than orange). The eighteen colors so derived were then graded into **shades** (darker values—cleverly created here by optical mixing with ever more closely placed black lines) and **tints** (lighter values, commonly created by adding white to a color or thinning the medium to allow the white of the support to show through, but here developed by wider spacing between the black lines).

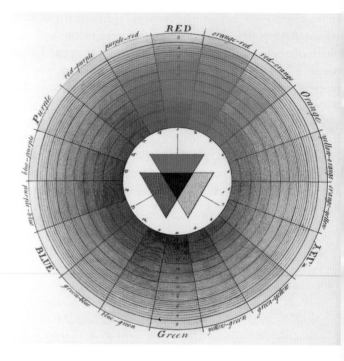

▲ **6.2 Moses Harris, Color circle from *The Natural System of Colors*, c. 1766**
Royal Academy of Arts, London.
From an initial set of three primaries, Harris derived a color circle with 18 hues, shaded with black as they approached the center.

Goethe

Johann Wolfgang von Goethe (1749–1832), the great German poet, thought his color theory would be of greater historical importance than his poetry. In 1810 he published his book *Zur Farbenlehre*, or *Theory of Colors*. In it he vigorously attacked Newton's theories of the physics of light, which were still controversial, and returned to the observational tradition of Aristotle and Leonardo. Contrary to Newton, Goethe concentrated on color as a visual phenomenon happening in the eye, rather than as an aspect of light. "The waking eye reveals itself as a living organism," he wrote. "The eye is not capable of remaining—cannot bear to remain—for even a moment in a state which is determined by the object looked at." It was Goethe who gave us extremely detailed descriptions of visual phenomena that are still of interest to artists, such as colored shadows, simultaneous contrast, and successive contrast.

With reference to colored shadows, Goethe observed that

strong midday sunlight produces a black or gray shadow on white—or a darker value of the surface—but that under other conditions, shadows will be the hue complementary to the hue of the light. These other necessary conditions were that the light be of some hue other than white and that the shadow be somewhat illuminated by a secondary light source. The stronger the colored light, the paler the shadow; thus the most brilliant-colored shadows result from the palest-colored lights. Roger Crossgrove's photographic study of colored shadows (**6.3**) employs a bank of red, green, blue, and yellow lights with rheostats for dimming the lights to increase the saturation of the shadows. Where the shadows overlap, you can see secondary mixtures, such as orange and purple.

Although Goethe gives instructions for producing colored shadows experimentally, he also describes their natural occurrence in scenes like the following, which took place in snow- and frost-covered mountainous terrain:

During the day, owing to the yellowish hue of the snow, shadows tending to violet had already been observable; these might now [at approaching sunset] be pronounced to be decidedly blue, as the illumined parts exhibited a yellow deepening to orange. … But as the sun at last was about to set, and its rays, greatly mitigated by the thicker vapors, began to diffuse a most beautiful red color over the whole scene around me, the shadow color changed to a green, in lightness to be compared to a sea-green, in beauty to the green of the emerald. The appearance became more and more vivid: one might have imagined oneself in a fairy world, for every object had clothed itself in the two vivid and so beautifully harmonizing colors, till at last, as the sun went down, the magnificent spectacle was lost in a gray twilight, and by degrees in a clear moon-and-starlight night.[5]

The Impressionists and Postimpressionists acknowledged these observations, adding color shadows to the bright hues of some of their work, as in Monet's paintings of Rouen Cathedral (3.13 and 3.14) and Van Gogh's *Still-Life with Drawing Board and Onions* (**6.4**). Here the shadows of plate and book are indigo, rather than simply a darker yellow as one might expect, and reflection off the gold borders of the book creates a secondary shadow of the complementary purple.

Goethe also described complex color sensations such as the "catotropical" colors seen when colorless light strikes a colorless surface, such as a spider's web or mother-of-pearl, and the colors seen in haloes around the moon. He suggested two models for relationships between colors. One was a circle with lines linking complementary hues super-

▲ **6.3 Roger Crossgrove, *Study in Colored Shadows*, 1987**
Photograph.
The cast shadows seen here are the complementaries of the lights used to make them, true to Goethe's observations.

imposed on two triangles delineating primary and secondary triads (**6.5**). The second was a triangle (**6.6**) with red, blue, and yellow at its outermost points and the secondaries green, orange, and purple in the middle. Dividing primaries and secondaries were further triangles denoting the less saturated, lower-value tertiaries that would theoretically result from mixing two secondaries with the adjacent primary.

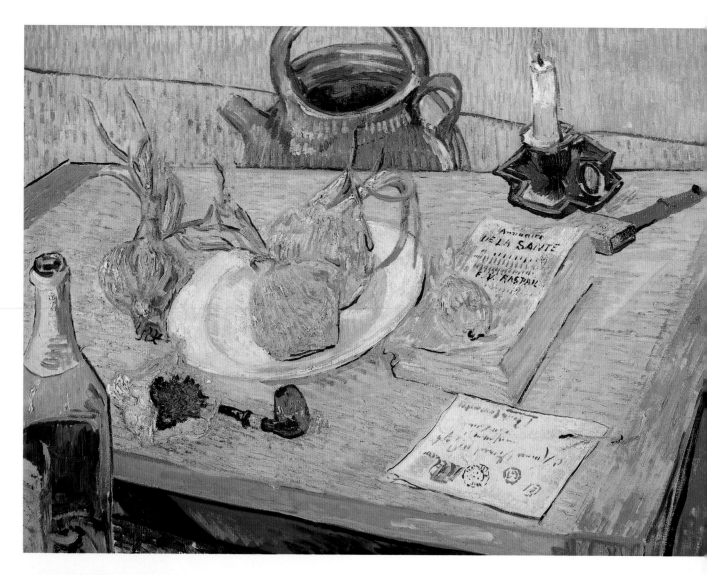

▲ **6.4 Vincent van Gogh,**
Still-Life with Drawing
Board and Onions, 1889
Oil on canvas, 19½ × 25¼ ins
(45 × 64 cm).
State Museum Kröller-Müller,
Otterlo, The Netherlands.
Van Gogh's use of brilliant
colors included color
shadows in this painting,
following Goethe's
observations that a colored
light will create shadows in its
complementary color.

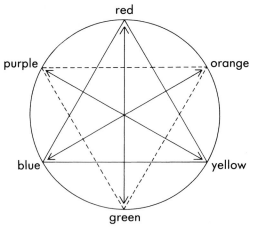

◀ **6.5 Goethe's color**
circle
Triangles join the triads of
primaries and secondaries
and, in this reconstruction,
arrows link complementary
hues.

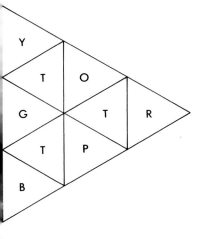

◀ 6.6 Goethe's color triangle

Goethe offered an alternative model in which the primaries red, blue, and yellow were the corners of a triangle, secondaries the sides, and tertiaries ("T") the mixtures of the three surrounding colors. The tertiaries were therefore probably of low saturation, but we do not have an actual colored sample of what Goethe envisioned.

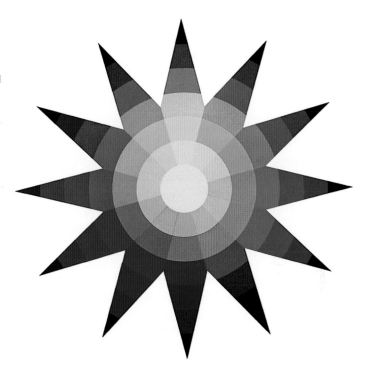

▲ 6.8 Johannes Itten, Runge's color sphere presented as a star

In Itten's version of Runge's model, certain color relationships—such as complementarity, value gradations, and close harmonies (analogous colors)—can readily be seen.

▲ 6.7 Philipp Otto Runge, Color sphere from *Die Farbenkugel*, Hamburg, 1810

Collection Faber Birren.

Runge presented his pioneering model of a color sphere from various angles to show its three-dimensional relationships.

Runge

The same year that Goethe published his *Zur Farbenlehre*, the German painter Philipp Otto Runge (1777–1810) published *Die Farbenkugel* (*The Color Sphere*)—the first attempt at a three-dimensional model of color. Runge presented color relationships as a sphere (**6.7**). Pure hues were displayed around its equator. Through the central axis was a gray value scale, from black at the bottom to white at the top. Across the surface of the sphere, the colors were graded from black to the pure hue to white, in seven steps. Intermediate mixtures theoretically lay inside the sphere.

One hundred and fifty years later, Johannes Itten, a great German teacher of the art of color, adopted and adjusted the same model, considering it "the most convenient for plotting the characteristic and manifold properties of the color universe."[6] Itten displayed the outer surface of the whole sphere at once by opening it into a twelve-pointed star, with the white top as its center (**6.8**).

Chevreul

Interest in codifying and understanding color relationships was so strong in the early nineteenth century that another major contribution soon appeared: *The Principles of Harmony and Contrast of Colors* by Michel Eugène Chevreul, a renowned chemist and director of the dye house for Gobelins tapestries in Paris. Chevreul (1786–1889) developed a finely graded two-dimensional color circle. His work with liquid dyes verified the usefulness of red, yellow, and blue as primaries and orange, green, and violet as secondaries. His greater contribution to the art of color, however, was his elucidation of the laws governing the visual effects of colors upon each other: simultaneous contrast, successive contrast, and optical color mixtures. From these he derived certain suggestions about how colors should best be used: the principles of harmony.

Chevreul noted that colors with little contrast, such as hues adjacent to each other on a color circle (**analogous hues**), will tend to blend optically. Highly contrasting colors (such as complementary colors lying opposite each other on the color circle) used in sufficiently large quantities will make each other appear more brilliant, without any optical change in their hue. If small areas of opposite colors are presented together, on the other hand, they will tend to blend visually and thereby create a duller overall color sensation, "want of vigor," as he wrote. These effects, to be explored in Chapter 9, led Chevreul to recommend that highly contrasting colors be used in large juxtaposed areas, whereas analogous colors should best be used in small, diffused amounts. He stated: "The contrast of the most opposite colors is most agreeable. … The complementary assortment is superior to every other."[7] When using analogous hues, Chevreul asserted that combinations worked best when the key hue was a primary.

Chevreul's book is full of such prescriptions. While they were of great interest to many painters of the times, such as the Impressionists and Postimpressionists, few consciously followed his recommendations for proper color harmonies. Monet rejected his theories; Pissarro read Chevreul's work but claimed there was no intellectual basis for what he was trying to do in his paintings. Georges Seurat, however (9.27), attempted to apply the laws of color theory precisely to the craft of painting. In doing so he relied not only on Chevreul but also on his successor, Ogden Rood.

Rood

Trained as an artist as well as a scientist, the American Ogden Rood (1831–1902) performed extensive research into the optics of color, declaring it to be "a sensation existing merely in ourselves" rather than an absolute fact of the physical world. He identified the three major variables that determine the differences between colors as purity (saturation), luminosity (value), and hue. Through painstaking experiments with spinning disks and other equipment, he demonstrated that pigment hues can be mixed optically to form the sort of luminous mixtures one would get when mixing lights.

Such optical mixtures would be blended by the eye if lines of color or "a quantity of small dots of two colors very near each other" were viewed from a certain distance. "For instance," he wrote in his 1879 classic, *Modern Chromatics*,

> *lines of cobalt-blue and chrome-yellow give a white or yellowish-white, but no trace of green; emerald-green and vermilion furnish when treated in this way a dull yellow; ultramarine and vermilion, a rich red-purple, etc. This method is almost the only practical one at the disposal of the artist whereby he can actually mix, not pigments, but masses of colored light.*[8]

Rood felt that it was important for artists to know exactly which colors were directly complementary to each other, so that they

> *are made to glow with more than their natural brilliancy. Then they strike us as precious and delicious, and this is true even when the actual tints are such as we would call poor or dull in isolation. From this it follows that paintings, made up almost entirely of tints that by themselves seem modest and far from brilliant, often strike us as being rich and gorgeous in color, while, on the other hand, the most gaudy colors can easily be arranged so as to produce a depressing effect on the beholder.*[9]

From his experiments, Rood developed the circle of contrasting colors shown in Figure **6.9**.

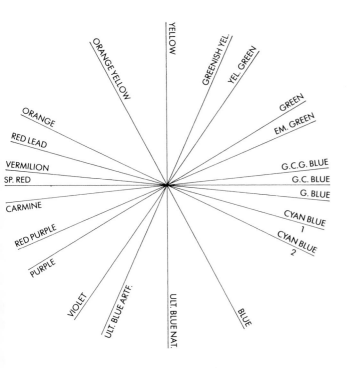

The circle is labeled with the following hues around its circumference:

YELLOW, GREENISH YEL., YEL. GREEN, GREEN, EM. GREEN, G.C.G. BLUE, G.C. BLUE, G. BLUE, CYAN BLUE 1, CYAN BLUE 2, BLUE, ULT. BLUE NAT., ULT. BLUE ARTF., VIOLET, PURPLE, RED PURPLE, CARMINE, SP. RED, VERMILION, RED LEAD, ORANGE, ORANGE YELLOW

▲ **6.9 Ogden Rood, Circle of complementaries from** ***Modern Chromatics*, 1879**
Rood's experiments with optical color-mixing contraptions enabled him to develop this precise matching of complementary hues.

Rood's work has been highly influential among artists, beginning with **Pointillist** techniques of optical blending. Yet he himself deplored the ways his theories were used, considering the results most unattractive. His son, an enthusiastic student of the Impressionists, described Rood's reaction to an exhibition of their paintings:

"… by a lot of Frenchmen who call themselves 'Impressionist,' some are by a fellow called Monet, others by a fellow called Pissarro, and a lot of others."

"What do you think of them?" I ventured.

"Awful! Awful!" he gasped.

Then I told him what these painters said of his theories.

This was too much for his composure. He threw up his hands in horror and indignation, and cried—

"If that is all I have done for art, I wish I had never written that book!"[10]

Munsell

For all his painstaking experiments, Rood himself was unable to devise a "scientifically accurate color-system," as he admitted to Albert Munsell. Working with reference to Rood's experiments to devise a system simple enough for school-children to understand, Munsell himself developed the standards for color notation still used as the basis for pigment specifications in the United States, Great Britain, Germany, and Japan. These were first published in 1905 in his book *Color Notation*.

Munsell used three dimensions for describing color variations: hue, value, and chroma (saturation), each graded in equal steps, as measured by a photometer. These dimensions form an irregular three-dimensional "tree" (see Figures 2.13 and 2.15) rather than the perfect sphere proposed by earlier theorists, for the hues reach maximum saturation at different steps of value and also vary in the number of steps from neutral gray to maximum saturation (**6.10**). Munsell gave each step in each direction a distinctive number reflecting the three dimensions: vertical (value), horizontal (saturation), and around-the-circumference (hue). His numbers replaced the imprecise vocabulary of popular color names, such as "hellish blue" and "celestial blue." As we noted in Chapter 2, Munsell departed from tradition by using five primary hues—red, yellow, blue, green, and purple—instead of three, thus placing rather different hues opposite each other as complementaries. Whereas Rood had emphasized the truth of visual sensations, without being able to derive a mathematically logical system from his observations of color realities, Munsell sought an objective standard for precise pigment specifications.

Ostwald

Another early twentieth-century color theorist, the German scientist Wilhelm Ostwald (1853–1932), won the Nobel Prize in 1909 for his work in chemistry, and his color model bears the stamp of a highly scientific mind. To quantify color variations, Ostwald based them on mathematical steps from black to white, in geometric rather than arithmetical progression, and on an analysis of the light apparently reflected or absorbed by a surface. Arithmetical progression, in increments of one—1, 2, 3, 4, 5, 6, and so on—does not give the

PLATE I.

Y

R

B

G

P

Light Values

Middle Values

Dark Values

P   B   G   Y   R

Y

G

R

B

P

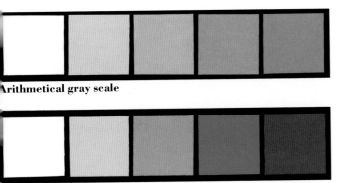

Arithmetical gray scale

Geometric gray scale

◀ **6.11** Following the work of Gustave Fechner, Ostwald made use of the visual fact that to achieve optically equal steps in value gradation, one must use geometrically rather than arithmetically changing pigment percentages.

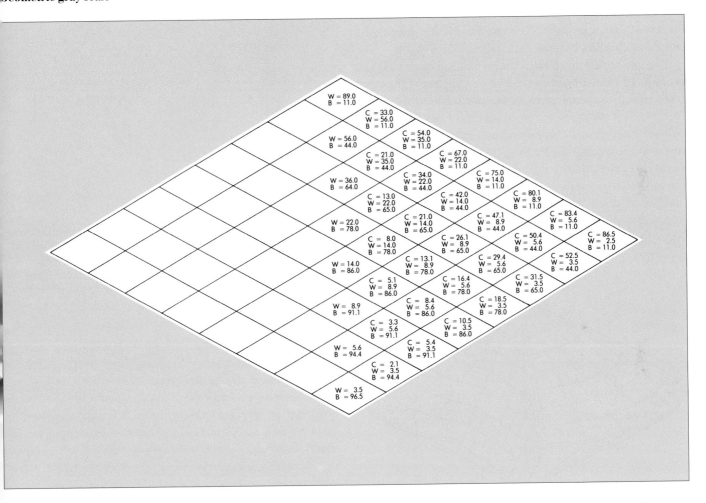

▲ **6.12 A generic slice through the Ostwald solid**
Ostwald's notation gives the mathematical percentages of "pure color" (C), white (W), and black (B) used as a basis for his model.

visual appearance of equal distance between steps. This effect is obtained instead by increasing the value geometrically—1, 2, 4, 8, 16, and so on. Both are illustrated in Figure **6.11**.

Ostwald's system of color specification was portrayed as a three-dimensional series of triangular cross-sections. White formed the upper pole or top of the triangles, black the

◀ 6.10 Albert Munsell, Diagram of equal steps to maximum saturation

Munsell noted that different hues reach maximum saturation at different steps of value, and that they also differ in the number of equal steps from neutral gray to maximum saturation.

lower pole, and 24 pure hues circled the equator (**6.13**). To create the 12 double triangular charts from which the solid is constructed, Ostwald mixed the fully saturated hues with measured amounts of black and white and gave each sample a notation with percentages of color (C), white (W), and black (B) (**6.12**). Moving diagonally toward white from the equator, the amount of black is held constant as white increasingly takes the place of the original hue, which Ostwald called the "full color." This process is called **tinting**. The opposite process, called **shading**, adds black and decreases the full color while white is held constant. Moving directly toward the center is called toning; here both white and black increase while the full color is decreased, thus graying it. Colorist Faber Birren devised a simplified diagram to show these relationships (**6.14**).

Ostwald's addition of black and white is a quite different procedure from Munsell's system of graying hues by mixing them with their complement. In practice, different white pigments vary in tinting power, so no standard Ostwald chart can be used with accuracy unless one uses exactly the same pigments as those used in preparing the chart. Moreover, some artists have rejected Ostwald's model as being too scientific to use in the actual creation of art or to represent the dynamic realities of color. The colorist Adolf Holzel was strongly opposed to the limitations of trying to make all color differences fit into variations of black and white content. Holzel

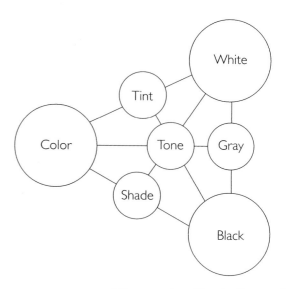

▲ **6.14 Faber Birren's Color Triangle**
Like Ostwald, the color theorist Faber Birren did not analyze colors in terms of hue, value, and saturation. Rather, as in this simplified diagram, he claimed that "there are only seven forms in the world of color—pure hue (red, yellow, etc.), white, black, gray, tint, shade, tone. … All colors seen in the world will find classification on this chart."[11]

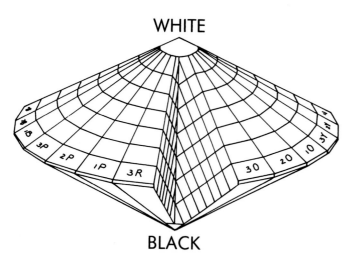

WHITE

BLACK

▲ **6.13 Wilhelm Ostwald, Color solid from** *Color Science*, **1931**
Ostwald's double pyramid model is based on a series of double triangles in which pure hues form the equator, and black and white the poles. Within this framework, mixed colors are derived in quite a different manner than in Munsell's model.

himself held that colors contrasted with each other in seven ways: hue, saturation, area, value, complementarity, warmth and coolness, and simultaneous contrast. The artist Paul Klee was particularly disturbed by what he considered Ostwald's "negative reaction to color."[12] Nevertheless, Ostwald's symmetrical system well suited certain rational approaches to art, such as the Bauhaus attempt to merge technology with the arts and crafts.

Ostwald originally provided for 30,000 graded colors, but upon recognizing that the distinctions between one and the next were so slight that he thought people could barely distinguish them, he devised an abridged version of his color model with 680 "psychologically equidistant" colors, which he thought would be sufficient for most artists. His system has been useful in grading colors for printing processes, one of the subtractive methods of color mixing explored in Chapter 8.

7 Color, Light, and Computers

● ● ● ●

People were being quite emotionally overcome [by her virtual reality installation] but I don't really have anybody's response because none of them could talk.

CHAR DAVIES

OUR sun is the source of all the colors we see on our planet. Overly generous with its radiant energy, it offers us an entire electromagnetic spectrum: microwaves, radio waves, radar, television, X-rays, ultraviolet light, and infrared light. Only a very small percentage of the total solar spectrum is devoted to our most precious commodity: visible light (see 2.3). Yet within visible light, we continue to be astounded with its offerings.

Peter Erskine decided to celebrate this fact for the millennium in Rome. He placed laser-cut, heliostat-oriented prisms among the ancient Roman ruins to follow the sun's beams as they played across the surfaces, refracting them into ever-changing patterns of brilliant colors (**7.1**).

Even artificially created lights have in the past not been widely used as art media, although they have been extensively studied by scientists. Now, however, technology is redefining how we use our luminous palette. Installation artists use the lights of neon and lasers for their artwork; holograms extend the color range of two-dimensional work. Video art, film, and animation are sharing techniques; the music world joined with the film industry to bring us music videos, and video artists are utilizing all these techniques. Even camera cell phones are changing the way people think about photographs, as the slightly blurred

▶ **7.1 Peter Erskine, *New Light on Rome*, 2000**
Laser-cut prism installation in the cryptoporticus of the Domus Transitoria of Nero. The cryptoporticus was a cool underground walkway, lit by natural light through slots which Peter Erskine strategically appropriated for prismatic displays of spectral colors.

images taken quickly can become a "living in the moment" journal. Computers have expanded their capabilities with Digital Video Discs (DVDs) and Compact Discs (CDs), showcasing a wide variety of artistic talents involving movement and sound. With tools such as MP3s,[1] which compress musical files for storage, a computer has a full range of musical sound as well as color images. The uses of color, combined with technology, are endless in variety and the discoveries are ongoing.

Transmitting Color Electronically

The term video is used both for electronic light signals broadcast to television sets and for images displayed on television monitors directly from videotapes, CDs, or DVDs. These visual images are usually recorded electronically by video or digital cameras, which scan a scene to analyze and communicate its light patterns. The light received in the camera is divided by a system of mirrors into the three light primaries—red, blue, and green. For transmission, these are then converted into two signals indicating **chrominance** or **chromaticity** (a combination of **dominant wavelength**, or hue, and **purity**, or saturation) and **luminance** (the light-mixture equivalent of value in pigments).

This information is broadcast through the air or fed electronically to a receiving monitor, which decodes the video signals corresponding to the light primaries. These are sent through electron guns, usually one for each primary. Each sends beams to the screen of the picture tube, the inside of which is coated with hundreds of thousands of tiny dots of red, green, and blue fluorescing powders, called phosphors. When hit by electron beams, they give off a certain amount of light, depending on the luminance signal. In many television sets, a **shadow mask**—a metal plate with thousands of small holes—is used to keep the electron beams focused only on one triad of phosphors at a time, preventing them from spilling over into other areas (**7.2**). The electron guns rapidly scan all the phosphors, traveling along horizontal lines, and thus rebuild the image on the entire screen just as it was when originally scanned by the video camera. This process occurs 30 times a second in a standard screen in the United States, which is composed of 525 scanning lines. The European system uses 625 lines, scanned 25 times a second. The persistence of our vision keeps the image from appearing to flicker.

▲ **7.2 Phosphors and electron beams in a color television tube**
The upper picture is a considerably enlarged diagram of the mosaic of red, green, and blue phosphors on the screen of a television set built on the shadow-mask system. Below is an enlarged diagram of the shadow mask, showing its use to focus the electron beams on one triad of phosphors at a time during the scanning process.

Red, blue, and green are used as primaries in video transmission because they can produce the widest range of mixtures. It comes as a great surprise to many people that there is no yellow in a television tube. The yellow that we "see" on a television screen or monitor is actually an optical mixture of tiny dots of green and red. Green and blue juxtaposed in space or flashed quickly one after the other will produce a cyan sensation; red and blue juxtaposed in time or space will appear magenta. Black areas have no light coming through; white areas are a mixture of all three primaries. Luminance (value) differences are controlled by the amount of light and 8.7) to illustrate the parameters of modern computer graphics color capabilities. Chromaticity coordinates for the red, blue, and green primaries in a standard computer monitor form a triangle that is much smaller than the flat-iron shape formed by the whole range of spectral colors. The purest spectral colors fall along the outer edge of this shape, with saturation decreasing gradually into the central point of equal energy (E), where x and $y = 0.333$. This point represents neutral colors, from black to white, with their value depending upon the degree of luminance, which is not shown in this two-dimensional diagram.

The primaries do not reach the corners of the flat iron because the phosphors are not as pure as spectral hues. Moreover, nothing outside the triangle can be mixed using the three primaries. Along each edge, hues are pure mixtures of the two connected primaries; within the triangle, all three primaries are involved to some extent in the mixture, until finally they all mix to a neutral in the center. The only way to mix a color outside the triangle is to have negative hues available as mixers—such as a minus blue which would subtract enough blue from the green and red to produce a pure yellow.

These limitations are actually not apparent to the average eye, which finds the outer limits of computer graphics colors brighter and more saturated than any pigment colors, as indeed they are. Furthermore, computer graphics programs for color mixing are becoming increasingly sophisticated and are now able to create very fine gradations of hue, value, and saturation.

Choosing and Using Color on the Monitor

Popular desktop graphics systems offer two simple ways of creating over 16 million colors, far more than the eye can actually distinguish. Firstly, the user can hold a "dialogue" with a color map, such as a wheel divided into hues with concentric circles showing gradations in saturation. Using a "mouse" to position a pointer on the screen, the computer artist can point to a place on the wheel and it will be displayed in a box. Placing the pointer close to yellow in the red area, for example, will bring up an orange. Slight movement of the pointer will make the color chosen more red or more yellow. The brightness (value) of the whole wheel can be changed by another maneuver.

▲ **7.3 Chromaticity coordinates of the red, blue, and green primaries on the standard computer graphics monitor**
Printing inks can reproduce only a comparatively small portion of the visual spectrum. Color film can reproduce a larger range than a television or computer monitor.

released. The saturation and balance of colors between the three primaries can be controlled to the viewer's taste by adjusting controls on the monitor. Computer graphics use monitors that are essentially the same as television screens. They use the same red, blue, green primary system of phosphor activation, though they are capable of slightly higher saturation. Video and computer graphics have within their range a greater degree of saturation in colors than is possible with any subtractive medium, for they are based on the purity of colored lights. However, phosphors are not as pure as they theoretically might be, and the trichromatic mixing system means certain mixtures are not possible.

Figure **7.3** uses the C.I.E. chromaticity chart (see p. 94

◄ **7.4** The Photoshop program offers several different ways of selecting and changing colors in an image on the computer monitor.

The second way of choosing a color is numerical, by specifying saturation and brightness on a scale of 0 to 65,535 for each of the primary hues. The box showing the first color chosen may have a split screen; to change it slightly, one could choose a slightly different number to see the result, whose color is displayed next to the first color on the split screen. The ease of color mixing with such a system makes color relationships fascinating and fun to manipulate.

Adobe Photoshop, a popular graphics program, presents a display on the monitor with a variety of ways of selecting a specific color. As shown in Figure **7.4**, the computer artist can move a small circle through a field of variations on a hue to select the one desired, or move arrows along a linear display, or type in the subtractive CMYK or additive RGB or **HSB** (hue, saturation, brightness) numeric values of the color. Once the hue is chosen, the numeric CMYK notation calculated by the computer can be used in specifying printing inks.

In addition to using on-screen color-choosing devices, those with engineering training can program color mixtures numerically. Colorist Nathaniel Jacobson and computer specialist Walter Bender of the MIT Media Lab have collaborated to try to create computer color maps based on the Munsell system of color classification. The colors shown in

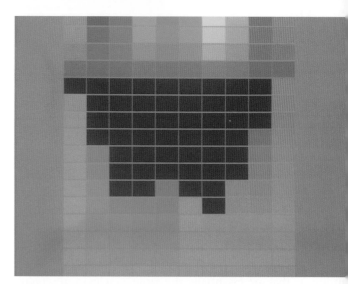

▲ **7.5 Nathaniel Jacobson and Walter Bender, MIT Media Lab computer graphics color map**

this custom computer palette (**7.5**) are deliberately muted to approximate the softness of pigments rather than the glare of phosphors; none are shown at the maximum saturation possible for the monitor. In addition, they are programmed to vary in visually equal steps, as in the Munsell system. One might think this would be easy on the computer, but it is, in

▲ **7.6 Ed Manning, Watson and Manning, Inc.,**
The Mona Lisa Blocpix Image
Spatially quantized transformation.
The last frame is the painting itself—not a computer image.

fact, quite difficult, for mathematically equal amounts of light energy do not create visually equal steps in value. They must be measured by the most sophisticated of visual instruments: the human eye.

Colors can be added to computer drawings by using an electronic drawing pad, a light pen to touch areas on the screen, or a pointing device such as a mouse to "click" the colors into place. They can also be programmed to develop along with computer-generated imagery such as the fractal image displayed in Figure 2.8.

Another approach to color in computer graphics is to digitize or quantize an existing image. This basically means electronically scanning and converting it into numbers that correspond to points on the x and y axes of the monitor screen as graphed in Figure 7.3. Computers with graphic capabilities have screens divided into **pixels**, which are individual picture elements, like mosaic tiles. The more pixels, the finer the possible resolution in the image. Figure **7.6** demonstrates the visual results of digitizing the *Mona Lisa*

▲ **7.7A** Douglas Kirkland's original photograph of Audrey Hepburn.

▲ **7.7B** A version of the same photograph, digitally manipulated to appear as a high-contrast image of bright, flat colors.

with increasing numbers of pixels. The color variations—averaged for each pixel—become finer and finer mosaics of colored blocks. It is possible to render an image with what appear to be continuous gradations in tone if the computer has a substantial memory. The larger the computer's memory, the more pixels it can support.

Once the image is scanned into the computer's memory, it can be manipulated endlessly. Colors can be added and changed in hue, saturation, and brightness at will; shadows, highlights, and midtones can be added wherever the artist wants them. Figure **7.7A** shows the original photograph of Audrey Hepburn which Douglas Kirkland used as the starting point in a manipulation process that resulted in the final piece shown in Figure **7.7B**. Among other changes, Kirkland converted the image to high contrast, burned in certain low-value details from the original that would have been lost in high contrast, and then used a limited palette of six colors to replace those in the original. Kirkland observes that, in using powerful computer programs:

You have to know when to blow the whistle on yourself. We have this incredible wide-open possibility, but we have to learn when to say no and when to say yes. It's like having a wonderful musical instrument that can make any sound in the world—but you have to put those sounds together to make a beautiful song.[2]

In Adobe Photoshop, a user-selected range of color choices in the image are displayed side by side to help in making aesthetic choices. The "current pick" is juxtaposed with other possible choices as one works with alterations in hue, value, or brightness in the shadows, midtones, or highlights. The entire original may be shown in reduced size in many variations side by side on the monitor, or the image may be "cut" into "test strips," as in Figure **7.8**. This allows the computer artist to apply separate color treatments to each section and view the result before printing, like a traditional photographer making test strips with different color filters.

To avoid obvious jumps between different hues and values used in representing gradations across a three-dimensional form, the PostScript program offers up to 256 gradations

▲ **7.8 Test strip sample**

between two colors, for the equivalent of an airbrushed effect. This number of choices is not necessary in a small area, but if a program had only 50 choices and if they were stretched across ten inches, there would be only five bands of color per inch. In such a case, the bands themselves would be noticeable as hard-edged shapes, an effect that an artist might not desire.

A person with normal color vision can distinguish approximately 150 different hues in the visible spectrum. Scientists calculate that when differences in value and saturation are factored in, our eyes can probably distinguish about seven million different colors. But high-end computer work-stations can generate a palette of 16.7 million colors on the screen—almost ten million more than we can actually see. Is this pointless extravagance? Perhaps not, for this tremendous ability allows for very gradual gradations between colors. We can visually detect very small differences between certain hues, but not between others, so such abundance of differences is necessary to ensure that nowhere in the even subdivisions of color choices can we detect unwanted jumps.

Digital Art

New terms are being created to define the variety of computer-generated artwork, since no one term seems to fit all the types of art associated with it. In fact, we are still trying to

▲ **7.9 Ursula Freer, *Reflections***
Digital print.
Digital artist Ursula Freer uses the computer in a "painterly" way, and markets her prints through galleries and her website.

decide whether some of it is really art, rather than manipulated engineering feats. Nevertheless, there are many artists who are at the forward edge of what we broadly refer to as digital art, who are exploring new methods of working with this additive mixture of light. They are altering photographs, drawing or painting with the computer, utilizing mathematically oriented things like fractals to create a mechanized type of art, or using a combination of music and movement for interactive pieces. There are software programs to assist with a wide variety of efforts. Digital art is outsourced through a digital printer, which we go into further in the next chapter, where we discuss more about inks and subtractive (pigment) issues. Here we deal with the computer and with "light" issues.

New Mexico artist Ursula Freer has been creating digital art directly from the computer since the late 1990s. In *Reflections*

(**7.9**), we can see the influence of her traditional painting background in the landscape format, although this piece does take on a new character in the luminous transparency of the colors. Using digital photographs from her camera, software and filters, a digital graphics tablet, and her inkjet printer, she now produces made-to-order digital prints which she markets through galleries and her website. She states:

> *It has totally changed my way of creating art. The medium is quite amazing; there seems to be no end to the possibilities for creative expression and great freedom for communicating ideas.*[3]

Another painter who uses the computer as a tool is painter/illustrator Pam Zagarenski. For *Sunday Drive* (**7.10**) she scanned a photographic print of her painting into the computer and embellished it with her drawings to create a new composite illustration. She elaborates:

> *I have recently discovered the pleasures of marrying the two worlds of fine art/illustration on paper with computer illustration. I am able to teach myself a lot about color and composition using the computer as*

a tool. Changes are made quickly and efficiently. I scan all my images out of my journals and all my paintings. I use those images in new computer-generated "collages" that would otherwise have been impossible to create. Don't be afraid to play with images… you'll be pleasantly surprised by your "mistakes."[4]

When Robert Silvers was a graduate student at Massachusetts Institute of Technology in 1995, he invented the Photomosaic process, so named for the hundreds of tiles of computer-stored images he had compiled to make a final image. He founded Runaway Technology to create fine art and high-end commercial images using his patented process. He considers the colors, brightness, and shapes within each of the small images in order to decide their placement within a large reference image of his choosing. To make his composite image *Dove* (**7.11A**), a symbol of peace, he used photographs of ordinary people going about their everyday lives, rather than of people well known for their work in the peace movement, thereby creating a com-

pelling statement of what peace is for all humankind. When viewing this image close up, we can clearly see the variety of detail in the photographs that compile the image, and are drawn into the work in spite of wanting to get far enough away (**7.11B**) to see the whole work clearly. There is a push/pull effect, and when we see a repeat of a photo among the tiles, it becomes an enticement to find more such repeats, a visual game. Silvers has been commercially successful with his patented process, having completed a wide range of projects to date, from portraits to magazine covers to wall murals. His TV commercials use fully animated photomosaics, and in music videos like the B52's "Debbie," each individual tile is a music video of its own that can be played on Quicktime if you click on the tile. Like Chuck Close, he has continued to expand the color theories of the Pointillist Movement, but with an evolving twenty-first century style.

In *Pixels from a Scan of My Fingertips* (**7.12**), artist Ron Lambert has let the computer itself be the arbiter of taste in allowing it to make its own choices of colors. As Lambert explains:

After scanning a black and white image of my fingertips into the computer, I zoomed in until all that could be seen were the color pixels. This removed the images from any context where they are recognizable as fingerprints. The viewer is meant to initially notice only the aesthetics of color, an aspect of the work that is a façade. Although the images are unique to my person, the visual clues, the colors, were determined by the computer, therefore having no basis in truth.[5]

Color in Website Design

For those thinking about creating websites, or improving existing ones, there are certain issues pertaining specifically to web color choices that are worth mentioning. If you have heard of the "browser-safe" palette, Netscape palette, 216 palette, web palette, or 6 x 6 x 6 color cube, then you need to know that they are all referring to the same thing.

In the early years of web design, the number of colors a computer screen could show was 256 (also known as the 8-bit system). The majority of computers in the mid to late 1990s were still using 8-bit systems, but because PCs and Macs used a different numbering system for their colors,

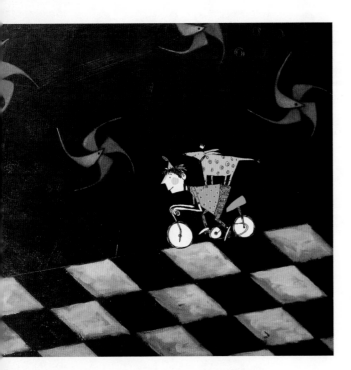

▲ **7.10 Pam Zagarenski, *Sunday Drive*, 2005**
Computer illustration.
With a scanner, her own paintings and drawings, a Mac computer, Adobe Photoshop, and Adobe Illustrator, the artist creates her own new multi-media style.

▲ **7.11B Robert Silvers,** *Dove*
This is the complete work from which the detail in 7.11A is taken.
Like looking at magnified pixels, one needs to see the tiled
image from a distance in order for the squares to blend into a
smooth image.

web images did not always appear as the same color on both of them. There were 40 colors that would routinely show up in surprising ways when going from a PC to a Mac, or vice versa, so those colors were dropped—hence the 216 colors. Netscape, Internet Explorer, and Mosaic used this "browser-safe palette" within their browsers. The name was coined by Lynda Weinman, who was the first author to identify and publish the colors that were being used in this system.[6] Those 216 colors were based on mathematical choices, not aesthetic ones, which limited earlier users to a palette that leaned toward overly saturated

◀ **7.11A Robert Silvers,** *Dove* **(detail)**
Photomosaic.
We are fascinated with the "imagery within the imagery" in
Robert Silvers's work.

colors. Many users would have preferred more muted tones, with a greater variety of values, to the chosen colors, but limiting the palette was the necessary first step toward gaining some control over color compatibility between monitors, and it was widely accepted and used by all. (Color management in reference to printing is discussed in the next chapter.)

Most software programs that support designers, such as Photoshop, Illustrator, Dreamweaver, Paint Shop Pro, GoLive, and Freehand, now have built-in, browser-safe palettes. With the continuing rapid advancement in computer capabilities, however, the original importance of the 216 color choice has sharply diminished. Many computers have built-in color-management settings (Windows uses ICM, Macs use ColorSync) and monitors and computers can be set to see "thousands" or "millions" of colors—the colors are no longer limited to 256. When a machine is set for that extended range, all colors display properly. As older machines are phased out of circulation, using the 8-bit or 256 (or 216) system becomes less of an issue.

There is still an issue with the degree of contrast of gray values in an image (known as gamma values) but these can also be reset within your computer. Gamma adjustment would be important if you were using images in which the exact color value was essential, such as reproducing fine art or black-and-white photography on a website, or in medical diagnostic imaging. Default settings for PCs and Macs are different—PCs are 2.2 target gamma, and Macs are 1.8 target gamma, which means that a Mac-generated image will show up darker and with more contrast when seen on a PC monitor, and Windows-generated images will show up flatter and more washed-out on Mac monitors. Designers get around this by opting for a middle ground when setting the gamma targets—lightening a little if they work on a Mac, and adding a little more contrast if they work in Windows.

When it comes to designing for other online devices, such as cell phones and PDAs (Personal Digital Assistants), the browser-safe palette comes back into play, as most of those systems are still 1-bit (black and white) or 8-bit (256 colors). There is no way of knowing how advanced those systems will be by the time this book is published, but at the least a familiarity with the "browser-safe" colors would be helpful if you wanted to create a website targeting the widest variety of digital devices.

▲ **7.12 Ron Lambert,** *Pixels from a Scan of My Fingertips No. 2,* **2000**
Inkjet print, 6 × 6 ins (15.2 × 15.2 cm).
Letting the computer create the color scheme is the final touch in removing the personal origins of this piece.

Dynamic Imagery and Virtual Reality

Computer graphics enable artists to create computer animation using color change through time as well as space. Internet websites now often employ animated graphics in color to catch attention. The technology can also be used for fine arts applications, such as video art. Herbert Franke's *Metamorphoses* (**7.13**) tells a color story with a surprise ending as the background shifts from a subdued red-purple to a strong red. When this sequence was created in 1984, number-crunching was required to program the computer to display such changes. At that time, this highly technical process was intimidating to many visual artists. Herbert Franke suggests that the same thing happened when photography was first introduced:

An experience made at the beginning of the photographic work repeated itself at this point: we thought at first that it would be painters who made use of the new medium, leading it into branches of art; in reality, such people showed a lack of interest and a new branch of the arts came into existence. Computer graphics have also been largely ignored by exponents of the visual arts. The people who are today concerned with computer animation come only to a small extent from the ranks of the visual arts. A much larger proportion of them rely on training as photographer or cameraman, mathematician or programmer. It is obvious that artistic possibilities opened up by computer graphic systems are leading to the formation of a new profession, standing somewhere between art and technology.[7]

Mark Napier packed up his paints in 1995 and focused exclusively on projects for the web. His *Shredder* was an interactive piece allowing anyone to send information from any website and watch it being shredded. In spite of the playful quality of this work, it brought up copyright

▲ ▶ **7.13 Herbert W. Franke,
Stills from computer film
Metamorphoses, 1984**
DIBIAS picture processing system.
Computer graphics can be used to
develop color stories varying through time.

issues of tampering with websites, which the 1998 Digital Millennium Copyright Act had established. The issue of infringement is an ongoing one in today's fast-paced art technology, as we try to reconcile our artist ownership/autonomy with control over the process. Napier feels "letting go" to be a vital part of the creative process. His interactive piece *The Waiting Room* (**7.14**) featured at Bitforms Gallery in New York City was well received:

> *beginning April 6, 2002,* The Waiting Room *is Napier's latest achievement. The* Waiting Room *is a multi-user space with a "language of shapes" that operates like a chat room of people networked together, all of whom can alter the piece with real-time effects occurring on every participating terminal. Napier aimed for a variety of aesthetic qualities with the piece, from architecturally inspired shapes to more ephemeral ones. As many as 30 shapes can be evoked simultaneously, each with a corresponding sound which decreases in volume during the one-hour life span of each shape.*[8]

In his explorations into standard-sized industrial fluorescent lights, Dan Flavin blended a painter's sense of color with a sculptor's awareness of space. Flavin was well known for his Minimalistic body of work that spanned the decades between the early 1960s until his death in 1996. His visual light statements continue to provide us with unique visions of spatial color effects, whether they are his "barrier" series of long freestanding light structures, or wall pieces. He loved to utilize corner spaces, as in *Untitled (to Janie Lee) One*, a work that brings boundaries into play (**7.15**). Where are the edges to this work? What happens to the space so encaptured? Do the colors change and move as we move? Minimalist work by its very nature invites questioning.

Slawomir Brzoska, with his *Lumenosphaera* (**7.16**), made a site-specific installation in a chapel on the grounds of the Center for Polish Sculpture in Oronsko, Poland. He blocked all the windows to keep out any other light, and fixed pale strands of fibers at regular intervals from the walls to the floor. The thin fibers glowed under soft black lights within the space like colored sunbeams, creating their own Op Art patterns.

◀ **7.14 Mark Napier,** *The Waiting Room*, **2002**
Interactive video.
Collaborative prints of this particular piece have sold for $1,000 each, although Napier is well known for his free interactive works posted on the web.

encountered is in constant flux. Seeds explode into light, night turns into day, rocks pulsate. The objects in these ephemeral landscapes are, moreover, transparent and permeable rather than solidly opaque. With her background as a painter, Davies says she

> *worked with transparency and textured shadow-casting to create spatial ambiguity, merging objects and space, figure and ground. . . . Just as the invention of film—through the technology and craft of photography—extended the stillness of painting into the flow of time, the technology associated with immersive virtual reality extends beyond the two-dimensionality of painting and film, into enveloping "circumferal" space. . . . In works such as these, perceptual boundaries between inside and out may be experienced as permeable as the virtual and immaterial are confused with the bodily-felt, experienced as strangely real.*
>
> *The visuals in these works are soft, luminous, and translucent, consisting of semi-transparent textured three-dimensional forms and flowing particles: the three-dimensional forms have been designed to be neither wholly representational (i.e. recognizable) nor wholly abstract, but to hover in between, creating perceptual ambiguity. By animating these forms, and by enabling the participant not only to see them but to float through them as well, it is possible—because of their varying degrees of transparency—to create spatially ambiguous figure/ground relationships. . . . In my work, ambiguity is the key to softening, lessening the distinctions between things.*[10]

▲ **7.15 Dan Flavin, *Untitled (to Janie Lee) One*, 1971**
Installation.
In keeping with Flavin's Minimalistic viewpoint, he stated that his work "is what it is and it ain't nothing else."[9]

By now, computer skills have become common among artists, and more user-friendly software makes it far easier to develop dynamic as well as static computer graphics. And no longer does computer-generated imagery seem to sit on a flat screen—now **virtual reality** works give the impression of surrounding the viewer in a participatory experience in which the environment is composed entirely of light. In Char Davies's *Ephemere* (**7.17**), participants don a stereoscopic headset and a chest-mounted device that translates their body movements and breathing into a virtual journey through virtual landscapes. These consist only of computer-generated lights creating the impression of a surreal three-dimensional world. Since the subject of this virtual reality "immersion" is the fleeting nature of time, everything

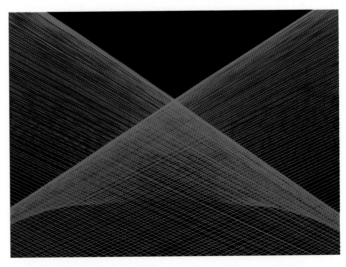

▲ **7.16 Slawomir Brzoska, *Lumenosphaera*, 2000**
Site-specific installation.
This installation, with its haunting use of black lighting, gives us a three-dimensional version of an Op Art painting.

▲ **7.17 Char Davies, still from *Ephemere*.**
Virtual-reality installation.
Davies's painterly approach makes virtual reality a truly immersive experience in semi-abstract landscapes of shifting colors and forms.

Laser Art, Holography, and Multi-Media

Artists are using all types of lights—fluorescent, neon, laser, black and colored—taking light off screen and out of containment, and reforming it into new images, of pure color, pure luminescence. Laser lights are relative newcomers to the field of art, having been developed in the 1960s for scientific purposes. Prior to that it was impossible to work with **coherent light**—light in which waves are all of the same length, in unchanging relationship. Laser light approaches this ideal. It is generated by an oscillator, which creates pulses in a thin tube filled with some electrically excitable medium, such as helium and neon. Light projected into this cavity is reflected many times from one end of the tube to the other by a system of mirrors, creating standing waves of energy. The medium used determines the spectrally pure color that results from this process. A helium and neon mixture gives a coherent red light of 633 nanometers.

Laser sculptures can be created by setting up reflecting materials in the path of the thin laser beams or by projecting the beams through a smoky atmosphere so that they can be seen. For laser light shows, the beams may be moved so quickly that persistence of vision causes viewers to perceive lines of colored lights on a screen rather than moving dots of light. Their movements may be coordinated with music,

either manually or electronically. Incorporating colored lights within the performing arts is not a new effort, although lasers have certainly taken the attempts to amazing heights. Composers, writers, and artists of the late nineteenth and early twentieth centuries became fascinated with the ability to see colors when hearing music, or hearing music when viewing colors (the painter Kandinsky was involved with this), a process known as synesthesia, which we wrote about in Chapter 3. The term applies to other sense cross-overs as well, such as seeing the alphabet or numbers in color, and having smells associated with color. The Russian composer Alexander Scriabin wrote his "Symphony No. 5, Opus 60, Prometheus: Poem of Fire" and included a part written for a "*clavier à lumières*," which instead of playing notes when the keys were hit, projected colors on a screen. It was seldom included in the performance of the symphony, however. But fast-forward to the mid-1970s, to discoveries within the field of lasers, and "Prometheus" truly came into its own through the efforts of musician Lowell Cross and physicist Carson Jeffries, in their multi-media symphonic production of the work, "Video/Laser III" (**7.18**). Although few people have the synesthete's abilities, it is a fascinating phenomenon, and perhaps laser art comes closest to allowing those of us who do not have music/color cross-overs to see what it might be like if we did.

Advances in laser technology have also made **holograms**

◀ **7.18 Lowell Cross,
Kinetic laser imagery**
Laser deflection system
Video/Laser III. University of Iowa.
University Symphony Orchestra
conducted by James Dixon.

possible. These are two-dimensional images formed by wave fronts of light (or sounds or electrons) that reconstruct the visual impression of a three-dimensional object. To create this effect, a laser beam is split. Part of it—the object beam— is reflected onto an object from an angle; the other part—the reference beam—is projected onto photographic film. The light waves bouncing off the object from the object beam intersect this non-reflected light on the film, creating an optically three-dimensional interference pattern. When the resulting hologram is viewed from different directions, the part of the image seen changes, just as it would if one were moving around a three-dimensional object.

Although this technology is being employed in many nonaesthetic ways—such as difficult-to-forge images on credit cards—some artists have adopted the hologram as a means of creating imagery with the glowing purity of pure spectral lights. Some would maintain that lasers and holograms reveal the essence of color: having no substance, they are an optical phenomenon resulting from the eye's response to the reflection and refraction of clear light.

Contemporary electronic possibilities have led to entirely new kinds of aesthetic experiences—multi-media installations in which computer-controlled sounds, laser light displays, holograms, video art, and virtual reality setups surround and perhaps interact with the viewer. These possibilities are requiring revamping of museum and gallery spaces so that participants can explore ephemeral worlds of pure light.

Video artist Nam June Paik took over the entire Guggenheim Museum in New York for a multi-media show (**7.19**) including a "waterfall" of zigzagging laser beams, a circle of video monitors on the ground floor beaming video clips upward, and flat screens around the spiralling ramps displaying rapidly-changing video montages. Spectators became part of the spectacle, as projected colors played across their own bodies, movements of which also interrupted and distorted the projected light patterns. Art critic David Joselit observed:

The excess Paik produces in his art, both its carnivalesque euphoria and its melancholic distraction, engages a bigger problem than does much recent media art: the problem of television and its role in our world. Paik pummels the television set, extracts its guts and spills them on the floor. But at the same time, he teases out of the monitor a hybrid video stream composed of diverse elements, synthesized and reordered. In other words, Paik sees television as both a set of institutions and a language that is probably the most widely "spoken" in the world.[11]

▲ **7.19 Nam June Paik,** *Modulation in Sync: Jacob's Ladder*, **2000**
Laser light, waterfall, mirrors, steel armature. Bohen Foundation Collection, promised gift to the Solomon R. Guggenheim Museum, New York.
Nam June Paik employed an array of light technologies to create this installation as part of a retrospective of his work that occupied
the entire Guggenheim Museum.

8 Inks, Dyes, Pigments, and Print

Do you know a painter who has invented a color different from those that compose the Solar Spectrum?

ANDRÉ DERAIN

ONE of the most complex aspects of contemporary color use is the mixing and specification of precise colors. Until the nineteenth century, painters and dyers mixed their own colors from private recipes. However, with the growth of industry and the availability of premixed oil paints, the need arose for precise means of communication between suppliers and users of pigments. "Cadmium red medium" from one paint company differed from another company's "cadmium red medium." Furthermore, industrial processes brought expectations that colors could be precisely replicated in printing and dyeing or matched exactly to a sample. To standardize ways of specifying and mixing colors, a number of systems have been developed. None is as sophisticated as the human eye. Under optimal lighting conditions, an average human being can distinguish up to seven million different colors. But matching colors by eye is a subjective matter, for different people see colors somewhat differently. Nonetheless, standardization of prepared pigments diminishes the amount of guesswork in pigment mixing, which remains a complex art.

Dye and Pigment Sources

The major subtractive colorants—those whose apparent color depends on the wavelengths they reflect—are dyes and pigments. **Dyes** are coloring materials dissolved in a liquid solvent; **pigments** are bits of powder suspended in a medium such as oil or acrylic. Materials to be colored absorb dyes, whereas pigments sit on the surface. **Lakes** are pigments made from dyes, extending the range of pigment colors.

Since the end of the Ice Age, humans have used natural plant and animal materials to form dye solutions into which fabrics were dipped. Berries, fruits, leaves, lichens, and roots were found to have different coloring properties. The root of the indigo plant was for centuries the only source of blue dye. The stigma of the crocus yielded a yellow dye called saffron. Cochineal, a brilliant red dye, was created from the dried bodies of certain female scale insects that fed on cactus plants, and was once exported on a large scale from huge cactus plantations in Mexico. And royal purple dye used in Greek and Roman courts was derived from the glandular mucus of a certain sea snail.

Synthetic dyes first appeared in 1856, with the discovery that the addition of alcohol to coal-tar yielded a purple that could dye silk. These synthetically derived dyes are called **aniline dyes**. They rapidly became popular for their range of colors, potentially high saturation, even consistency, and convenience. A few years later, a more colorfast, vivid, multi-hued family of dyes called **azo dyes** was developed synthetically from petroleum. Farms producing precious natural dyestuffs, such as madder roots in Europe and indigo in India, were largely put out of business by these new discoveries. Experimentation with synthetics continues apace. Over three million synthetic dyes have been discovered and several new ones are announced every week.

The colors produced by pigments and their mixtures are more difficult to predict than dye colors, for light is reflected

▲ **8.1 Main hall ("Hall of Bulls"), Lascaux, France, c.15,000–10,000 B.C.**
Early cave-dwelling humans in the Lascaux area apparently painted with pigments from natural materials such as red earths, red and yellow sandy ochers, manganese oxide for browns and blacks, and calcite for white.

Cadmium Yellow	Cadmium Red	Alizarin Crimson	French Ultramarine	Cerulean Blue	Viridian

Burnt Sienna	Raw Sienna	Yellow Ochre	Burnt Umber	Ivory Black	Purple Lake

from the surfaces of the pigment particles. While natural dyes were substances that would dissolve in water, those used as pigments were usually insoluble. The earliest pigments were minerals extracted from the earth, used by cave dwellers for unsaturated yellows, browns, reds, and black (**8.1**). As early as 40,000 B.C., however, some were heated to increase the range of colors available. Yellow ocher, for instance, was heated to obtain red. Over the millennia, color palettes were extended by the creation of the deep blue of ultramarine from lapis lazuli, the Romans' bright cinnabar red from a sulfide of mercury, the cadmium yellows and oranges from greenockite, and green from malachite.

The next major progression in pigment palettes occurred during the Middle Ages, when pigments were chemically combined or changed to form new colors. The green of verdigris was the result of hanging copper plates over vats of vinegar to form a green crust on the copper. Certain blues were copper-ammonia compounds made from this verdigris. Zinc white is an oxide of zinc.

As in dyes, modern laboratory experimentation with petroleum has yielded a vast array of artificial pigments whose saturation, purity, and durability often exceed those of natural pigments. This was not necessarily so at first. The bright pink lakes used by Van Gogh in 1888 and 1889 have turned blue, as have rose lakes used by Gauguin. Countless works by Postimpressionists and Fauvists in the late nineteenth century have thus changed in color. Only in the early twentieth century did the fragile synthetic lakes give way to more costly synthetic pigments which were more resistant to light, humidity, and temperature fluctuations. These are now available to painters in premixed tube colors, some of which are labeled to reflect their resemblance to natural pigments, as in the sample palette of paint pigments shown in Figure **8.2**.

Today, the same pigments are used in many forms—oils, acrylics, chalks, egg tempera, watercolors. Only the media, binders, and range of pigments used differ among these forms. We explore the complexities of pigment mixing in two popular media—oils and acrylics—below, after first exploring attempts to standardize ways of examining colors and specifying desired pigmentation.

◄ **8.2 Contemporary paint pigments**
The original tube colors are at the top of each strip, with progressively lighter tints below.

Lighting

In addition to the sources of coloring material, the apparent color of a reflective surface will also depend upon the light falling on that surface. For **critical color matching**—the technical term for mixing colors to match a given sample—natural daylight from the north (in the northern hemisphere) is used as a standard. As shown in Figure **8.3**, north sky daylight at 7400 Kelvin (a measure of the color temperature of the light source) contains a balanced combination of

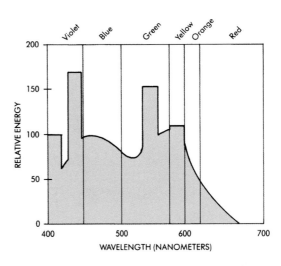

▲ **8.5 Relative energies of wavelengths in ordinary fluorescent light**

all visible wavelengths, with a tendency toward the blue end of the spectrum. By contrast, incandescent lighting is high in red and yellow wavelengths, with relatively little energy from the greens, blues, and violets (**8.4**). As indicated in Figure **8.5**, ordinary fluorescent lights have sharp peaks in certain areas of the visible spectrum. These color distortions in incandescent and fluorescent lights will obviously affect the colors seen.

Because optimal north sky daylight is not reliably available, critical color matching must be done under special lights. Some fluorescent lights attempt to provide a fuller spectrum of wavelengths; filtered tungsten lamps and quartz halogen lights are said to approximate north sky daylight more closely. However, because many colors will actually be viewed under regular fluorescent or incandescent light, colors are often compared under equivalent lighting conditions.

The Munsell Notation System

The most widely adopted way of communicating about colors is the system developed by Albert Munsell and subsequently refined and recognized by the National Bureau of Standards, the Munsell Laboratory, and the Optical Society of America. It is the basis for standards used in the United States by various official color councils, by the Japanese

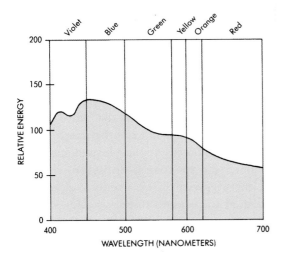

▲ **8.3 Relative energies of wavelengths in natural daylight**

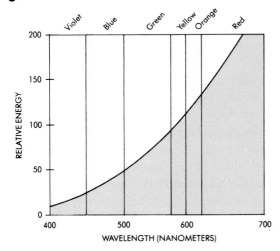

▲ **8.4 Relative energies of wavelengths in incandescent light**

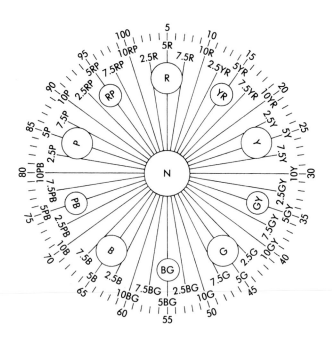

▲ 8.6 The Munsell 100-hue circle
Two ways of specifying hues are provided—the numbers from 1 to 100 around the circumference, and the letter and numbering system in the inner circles.

Industrial Standard for Color, the British Standards Institution, and the German Standard Color System.

As we saw in Chapter 2, Munsell graded colors in equal visual steps along three variables: hue, value, and chroma (saturation). Hues are divided into 100 equal steps and displayed around a circle (**8.6**) based on ten major hues: red, yellow-red, yellow, green-yellow, green, blue-green, blue, purple-blue, purple, and red-purple. Each is designated by its beginning initials in the inner circle and in some Munsell notations. Between each of these major hues are many intermediate hues, indicated by an infinitely expandable decimal system. As shown here, these can be expressed as points from 1 to 100, as on the outer circle. Alternatively, they can be labeled according to hue families, as in the intermediate circles, with the hue initials included in the designation. The number 5 indicates the midpoint in each hue family. The central N represents neutral gray.

In the Munsell system, values are expressed numerically as steps from absolute black (0/) to absolute white (10/), with the symbol 5/ used to indicate middle gray and its value equivalent in all the chromatic hues. In reality, absolute

white and absolute black are never seen in material form.

The third designation in the Munsell color notation is chroma, conceived as equal steps from neutral gray to the greatest saturation seen in each hue at that level of value. The complete notation combines all three variables as hue/value/chroma. A brilliant vermilion red might be designated as 5R 5/14, whereas a less saturated "rose" red of equal value might be 5R 5/4. Finer distinctions in each variable can be indicated by decimal division (that is, 4.5R 4.3/11.8).

The C.I.E. System

To standardize color notations further, the 1931 International Commission on Illumination (*Commission Internationale de l'Eclairage*, or C.I.E.) developed a visual means for precise color matching that relied on mechanics rather than subjectivity. This system is based on lights and is therefore only indirectly applicable to pigments.

A computerized **spectrophotometer**, which measures the light energy given off by a reflective sample or light source, is used to measure three variables. One is **luminance**, the intensity of the light given off. The other two, of relevance to subtractive mixtures, are hue and saturation. Together their values determine what is called the **chromaticity** of the color. In the horseshoe-shaped **Chromaticity Diagram** developed by the C.I.E. (**8.7**), pure spectral hues are placed by wavelength around the perimeter, with non-spectral purples represented by a straight line across the bottom. The center is the neutral sum of all hues. This point is white in light mixtures; in pigment mixtures, adding hues to each other "subtracts" light, creating a darker mixture that reflects less light.

Note that the areas covered by certain wavelengths in the C.I.E. diagram—particularly the blues and greens—are far larger than the yellow, orange, and red segments. This is so because the shape of the diagram is based on the color visibility or **Spectral Sensitivity Curve** shown in Figure **8.8**. According to scientific research, a person with normal vision looking at colored lights of equal energies under good illumination will perceive the yellow-green part of the spectrum (peaking at 555 nanometers) as brighter than all other parts. The visibility of lights drops off sharply toward each end of the spectrum. However, as we have seen, human

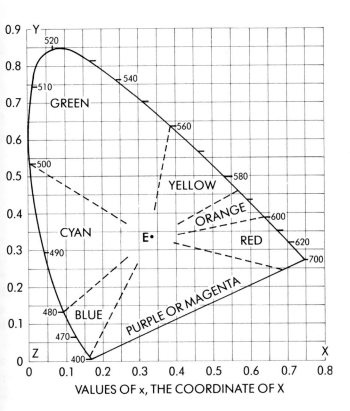

▲ 8.8 Spectral sensitivity of the normal eye
Cone vision is used to assess the relative brightness of colored lights of equal energies but varying wavelengths. Yellow-green is perceived as the brightest color.

▲ 8.7 The C.I.E. chromaticity diagram
The purest spectral colors are located on the outside of the flat-iron shape, with non-spectral purple across the bottom and the neutral sum of all hues (E = equal energy) in the center.

visual perception is also capable of distinguishing very keenly between different colors, so this spectral sensitivity curve is an exaggeration of visual truth. The concept of *just-noticeable difference* is important in some color-matching situations; one may have to know how many steps of just-noticeable difference are allowable in approximating the color of a given sample.

Despite its limitations in representing the degree of noticeable difference between colors, the C.I.E. system offers a standard which is objective and does not depend on the permanence of pigmented swatches used as a control. The sample-based Munsell and Ostwald systems have now been improved by the establishment of C.I.E. values for the standard swatches; if these fade, new ones can be prepared.

Interestingly, the fact that C.I.E. measurements are based on wavelengths rather than actual color composition means that the same color can be created from many different mixtures. If a paint company wants to make sure that a new batch of a certain red-purple matches its previous batches, it can analyze the new batch with a spectrophotometer. If the new batch deviates numerically from the standard values of luminance, hue, and saturation for that red-purple, quantities of pigment can be added until the new batch is the numerical equivalent of older ones—even though its actual pigment composition may be different!

Mixing Oils and Acrylics

As an artist, you can apply this same scientific principle of considering many possibilities for mixing a desired color in subtractive work. But you cannot mix colors using traditional two-dimensional color circles (2.6) for reference because they typically show all hues at maximum saturation—and therefore different steps of value.

As a tool to guide paint mixing, Binney and Smith, suppliers of Liquitex® oils and acrylics, have prepared color maps that display hue, value, and saturation relationships two-dimensionally (**8.9**). To offer a broader mixing palette than that based on the ten-hue Munsell system, the Liquitex® color map adds yellow-orange and yellow-green, for a total

▲ **8.9 The Liquitex® acrylic color map**
Hues are represented horizontally and values vertically, with two steps of decreasing saturation given on each paint chip. The Liquitex® oil color map is almost identical to this one.

of 12 basic hues, arranged horizontally. Vertically they are graded by value. Changes in saturation are represented within each color chip. Each starts on the left with the most saturated form available at that level of value (many of which are available premixed as tube colors—those that must be mixed by the artist have a palette knife symbol below). The effects of mixing increasing amounts of a neutral gray of the same value, thus lowering the saturation of the color, are

then shown in two steps. Less saturated versions of a hue can also be mixed by adding amounts of its complementary; doing so tends to "muddy" the mixture, as shown in Figure **8.10**. Some colors opposite each other on various color wheels may not be exact complementaries, and thus do not produce a neutral gray when mixed. However, an imprecise, softened, or muddy mixture may be what is desired.

To mix hues not immediately available in premixed tubes, there are at least three possibilities, as indicated in Figure **8.11**: adjacent diagonals, a horizontal mixture, or a vertical mixture. To mix a yellow 5 (light brown), for example, one could mix yellow-green 6 and yellow-orange 4, or yellow-orange 6 and yellow-green 4, or yellow-orange 5 and

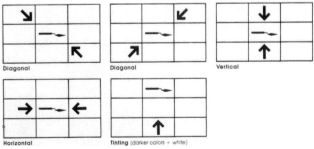

▲ **8.10** If its true complementary is added to a hue, they will lower each other's saturation until a neutral gray of lower value is formed. Another method of lowering saturation is to add a neutral gray.

▲ **8.11** To mix hues with reference to the Liquitex® color map, the best results are usually achieved by mixing colors nearest to the desired mixed color, diagonally, vertically, or horizontally.

yellow-green 5, or yellow 6 and yellow 4.

The color map can be bent into a cylinder, just as Newton bent the straight spectrum into a circle, thus juxtaposing the red-purple end and the purple end for mixing purposes. Any of the adjacent combinations will yield an approximation of the desired color in the middle, depending on the exact amount and characteristics of the mixing colors used.

Tube colors vary in permanency, clarity, intensity, and tinting strength. The natural form of chrome yellow, for example, turns green or even greenish black over a long period of time; natural cadmium yellow is far more permanent but harder to use since it quickly dulls when mixed. Tube colors also vary in cost and toxicity, factors one may

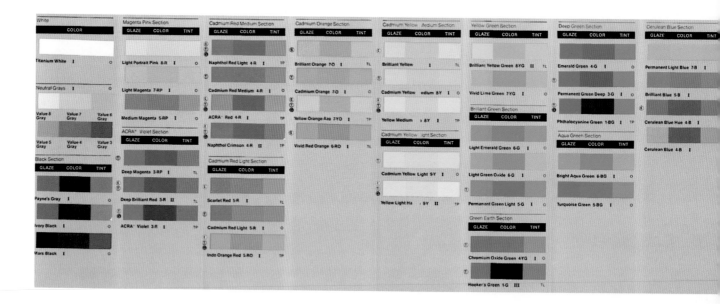

▲ **8.12** Tube colors vary when used as glazes or tints. Each is shown in its original form in the central swatch, with its appearance when used as a glaze indicated on the left and as a tint on the right.

need to consider before purchasing a basic palette. However, many costly and/or toxic natural pigments have been replaced by synthetic ones.

Although many color theories posit that all colors can be mixed from three primaries, in practice this cannot be done with paint pigments. Yellow is a particular problem, for a high-value maximum saturation yellow cannot be created by adding white to a value 5 yellow, since this will decrease its saturation while lightening its value. Furthermore, if black is added to a high-value yellow to lower its value and saturation, the result is greenish, no matter what brand of paints is being used. Contrary to the idea that yellow is a primary color that cannot be mixed, we find that it can be mixed from the hues around it on the color map, as indicated above. To mix all the colors in the color map, we therefore recommend that students start with a basic set of 12 tubes of oils or acrylics: value 5 of red-purple, red, yellow, green, blue, and purple; value 8 yellow; value 3 red; base value blue-green; base value 75 blue-purple; Titanium White; and Mars Black. Higher values can be created by mixing in some white; darker values can be mixed by adding black or the appropriate base value—a very dark

step in the hue. These measures will tend to lower the saturation of the brilliant tube colors. Saturation can also be lowered by mixing complementaries or adding neutral gray. To lower saturation without lowering value, some white may be added to the mixture.

Additional hues can be mixed from adjacent colors in any of the four possible directions mentioned above. However, if the mixed pigments are of equal value, they will produce a result of lower value, for pigment mixing is a subtractive process. It may be necessary to compensate by starting slightly higher in value in one or both hues.

Various tube colors respond differently when thinned to transparency with a medium, forming a **glaze**, or when mixed with white to form a **tint** (**8.12**). The differences between some tube colors are then more apparent than when they are shown at full strength. The colors labeled by Liquitex® as "Deep Brilliant Red" and "Cadmium Red Deep," for instance, look almost identical in the tube form, shown in the central patches. But note how different they become as glazes or tints.

When mixing paints, the **Weber–Fechner Law** must be applied if colors visually equal in value are to be mixed. If we add equal parts of white or black repeatedly to raise or lower value, the rate of optical change will decrease. To create an optically equal series of differences, geometrically increasing parts of black or white must be added. The Weber–Fechner Law, formulated by Weber and Fechner in the nineteenth

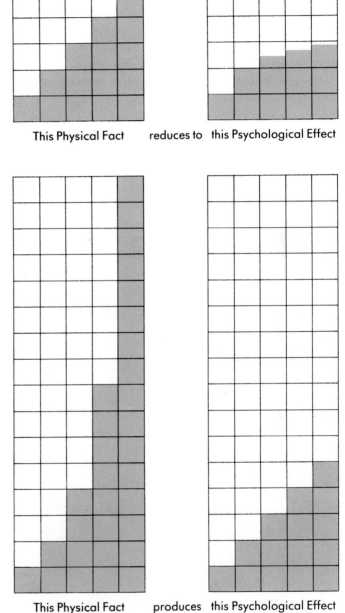

This Physical Fact   reduces to   this Psychological Effect

This Physical Fact   produces   this Psychological Effect

▲ **8.13 The Weber-Fechner Law**

century, is stated thus: "The visual perception of an arithmetical progression depends upon a physical geometric progression." The difference between adding arithmetically increasing parts (1 + 2 + 3 + 4, etc.) and adding geometrically increasing parts (1 + 2 + 4 + 8, etc.) is shown graphically in Figure **8.13**, and in value steps in Figure 6.11.

All the above comments on paint mixing can be applied to both oils and acrylics. The pigments used today in both forms are the same; only the media are different. This is not to say that the two have the same visual effect. Oil is typically more glossy; acrylic tends to have a more matte finish, unless a lot of the medium is used. Oils can be blended wet-to-wet since they dry slowly; acrylics dry quickly. Over a long period of time, a quality acrylic paint should retain the original color of its pigment, for the medium dries as clear as glass, albeit somewhat darker than the wet tube paint. Oil paint tends to darken somewhat as it dries, and yellow as it ages.

Another problem can sometimes be seen in old oil paintings. The upper layers which were once opaque may become rather transparent, revealing the underpainting, an effect so well known that it has a name: pentimento. Recognizing that the ground and underpainting may sooner or later be seen in the painting, artists have therefore learned to keep the ground and underpainting of oil paintings as light as possible, and build up colors with the addition of dark colors over light ones.

Ceramic Glazes

Ceramics employ clays which naturally vary in color, from reds, browns, and grays to the white-firing clays used for the finest porcelain. In addition, ceramic objects are often given one or more coatings of glaze, which is brushed, dipped, poured, or sprayed onto the piece and then fired to water-proof, often glossy, hardness. Glazes are made of chemical combinations known as silicates. Their fired color may not be apparent until after firing, so potters typically make or consult glaze samples for color references. If a transparent glaze is used, the color of the clay itself will show through. A matte glaze has a dull, nonreflective, opaque surface when fired. Fritted glazes have shattered bits of water-soluble, molten chemicals added, increasing their color clarity. Methods of firing will also affect ceramic colors. Old traditions are being revived by contemporary ceramic artists for

CONE 04 OXIDATION

CONE 5 OXIDATION

CONE 10 REDUCTION

▲ **8.15** Susan Peterson's glaze tests demonstrate the effects of different firing temperatures on glaze colors.

their special effects. Heidi van Veen-Kiehne used the sixteenth-century Japanese technique of raku firing—brief placement in a hot kiln and then smoking in a bed of natural organic matter—and also threw soda into the kiln during the firing to create the serendipitous color effects shown in Figure **8.14**.

Students new to ceramics may work with commercially prepared glazes to lessen the uncertainties and chemical hazards of the process. Glazes must be matched with the clay body used, considering both the temperature at which they mature when fired and the degree of shrinkage during cooling.

Many experienced potters prefer to compound their own glazes from a variety of chemicals (see Figure 3.8). Recipes for those that work well are highly prized. Glaze consist

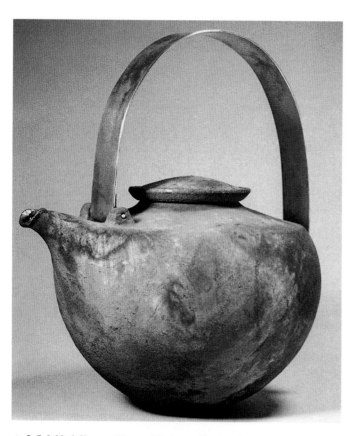

▲ **8.14 Heidi van Veen-Kiehne, Teapot**
Copper handle, 7 × 11 ins (17.8 × 27.9 cm).
Soda-raku fired, grass reduction.

mostly of silica, which is also the main constituent of clay. Silica has a high melting point by itself—around 3090°F (1700°C), but when a "fluxing agent" is added to it (boron, sodium, or potassium are a few that might be used), it is coaxed into melting at a much lower firing temperature. Alumina (which is also present in varying amounts in clay) is added to the flux material and the silica to give the glaze mixture stability and good adherence qualities. Variations in the proportions of these three main ingredients—silica, alumina, and flux—plus variables of other added elements such as iron, zirconium, calcium, copper, nickel, titanium, and zinc, will affect the ultimate color, opacity, glossiness and texture of the finished pot. Other glazing variables include the thickness of the glaze, how it is applied to the pot, and the firing temperature. Test chips of glazed clay are fired in order to study the effects of firing time, temperature, and clay body used. Figure **8.15** shows part of a series of tests by potter Susan Peterson, in which she shows the color effects of firing the same opaque glaze formulation at three representative kiln temperatures: low (cone 4), medium (cone 5), and high (cone 10). The results show that hues are mostly saturated at low firing temperatures.

Colored Glass

From the third millennium B.C., the people of Mesopotamia knew how to create objects of colored glass. When soda, silica, and lime were heated together, the glass was usually of blue-green hue because of the iron impurities in sand, which took the form of silica in the formula. The Romans learned to neutralize such impurities by adding manganese or antimony to produce a colorless clear glass. Brilliant hues could be produced by adding metallic oxides, with the results affected by the temperature of the firing. Copper was used at different temperatures to produce turquoise, dark green, or deep reds.

Very small portions of metal oxides produce highly saturated hues in glass. An intense blue results from adding only one part of cobalt oxide to 10,000 parts of the base glass. These jewel-like colors are made even more brilliant by the light that passes through transparent or translucent glass. Glass artists are also able to juxtapose hues of varying colors by techniques which allow the fusing of bits of differently colored glass to the main form. Threads of contrasting colored glass may be trailed over the piece, or bits of colored

◀ **8.16 Dale Chihuly, *Macchia*, 2005**
Glass.
Chihuly, a key figure in the studio glass movement since the late 1960s and co-founder of the Pilchuck School in Stanwood, Washington, is well known for his large and complex sculptural installation pieces, as well as for smaller, brightly colored works such as those in the *Macchia* series.

glass may be picked up as the piece is being formed, thus incorporating them into the surface. After the base and colorants are fused, the additions may be left to stand in low relief or flattened for a smooth surface. Dale Chihuly's inspiration for his *Macchia* series (**8.16**) (*macchia* means "spot" in Italian) came to him one day while viewing daylight through stained glass windows. He noticed that the part of the glass seen against something white, such as a cloud or fog or building, rather than blue sky, stayed a fully saturated color. He experimented with this color phenomenon in his studio by putting a layer of white glass over a highly colorful glass, and then putting another contrasting hue over that. This allowed the inside of a shape to be a different color from the outside, and both sides could thereby maintain their full intensity without leaking colors through to the other side. He then added a third contrasting color as a lip wrap, for a final punch of color. In Chihuly's glass hot shop, each of the *Macchia* pieces would take six or seven different glassblowers about an hour to make, each adding color to it at different times, sometimes with Chihuly spontaneously adding another color that wasn't on the chart he made for the blowers to follow. With over 300 color rods available, the combinations of the two colors, inside and outside, plus all the spots that could be added to any layer, were almost endless. Chihuly has said "I'm obsessed with color—never saw one I didn't like."[1]

Color Printing

Inks, like dyes, are colorants dissolved in a medium. In graphic design, they are generally used for mass reproduction of artworks originally created in some other medium. There are two ways of doing this: four-color process and flat (or match) color.

In **four-color process**, it is possible to mix most colors from three primaries plus black and the white of the paper (if it is white) by printing the same surface four times in the process, or primary, ink colors. These ink primaries are cyan, magenta, and yellow. In four-color process printing, tiny dots of these hues are juxtaposed so that they will be mixed visually by the viewer's eye. Black dots are added to deepen the dark areas and increase contrast. This system is therefore often referred to as **CMYK**, for cyan, magenta, yellow, and black (or "key").

Four-color process is typically used for the reproduction of **continuous tone** artworks (in which there are unbroken shifts in value, as opposed to shifts in value reproduced by dots), such as paintings and watercolors or, preferably, photographed transparencies of such reflective art. The process begins with photographic or electronic **color separation** of the original continuous tone work. That is, the work is photographed or scanned through filters in the additive primaries—red, green, and blue. The red filter allows only blue and green to pass through, creating cyan. The green one allows only red and blue, creating magenta. And the blue filter allows only red and green light to pass through, creating yellow. The positives printed from these filters are also **screened**, turning values into varying densities of tiny dots. They are then printed one color at a time, starting with yellow, building up to a print that closely resembles the colors of the original even though, when seen under magnification, it is quite different (**8.17, 8.18**). The screens for each color are set at varying angles to each other, rather than being directly printed one atop the other or set at regular angles that would cause undesired geometric moiré (wavy) patterns. When printed, the tiny juxtaposed dots give the illusion—if not the reality—of smooth transitions in values and hues.

It is difficult to match colors precisely with four-color process. For one thing, printing inks are not yet totally pure, so each of the primaries absorbs some of the light it is supposed to reflect. Various means of correcting color imbalances caused by this imperfection are therefore used by printers when high-quality reproduction is desired. Another problem is the impossibility of using the four colors to reproduce certain colors accurately—such as turquoise (which is warmer than cyan), orange-reds, lemon yellow, and fluorescent colors. An expensive option, when high-quality reproduction is needed, is to add one or two more process colors, such as lemon yellow, to increase the range of possibilities. Some specialized printers therefore have six- and even eight-color presses for fine-art work.

A typically less expensive way of introducing broad areas of color into a printed piece—such as a poster or advertisement (as in Figure 9.10)—is the **flat color** method. Here the designer may prepare transparent overlays indicating areas to be printed in one to four colors, or may simply mark

▶ **8.17** An enlargement of an area of Peter Good's poster (8.18), revealing the underlying dot structure of the screens.

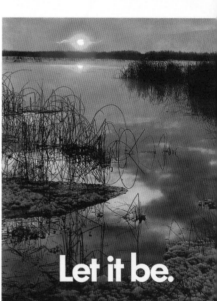

▲ 8.18 The color separation process

Color separations from a 1970 poster by graphic designer Peter Good, employing a photograph by Bill Ratcliffe.

The image has been separated by the printer— The Hennegan Company—into 200-line yellow, cyan, magenta, and black screens. They are overprinted in that order—as shown in the bottom line—to reproduce the final image.

regions of a single original for the printer to print in different colors. There are two ways of choosing and communicating these flat ink colors to the printer. One is based on the process colors. Tint charts (a sample page of one is reproduced in Figure **8.19**) have been developed with varying percentages of yellow, magenta, and cyan. Usually these charts hold magenta and cyan percentages constant and vary the amount of yellow from 0 to 100 percent through a series of charts. The one shown here mixes a 30 percent screen of

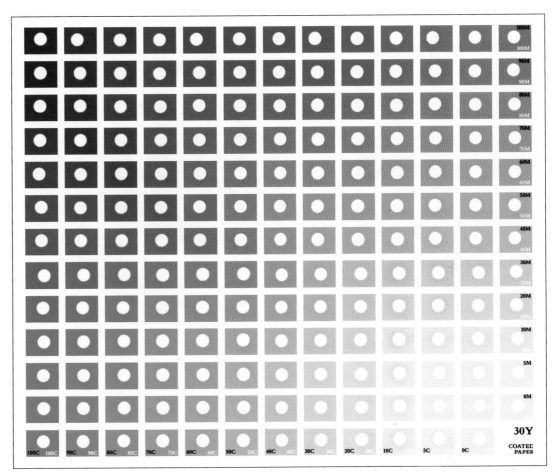

100M
90M
80M
70M
60M
50M
40M
30M
20M
10M
5M
0M

30Y

100C 100C 90C 90C 80C 80C 70C 70C 60C 60C 50C 50C 40C 40C 30C 30C 20C 20C 10C 5C 0C COATED PAPER

▲ **8.19** A page of color finder tints, in which the yellow part of the mixture is 30 percent throughout, with percentages of magenta and cyan varying.

yellow with all possible mixtures of cyan and magenta. As the dots get close together, resulting in a higher percentage of color in the mixtures, the value becomes darker. To gauge the effect of adding black as an extra color, the printing company that prepared this chart also offered a transparent acetate overlay with percentages of black. Colors are then matched with samples and specified in percentage terms. For example, one of the subtle, unnameable colors on this chart would be called 30%Y, 10%C, 60%M.

A second, commonly used method for color matching and specification is the Pantone Matching System (PMS). It is now based on nine "basic colors" carried by printers (**8.20**) plus black and transparent white, which are mixed according to PMS formulas to form a total of one thousand colors. To choose colors and communicate them to the printer, a graphic designer can use any of a number of tools displaying the PMS colors. Figure **8.22**, for example, shows the Pantone Color Guide in the form of a fan. Each page of

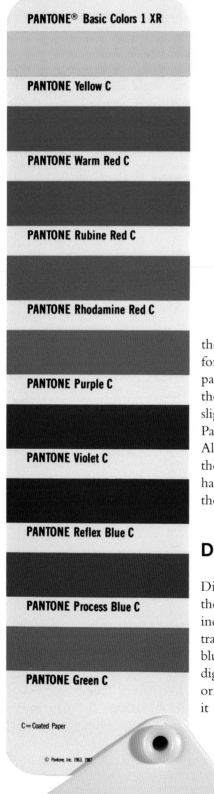

PANTONE® Basic Colors 1 XR

PANTONE Yellow C

PANTONE Warm Red C

PANTONE Rubine Red C

PANTONE Rhodamine Red C

PANTONE Purple C

PANTONE Violet C

PANTONE Reflex Blue C

PANTONE Process Blue C

PANTONE Green C

C = Coated Paper

© Pantone, Inc. 1963, 1987

paper

fuser roller

laser

transfer roller

magenta (m) toner

imaging roller

yellow (y) toner

cyan (c) toner

black (k) toner

◄ **8.21** In color laser printers, the laser beam charges a drum, attracting toner particles. They are then fused to the paper by heat.

the fan displays seven similar colors that vary slightly in formula for comparative purposes. Pages from different parts of the fan can also be compared side by side. To increase the number of colors available, the designer can specify slight alterations in the formulas. The C or U following the Pantone numbers indicate "coated" or "uncoated" paper. All colors are shown on both coated and uncoated stock, for they are considerably more brilliant on the former, which has been sealed with a clay covering so that inks will sit on the surface rather than be absorbed.

Digital Printing

Digital printing uses the same color base, CMYK, as the standard workhorse lithographic presses use in industry. The inks and dyes are known as "subtractive" colors, in contrast to the RGB (red, green, blue) colors of light that are within computer monitors. A digital printing process begins with the scanning of a fine art original or piece of commercial graphics into a computer, or it could begin directly with the computer in the case of

◄ **8.20 PMS basic colors**

computer-generated art or graphics. In the former, the CMYK gets converted to the RGB of the color monitor. In the latter, the artwork is created in RGB. The RGB colors of the monitor must change again to CMYK before printing can take place. Therein lies the newest problem of color management, which we discuss in the next topic section.

All printers use a form of dots, drops, or spots to create an overall image. The pixels (**pic**ture **el**ements) of the computer, referred to as **ppi**, or pixels per inch, become dot formations within the printer, or **dpi**, dots per inch, and these dots can be of different sizes and shapes, closer or farther apart, built up in layers on the paper, or sprayed out from the nozzle and joined up as a dot before reaching the paper. The dots can overlap, which creates tonality of hues. Some printer nozzles can produce multiple drops within a dot of color. Mathematically, this can deliver as many as 1.2 million colors per dot. When there are that many droplets in a dot, they can be as small as a red blood cell.

There are several types of printers on the market today, all using various methods to obtain a "continuous tone" print. Digital photo processing is what most photography developers use, whether they are minilabs, photofinishing labs, or online processors. It is a system that takes input from conventional film, digital camera, digital media, or prints (there is an onboard scanner for this step) and outputs to digital media or prints via wet-chemistry processing. The Fuji Frontier was the first digital minilab used in this way.

Color laser printers, also called "xerography" (meaning dry picture), use a laser beam to charge revolving drums of

◀ **8.22 The PMS fan**
With ink formulas for each of 1,000 colors, it is printed on both coated and uncoated paper.

▲ **8.23** Halftone screening (top) with frequency modulated screening (bottom), 30x magnification.

▲ **8.25A** An inkjet reproduction of an image, with 500 percent enlargement to show how the color is laid down in dot patterns.

◄ **8.24** IRIS print of variable-sized and over-lapping dots.

dry CMYK toner (**8.21**). The charged particles are drawn to the paper and fused by heat to the surface. Laser printers, along with other types of printer that produce continual tone prints, use a newer type of halftone screening called "frequency modulated" (FM) or "stochastic" (named after the type of random dot patterns) screening techniques to produce a near continuous tone where the dots are smaller and more random than halftone dots alone (**8.23**).

Dye sublimation (dye-sub) printers are used for high-quality photo and digital snapshot printing. They have a color ribbon that contains dye, and a heating head that runs the width of the paper. This head has thousands of tiny elements that heat up and vaporize (sublimate) the dye at that location, which is absorbed into the surface of the paper. Separate passes of CMYK ribbons build up the image,

▲ **8.25B** Laser reproduction of the same image, with 500 percent enlargement showing dithering of the dot patterns.

▲ **8.25C** IRIS (giclée) reproduction of the same image (with 500 percent enlargement), approaching continuous tone printing.

resulting in a layering of colors for a smooth, seamless final print. Some of these machines add a clear UV laminate as a final step. Dye-subs have a loyal following among those who prefer them to inkjet printers.

Inkjet printing can be divided into categories, depending on how the ink is applied to the print surface. Continuous flow technique, as in the IRIS/IXIA printers (see Figure **8.24**), uses electrostatic charging to recycle the part of the inks sprayed but not used in the image. Drop-on-demand types of printer use only the ink needed for the image, rather than a continual flow. Most desktop inkjet printers currently use this drop technology. There are subcategories within drop-on-demand: piezoelectric, or piezo for short, using an electric field that subjects certain kinds of crystals to expansion or contraction and forces the ink out of the nozzles by

pressure; thermal, involving the heating of a resister inside the printed chamber; or solid ink, where solid blocks of resin-based inks are melted by heat. This is, of course, an oversimplification of these processes, but might help explain the diversity among printers on the market today. Each process creates a slightly different effect, carrying its own issues of permanence of inks, what paper and ink combinations need to be used, and speed of printing.

Inkjet printing techniques are used for high-end printers, but also for the low end, which seems in itself a bit contradictory. However, the popularity of the IRIS 3047 printer, the high-end inkjet printer that started the inkjet revolution, may have been a driving force behind the development of desktop printers, because more and more artists began using the IRIS for smaller editions, and manufacturers saw a new market developing. The rush to fill that market continues.

When IRIS printers first came out, they were used for proofing and final comps for designers and printers. Even though they produced a smooth, continuous-toned print, with quality that was amazing for a proof, their inks faded within a year or two. As the decades passed, with improvements in inks and papers, a new industry of fine-art reproduction printing emerged using the digital technology of scanners and computers, and IRIS became more than a proofing machine. We often call continual-tone prints "IRIS prints" or "IRIS giclées," in spite of the fact that the new company CreoScitex has taken over the production of the IRIS, and the IRIS 3047 has been redesigned into the IXIA (**ick**-zee-ah, a word borrowed from the botanical genus for the iris family, and often shortened to **zee**-ah) by Improved Technologies New Hampshire (ITNH). The sidekick term "giclée" (zhee-clay), so often used interchangeably with IRIS, simply means "that which is sprayed." Back in 1991, Jack Duganne of Nash Editions in Los Angeles needed a new word to distinguish Diane Bartz's museum-quality prints for an upcoming show. He wanted to avoid reference to words like "digital" or "computer" since the art world was having a hard time accepting the new printing medium. Duganne used his pocket French dictionary to look up the word for "inkjet" (*jet d'encre*), then looked up "nozzle" (*le gicleur*), and then "to spray" (*gicler*) and decided on the feminine noun version, "*la giclée.*" The term was used for the first time in print to advertise Diane Bartz's work at the ArtExpo California, fall of 1991. Giclée, thanks to serigrapher Duganne, was a marketing word that caught on, and is now a standard in the industry when referring to a continuous-tone fine-art print. New terminology is being trademarked now, as in Tru Giclée™ by the Giclée Printers Association (founded in 2001), which requires its printmaker members to meet nine standards before they can display the trademark, and Tru Decor™ by the same group, which has a lower number of standards for the larger decor-art market.[2] Along with IXIA, there are other large-format inkjet printers being used, each of which has its own particular following. Figures **8.25A**, **B**, and **C** show the different results obtained from three types of printer.

"Hard copy" output from the computer screen may take the form of high-resolution film negatives and slides, as well as paper, textile, tile or canvas prints (variety depends upon the thickness of material that individual printers will accom-

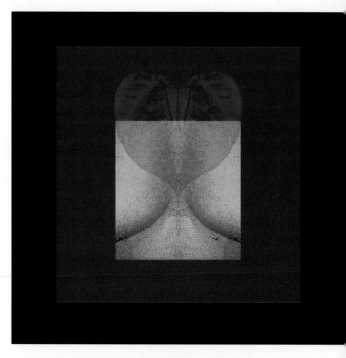

▲ **8.26 Janet Cummings Good,** *Gold icon, Heart Leaf*
Iris print, image 3¼ × 3¼ ins (8.25 × 8.25 cm), paper 8 × 8 ins (20.3 × 20.3 cm). Edition of five.

modate). Higher-quality desktop printers now allow artists to produce their own small-run editions. They still have the option to use commercial print companies for their final output, as in the case of Janet Cummings Good. On the processes behind the creation of her IRIS giclée prints such as *Gold Icon, Heart Leaf* (**8.26**), she says:

> *The computer has fed and fuelled my obsession with color since I got my hands on my first color monitor and printer in 1995. The analytical side of my mind loves the limitless possibilities for fine-tuning hue, value and saturation with the click of a mouse, the choice of a number, the sliding of a bar, the reshaping of a curve.*
>
> *Of course, the analytical is always at the mercy of the intuitive, which needs to ponder, contemplate, and react for no reason other than to come to a sense of personal sureness. Both approaches are facilitated by seeing the richness and subtlety of color that is produced by the miraculous little inkjet printer simply spraying pigment on paper.*
>
> *Any completed print is always preceded by a myriad of trials. And when the "final" print is established, I can choose to create one-of-a-kind or a series. The true "electronic original" is then archived away,*

remaining available to me as raw material to rethink, reform, reconfigure, and recolor. The wonder of the electronic file is that it stays fresh and pure, retaining forever its potential for being printed or recreated.[3]

Because of the ease of programming the computer over setting up the plates for a lithographic press, going "digital" allows for a wider variety of output at less cost to the consumer. There is still a need for standard presses, as digital printing does not meet all the printing needs for every job, at least not at the time of writing. And there are still issues that are ongoing with digital printing, the most notable being archival quality of papers and inks, although great improvements have been made since the first IRIS proofing machines were used. In fine-art printing, paper companies continue to experiment with coatings such as film laminates, liquid laminates, and sprays. There is now a new inkjet "infusion" formulation that is added as part of the paper-making process. Its inventor, John Edmunds, states, "This is the only type of built-in inkjet coating that actually increases the longevity of the paper and the inks that are applied to it."[4] Inkjet expert Dr. Ray Work is a firm believer in coatings. "Coating, or better yet, laminating with a pressure-sensitive lamination film, will give increased protection from moisture, which can interact with other variables and accelerate image degradation," he says. "Coating or laminating is also important for microporous, fast-drying papers that can soak up air pollution and cause rapid fading."[5]

While improvements in ink color fastness, intensity, and richness of tone continue, there is still no process using printing inks that can equal the brilliance of the hues created on the monitor screen with pure lights. The attempt to narrow the gap between RGB and CMYK, to control and formulate a consistency of color reproduction, has created the need for a new type of color management.

Color Management

The management of color has always been a primary concern in the printing industry, but there used to be a closed system, where all colors used throughout the input and output processes were CMYK-based. Pantone CMYK color spots or books gave formulas for consistency when inks and dyes had to be mixed. Scanners were set to CMYK colors. That is no longer the case, of course. We now face a diversely mechanized landscape, where our input and output machines have to convert and receive in RGB or CMYK, and be able to pass this information back and forth. And there are so many devices now in use: drum scanners, flatbed and slide scanners, monitors, a full range of digital cameras, and an assortment of presses using a variety of ink types on direct-to-plate printing, as well as digital proofers, film recorders, silk screeners, color copiers, and laser and inkjet printers. An even longer list would include all the different manufacturers of each of these machines, which makes for a very large group having compatibility issues when going from the light colors of RGB to the subtractive colors of CMYK. This is what makes color management such a complex issue, and it affects not only the entire process of printing, but also all those involved with getting the work to press. Graphic designer Keith Edwards explains:

Color management is an ongoing challenge in this industry. As technology continues to change within each facet of the design and production processes, we find ourselves having to adjust color at each step within that process to maintain consistent results. From the initial "comprehensive renderings" of design layouts/concepts to the finished printed piece, we rely on calibrated displays and color laser printing technology to provide us with something tangible to present to clients. Accuracy at this stage, however, can be as detrimental as it can be beneficial—clients' eyes tend to become "attached" to the laser printouts, which may not be color-accurate to the final printed piece. We find that even with the most high-end proofing technology that the printing industry has to offer, a final print might not match up perfectly to the colors from the proof, because the final medium is litho ink on paper as opposed to the inkjet, toner, wax, or dyes, etc. used for the proofing medium. In short, control of color gets better with each improvement in technology, but true management for us means anticipating the final medium—print or web respectively—to formulate something of a color "forecast." The more understanding one has of the final medium, the more useful the forecast.[6]

In the late 1980s and early 1990s, many companies that used device-to-device technology developed color-management systems to allow their printers, scanners, and monitors to work in tandem. These could solve the individual company's problems, but they were not compatible with any other company's system. Then, in 1993, Apple came out with ColorSync, building it into the

▲ **8.27** ColorVision SpectroPRO spectrocolorimeter.

Macintosh operating system. Apple started the ColorSync Consortium, which included other companies using the ColorSync system, and this group later became known as the International Color Consortium, or ICC. They used "profiles" in their system. Like a dictionary that translates one language to another, profiles changed colors into numbers which were plotted from the C.I.E. color chart (see Figure 8.7). RGB and CMYK could both be translated back and forth from these numbers. The concept is simple, but the technology is complex. The ICC soon came out with their ICC Profile Format Specification, which was a multi-vendor-friendly profile format that gave some standardization to color management.

The act of **profiling** sets up a record of how your computer, scanner, or printer is behaving, in a color profile, the type of color (RGB or CMYK), and what colors it can or cannot make are recorded. Calibration features are built into many computers now, so that you can change the computer's behavior to keep it in line with the color profile you have set up.

Profiles do not change the facts at hand, they record them; calibrations change things. In order to have monitors, scanners, and printers able to translate their information to each other, each needs a separate profile. Since this information is being transmitted in the form of numbers, screening algorithms are developed to convert the pixels of the com-

puter monitor into the dots of the printers. You can notice this every time the print window comes up on your monitor, enabling you to alter the ppi (pixels per inch) and the dpi (dots per inch) before you print something. Differences in those screenings will produce different tones in the prints (as in Figure 8.23). When you are a company dealing with large press runs, it is financially essential that all your machines be as closely color-matched as possible, so professional print shops usually calibrate their machines on a weekly basis to keep the profiles in sync.

There are now software packages on the market to improve this process, making it easier for anyone to get a good-quality print out of their desktop printer. In Figure **8.27**, a spectrocolorimeter acts as the link between the computer and the printer, measuring the colors on the target and fitting them into an ICC profile.

As in the case of any field of study, color management has its own language to help define it, and some familiarity with a few of the most basic of these terms helps when learning about CM. Trichromacy, which we wrote about in Chapter 3, refers to the three types of cone sensitivities we have in our retinas. There are cones that are sensitive to either long, medium, or short wavelengths, which gives us the ability to see red, green, and blue. This is similar to the three phosphor capabilities of the monitor screen. The rods in our retinas allow us to see in low-light conditions, but our cones carry the magic of color vision to our brain. Often the word tristimulus is used in relation to trichromacy, although they are two different things. Trichromacy refers to the theory that we have tricolor cone receptors. Tristimulus refers to measurements of three sources that are used to create a model for color management. Very detailed tristimulus are used by the C.I.E. as the basis for their color management. The term **metamerism** refers to the feature of our color vision that actually allows us to make color reproduction possible. In the simplest of terms, when a color sample is seen differently by two observers, yet the sample has the same recorded spectral value, that is a metameristic phenomenon. It is the same phenomenon that happens when two separate spectral hues can

▶ **8.28 Eliot Porter, *Pool in Brook, Pond Brook, New Hampshire*, 1953**
Dye-transfer print, 10¹¹⁄₁₆ × 8⁵⁄₁₆ ins (27.1 × 21.1 cm).
© 1990, Amon Carter Museum, Fort Worth, Texas, Bequest of Eliot Porter (P1989.19.23).

be made to look the same—most often by changing the light source, but also according to the color theory of "colors are affected by the colors around them" (see Figures 3.10 and 3.11). We have all experienced this. A single hue can change when viewed in either fluorescent or incandescent light, and be different once again in daylight. Metamerism can be when two samples look the same in a certain light, or when two samples look different in a certain light. Where does metamerism fit into color management? A scanner's sensory detectors might pick up a color and its detectors may match it, but when the sample comes out, our eyes see the colors as a mismatch. This issue of scanner metamerism makes it difficult to use scanners to create color profiles. The same thing happens in digital cameras. Engineers and color-management specialists are well aware of metamerism, but it is good for anyone working with color to be aware of it, since it plays such a basic role in color control.

There are other variables which are likely to affect the outcome of any color printing process. The paper's grain and absorbency will make a difference in the visual effect of inks applied to it, and of course its own color becomes one of the factors in the color mixture. The appearance of the inks themselves is affected by variables such as the sequence in which the colors are printed, the opacity or transparency of the ink formulation, the amount of water in the ink, the surrounding temperature, the size of pigment particles, the dryer used in the ink, its viscosity and tackiness, and the amount of ink used in the job. As the paper is passed through the press, the printing speed, humidity in the area, and drying time are among the many factors that can alter the final results and must be carefully controlled.

Color Photography

Black-and-white photography records differences in value, but color photography must also record differences in hue and saturation. The procedures and chemistry used to do so are complex and involve both additive and subtractive color mixing systems.

For both color prints and transparencies, the recording of colored images on film typically begins with an **integral tripack**: film with three thin layers of gelatin with sensitizing dyes. These dyes are now so sensitive that they can register light beyond the limits of the visible spectrum, from

▲ **8.29 Diane Althoff,** *Untitled,* **2000**
Chromogenic print mounted on aluminum, 144 × 30 ins (366 × 76 cm).

about 200 nanometers at the ultraviolet end to more than 1,300 nanometers at the infrared end. When the tripack is exposed to an image, it registers the image in the light primaries—blue, green, and red—by separating metallic silver grains from the silver halides. The result is invisible, however, until it is developed.

In the **color positive** or **reversal process**, used largely for transparencies such as slides, each layer is developed with chemical couplers that cause dyes to be released in unexposed areas in the subtractive primaries yellow, magenta, and cyan. When all three are superimposed, the area will appear black, the result of subtractive mixing. Areas of yellow and magenta will appear orange; yellow and cyan will make green; and magenta and cyan create blue.

In a **color negative process**, typically used for making color prints, dye-forming couplers are in the tripack itself. The first developer brings out the complementary colors in the exposed areas as a color negative. This color negative may then be printed onto special paper containing more dye-forming couplers in color-sensitized layers. The couplers in the paper will turn cyan, magenta, and yellow into their additive complements: red, green, and blue.

Many elaborate chemical adjustments and refinements are made to enable color reproduction by these methods to be as accurate as possible, without bias toward any particular area of the spectrum. This accuracy is often aesthetically desirable, for many photographers seek out interesting or beautiful color effects in the world around them and then attempt to record them on film, as in Eliot Porter's capturing of a fleeting moment of the vivid effects of sunlight on water (**8.28**).

However, sometimes the artist's purposes are better served by distortion of the colors of the original image. Photographed objects may become vehicles for color experimentation that has nothing to do with their original coloring. In her untitled chromogenic print (**8.29**), Diane Althoff has used the camera to record something whose identity is lost as she enlarges the image to a twelve-foot height. It becomes a surreal exploration of color and nebulous forms in space.

As a photograph is taken, manipulation of exposure time and choice of film will affect value and contrast but hue will remain largely unchanged. Colored filters placed over the lens will bias the results toward a certain color; diffraction filters will bend light into prismatic effects. Dramatic alter-

◀ **8.30 Frank Noelker,** *Untitled*
IIRIS print. Courtesy of the artist.
Frank Noelker travels around the world to photograph animals in zoo settings and then uses his computer to alter the colors, creating imagery that is at once convincingly natural and yet surreal.

ations in color may also be made in the darkroom, using techniques such as chemical toning, **solarization** (whereby the development process is briefly interrupted by exposure to low-intensity colored light, reversing the colors especially in high-value areas), and **posterization** (whereby continuous tone images are converted into distinct flat tones, in any color).

Colors can also be manipulated without limit in images scanned into computers before printing. In **8.30**, Frank Noelker has used the capabilities of the computer to readjust the colors in his photograph. Noelker finds that the computer allows him to make changes which are nearly impossible in traditional darkroom manipulation of photographs. He says:

> *I choose the digital process to print my documentary photographs because it gives me the greatest amount of control. Traditional color film cannot reproduce the color green in either hue or saturation with enough accuracy to suit my needs. I am able, through the computer, to reproduce all of the colors in the spectrum true to my original subject. I also love the different surfaces that I'm able to print onto in the digital process. I choose to print on rich watercolor papers instead of the plastic-coated papers that traditional photography is limited to using.*[7]

Fiber Dyes

The expanding world of fiber arts includes yarns, fabrics, basketry, and anything else created from linear materials woven together. Pre-dyed fibers can be interwoven to form patterns, or sheets of fabric can be dyed after they are woven.

With modern chemistry, the range of colors possible is so vast that *The Color Index* (**8.31**), a professional color specification list, includes over 8,000 dyes classified by chemical structure, properties, and applications (not all of which fall into the visual arts).

Traditional hand-dyeing of fibers—an art still carried on by many handweavers—begins with gathering of the dyestuffs. Practically any plant material can provide some colorant, but certain leaves, stems, berries, seeds, barks, and roots are known to work especially well as sources. The most common natural dyes are in the yellow and earthy brown range.

Natural dyes from plants are often quite different from their own color. Beets and strawberries, for example, yield only beige, and purple pansy blossoms give an intense blue-green dye. Moreover, colors will vary from dyebath to dyebath. Nevertheless, natural dyes are appreciated for the very features that make them unacceptable to commercial dye houses: Their subtle colors may or may not be replicated, depending on seasonal variations in the dye plant itself. A sampler of natural dyes with their sources, as prepared by handweaver Pat McMullan, is shown in Figure **8.32**.

Natural dyes will only adhere to natural fibers, such as wool, cotton, jute, linen, and silk. These materials' own natural color will, of course, affect the outcome. Before dyeing, the fibers are wound into hanks and scoured to remove foreign matter that would interfere with the dyeing. Often the fiber is then simmered in a **mordant** to help set the dye and perhaps affect the color. The mordant is a chemical, such as alum, iron, tannic acid, tin, or copper. The dyestuff itself is boiled in water to release its dye and the mordanted material is then simmered for a time in the

---

45370   **C.I. Acid Orange 11** (*Reddish orange*)
45370:1   (**C.I. Solvent Red 72**) is the free acid
45370:2   (**C.I. Pigment Orange 39**) is the aluminium salt

Dibrominate **Fluorescein** in aqueous sodium hydroxide and isolate as the sodium salt

Discoverer — Badische Co.
BIOS 959, 6, 26
FIAT 764 — Eosin H 8G
Am. J. Pharm. (Sept. 1942), 342 (see also *Coal-tar Color Regulations*, U.S. Food and Drug Administration. Sept. 1940, 13)

Slightly soluble in water (orange with faint yellow fluorescence)
Soluble in ethanol (orange with a greenish yellow fluorescence)
Soluble in acetone (pink with a yellow fluorescence)
Very soluble in furfuryl and tetrahydrofurfuryl alcohol
H_2SO_4 conc. — red yellow; on dilution — yellow brown with orange ppt.
Aqueous solution + NaOH — eosine red
Glycerol and liquid paraffin — good dispersion

▲ **8.31 Solvent dyes from *The Color Index***

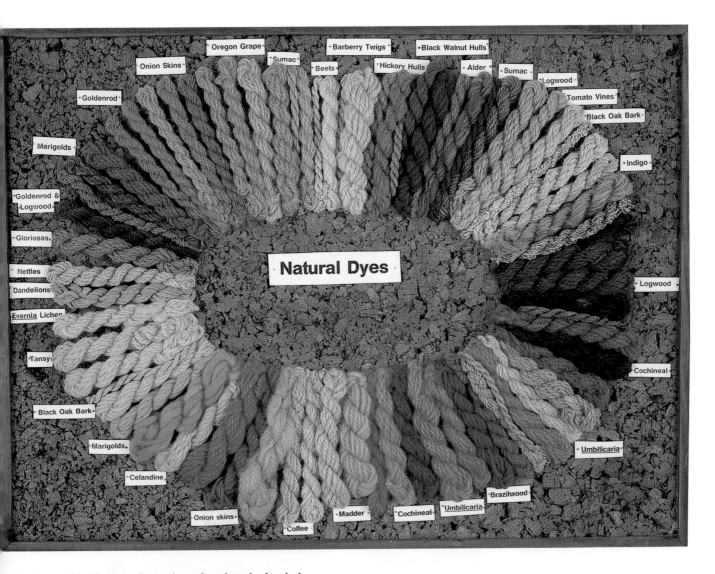

Natural Dyes

- Oregon Grape
- Onion Skins
- Sumac
- Barberry Twigs
- Black Walnut Hulls
- Goldenrod
- Beets
- Hickory Hulls
- Alder
- Sumac
- Logwood
- Marigolds
- Tomato Vines
- Black Oak Bark
- Goldenrod & Logwood
- Indigo
- Gloriosas
- Nettles
- Dandelions
- Logwood
- Evernia Lichen
- Tansy
- Cochineal
- Black Oak Bark
- Marigolds
- Umbilicaria
- Celandine
- Onion skins
- Coffee
- Madder
- Cochineal
- Umbilicaria
- Brazilwood

▲ **8.32 Pat McMullan, Sampler of natural plant dyes**
Most natural dyes are typically subtle, of low saturation, with exceptions such as cochineal, logwood, and umbilicaria (a lichen).

dye-pot. Longer dyeing typically deepens the value and may increase the intensity of the dye absorbed.

Dyestuffs are not usually mixed with each other directly, for the result tends to be a drab olive. If one therefore wanted to dye fibers green using goldenrod and logwood, one would first dye them with the goldenrod to be sure of getting a good yellow and then overdye some areas with the logwood, which by itself yields a purple or gray. Kitchen ingredients—ammonia, baking soda, vinegar, or cream of tartar—may be added to the dyebath to alter the color.

Adding vinegar to a purple grape juice dye, for instance, will turn it green!

This hand-dyeing procedure is a form of **direct dyeing**. Many artificial fibers, such as nylon and polypropylene, must be dyed by other means, since direct water-soluble dyes do not stick to them. **Dispersed dyes**, such as acetate dyes, are not soluble in water, but nonetheless disperse through the fiber when applied in a soap solution. **Reactive dyes**, such as henna for hair coloring and procions for dyeing cellulose fibers, bond chemically with the fiber. **Vat dyes** respond

within the fiber after it has been subjected to a certain treatment, such as being exposed to air and sunlight or an acid solution. Indigo is a vat dye, turning fibers blue as they are lifted out of the vat and exposed to air. Successive dipping and exposure will gradually deepen the color.

Such methods allow manufacturers of yarns to offer palettes of color, in both natural and synthetic fibers, that range from the subtle, unsaturated colors prized by many craftspeople to very bright, pure hues that are hard to obtain with most natural dyes. Figure **8.33** shows a great variety of contemporary commercial dye colors for mixing and use by fiber artists.

Xenobia Bailey has used a full palette of fiber colors in her *Sistah Paradise Great Wall of Fire Revival Tent* (**8.34**), a cross between a Southern Baptist Revival Tent and an African full-body mask with eyes. In her "aesthetic of funk," its rings of color are described as a "Mandala cosmic tapestry of energy flow."

Brilliant synthetic dyes for clothing have changed the human landscape. In India, peasant women have adopted saris of synthetic materials in highly saturated, almost fluorescent hues that add a rich and happy note in the midst of a life in the mud and dust. Such colors retain their visual impact even under bright sunlight, and unlike the short-lived dyes in natural cotton saris, they retain their brilliant colors without fading from washing and use. On the other hand, the toxicity of some petrochemical dyes—such as procions—may present serious environmental hazards and health risks to workers in dye plants.

Fading of Subtractive Colors

Fading from exposure to light has long been a problem with many dyes, inks, and pigments, both natural and synthetic. An example of the impermanence of the early red lakes can be seen in *The Virgin and Child Before a Firescreen* (**8.35**), where the less stable red has faded from the original purple robe, leaving behind the more stable blue.

Even with more colorfast pigments, sunlight and bright indoor lighting can damage artwork, so museums are careful

▲ **8.34 Xenobia Bailey,** *Sistah Paradise Great Wall of Fire Revival Tent*, **1999**
Hand crochet, cotton and acrylic yarns, height 10 ft (3.04 m).
Stefan Stux Gallery, New York.

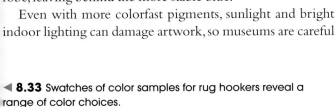

◀ **8.33** Swatches of color samples for rug hookers reveal a range of color choices.

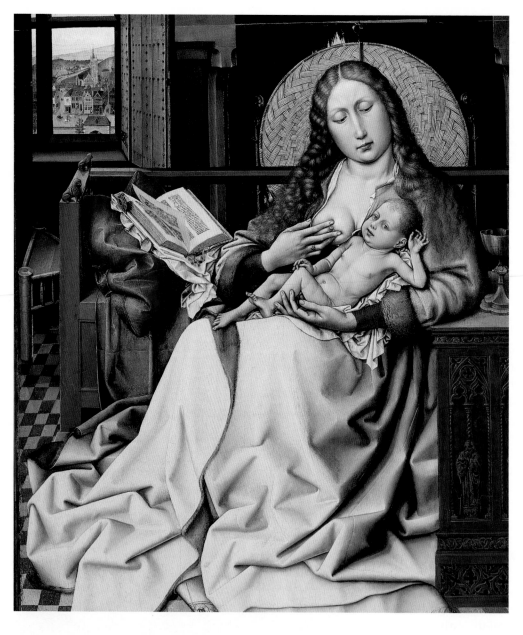

◀ **8.35 Follower of Campin, *The Virgin and Child Before a Firescreen*, c. 1440**
Oil with egg tempera on oak with walnut additions, 2 ft 1 in × 1 ft 7 ins (63.4 × 48.5 cm). National Gallery, London. Even with fading, this nearly 600-year-old medieval painting shows a masterful use of color. The robe still ripples in luxurious folds, while the details of a landscape can clearly be seen through the window in the upper left of the painting.

to display works with diffused lighting, and as new museums are built, or old ones renovated, attention is given to the choice of glass for windows, and to their overall placement in their gallery settings.

Both color and black-and-white photographs are susceptible to fading, and care should be taken in their display. At one time, collectors used to keep their watercolors and prints in drawers instead of displaying them, to prevent the colors from breaking down. Even with today's technological advances in paint chemistry, no paintings should be hung in direct sunlight. Fading happens gradually with some paints, so is often noticed after it is too late to correct the error. Museums and individual collectors, having paid high prices for their artworks, are naturally concerned that their purchases should last a long time. New advances are being made all the time to extend archival qualities of prints, especially in the field of continuous-tone printers that deal with art reproductions.

9 Color Combinations and Interactions

● ● ● ●

Give me mud and I will make the skin of Venus out of it,
if you will allow me to surround it as I please.

EUGÈNE DELACROIX

THUS far we have dealt with colors largely in isolation from each other. But in reality, we rarely see colors singly. Colors are surrounded by other colors, and they all interact in our perception. There are two ways of looking at this basic fact: We can seek pleasing or exciting combinations of color, if that is our aim, or we can study and exploit the ways that juxtapositions of specific colors affect our perception.

Color Schemes

The art of combining colors to create pleasing harmonies was approached as a science of sorts by many color theorists in the past. Certain color groupings were thought to be far more aesthetically appropriate than others, and attempts were made to list and prescribe the kinds of relationships that seemed to work best. Today, this approach is more typical of applied designers than fine artists; interior decorators are more likely to think in terms of color schemes than are painters. And in all the visual arts, effective color combining is more a matter of adding a pinch of this and a bit of that, to taste, than of following precise recipes. The underlying structures have been studied and understood, then used in intuitive and original ways.

The simplest color scheme is **monochromatic**. A single hue is used, often with variations in value and saturation to avoid monotony. Deborah Muirhead's *Nebula* (**9.1**) is painted almost entirely in varying values of bluish grays at

low saturation, with just subtle hints of grayed yellow-green. With all the colors available to the contemporary painter, why has she so limited her palette? Muirhead explains:

> *My work is about my continued interest in the ideas of elegy, memory, and mystery. In my paintings I try to evoke these sensations by creating an atmosphere of light with color. The reductiveness of my palette is not a limitation. In fact, it requires the viewer to participate longer with the painting in order to have color revealed and shrouded images emerge. The neutral grays of various tonalities of repressed hues are built up with thin glazes of paint in an attempt to suggest this ephemeral presence.*[1]

Whereas the flow of Muirhead's monochromatic color shifts occurs subtly, mysteriously, with no hard edges, sharp edges may often be distinguished between areas of very similar hues, as in Ad Reinhardt's monochromatic *Abstract Painting, Blue* (**9.2**). Although he has used only blues of low to medium value, the hue mixtures—a bit more green, black, or purple in the different blues—prevent the colors from flowing into each other visually. Each defines a distinct, hard-edged shape if viewed under proper lighting. Some of the shapes seem to come forward, as if they were sitting or floating on top of the surrounding color. Here the intentionally limited monochromatic color scheme allows us to give our full attention to these spatial effects and to the relationships of shape across the picture plane.

Variations on a single monochromatic theme obviously do not have to be boring. Often designers break up the inherent unity of a monochromatic scheme by using neutral

◄ 9.1 Deborah Muirhead, *Nebula*, 1991
Oil on canvas, 6 × 5 ft (1.83 × 1.52 m). Private collection.
Despite the abundance of colors available in the modern palette,
monochromatic variations on a single hue can be very effective.

colors—white, black, grays, and browns—as well as variations on the chromatic hue.

The next closest harmony is an **analogous** color scheme,
which uses several hues lying next to each other on a color
wheel. This is an imprecise concept, for color wheels can
have as few as six colors or as many as hundreds or thousands
of variations, depending on the size of the steps between
hues. On a six-hue wheel of pigment primaries and secondaries, blue and green lie next to each other. Based on such a
wheel, the azure-painted gravel paths and green gardens of
Daan van Golden's *Aqua Azul* (**9.3**) would be said to consti-
tute an analogous color scheme. However, in this context
they appear to be highly contrasting. The harmony would be
closer if there were more intermediate hues, such as a range
of blue-greens of varied values and saturations (as indicated
on the 12-hue color circle in Figure **9.4** and expanded in the
color map in Figure **9.5**). The colors would also seem more
closely related if there were less value contrast between the
high-value blue (a blue 7 on the color map) and the dark
green borders (value 4 green), and if the sole blue of the
gravel paths were not so highly saturated. It is clearly apparent that the artist was not intent solely on creating a quiet,
calming color combination, although the color choice is
actually a traditional one. In the seventeenth century, the
paths of this garden were, in fact, laid in blue tiles.

A high degree of contrast is expected in the third kind of
color scheme: **complementary**, in which the two principal
colors lie opposite each other on a color wheel. In a sense,
complementary hues are related like the two ends of a balancing device—they hold each other in equilibrium. If we
think in terms of warm and cool colors, a complementary
color scheme may provide a psychologically satisfying
balance between these two extremes. Goethe even felt that

► 9.2 Ad Reinhardt, *Abstract Painting, Blue*, 1952
Oil and acrylic on canvas, 75 × 28 ins (190.5 × 71.1 cm).
Carnegie Museum of Art, Pittsburgh, Pennsylvania.
Even in a monochromatic work, slight variations in hue and value
allow the viewer to see differences and therefore edges between
colored areas.

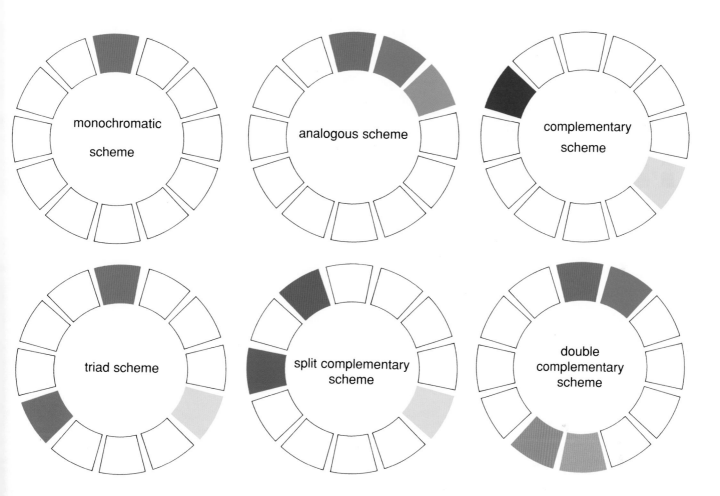

monochromatic
scheme

analogous scheme

complementary
scheme

triad scheme

split complementary
scheme

double
complementary
scheme

the eye hungers to see the complement. He wrote of "the demand for completeness, which is inherent in the organ,"[2] supplying after-images of the complement if it is not actually present. While providing psychological completeness, complementary colors used together also intensify each other's appearance, so the result tends to be stimulating, as in Van Gogh's *Peach Blossom in the Crau* (**9.6**), in which highly saturated purple and yellow are repeatedly juxtaposed.

Toning down the saturation of complementary hues—and raising or lowering their value beyond the level of

◀ **9.3 Daan van Golden, *Aqua Azul*, 1987**
Painted gravel on the paths of the Botanical Gardens, Amsterdam. Blue and green, an analogous color combination often used today, was deplored by earlier color theorists as offensive and vulgar.

▲ **9.4 Standard color schemes**

maximum saturation—lessens the visual contrast between them. Nevertheless, even at reduced contrast, complementaries may still subtly intensify each other's liveliness. Charles Emile Heil's *Lotus* (**9.7**) relies primarily on the contrast between green and red, both of which are painted at high value or relatively low saturation. This color scheme has been further balanced and varied by a secondary interplay of two other hues that are complementary to each other: yellow and blue-purple.

When two hues adjacent to each other on a color wheel are used with their respective complements, such as blue-green and blue with red-orange and orange, the scheme is called **double complementary**. Another scheme derived from the complementary pattern is **split complementary**, in which the hues to either side of the complements are employed, thus

◄ **9.5** Broad use of analogous colors might encompass three or four adjacent hues with many variants in value.

softening the contrast slightly. As used by Rufino Tamayo in his home outside Mexico City (**9.8**), a split complementary scheme offers a surprising juxtaposition of yellow, red-violets, and blue-violets. Tamayo enjoys the unexpected and had the ceilings of his home painted in chromatic hues—blue, mauve, yellow—while keeping the walls white. As he notes with amusement: "Usually it's the other way around." Although Tamayo strives to touch the universal in the human spirit, he does so by way of ancient pre-Hispanic and popular Mexican aesthetic themes, reflected in his color choices:

◀ **9.6 Vincent van Gogh, *Peach Blossom in the Crau*, 1889**
Oil on canvas, 25¾ × 32 ins (65.5 × 81.5 cm).
Courtauld Gallery, London (Courtauld gift 1932).

▲ **9.7 Charles Emile Heil, *Lotus*, c. 1912**
Watercolor on paper, 16 × 22 ins (40.6 × 55.8 cm).
Museum of Fine Arts, Boston.
An almost-black green provides a complementary foil to the high red of the lotus blossom, with toned-down complementary contrasts echoed throughout the painting.

I've used the colors of both my palettes here: those the village people use in their daily lives because they're cheap, like the blues and whites and ochers, and those bright colors they buy especially for fiestas.[3]

A broader range of contrasts is seen in the **triadic color scheme**, which draws on three colors equidistant from each

▲ **9.8 Rufino Tamayo, Part of living room with pre-Columbian pieces, near Mexico City**
Split complementary color schemes may offer unexpected color partnerships.

other on a color wheel. In his *Builders* (**9.9**), Jacob Lawrence has used the triad of pigment primaries—red, blue, and yellow—interwoven with brown, black, and grays. These "neutral" colors are visually interlocked with the chromatic hues, like flat shapes in a jigsaw puzzle, so that they are not mere background foils for the other colors. If anything, it is the black head of the hammer that most immediately draws our attention in this busy scene. Although the colors have been painted evenly, rather than with the value gradations associated with three-dimensional form, careful use of lines of one color extending into another—such as the blues enhancing the outline of the foremost worker's bent leg and the contours of his head—help us to recognize a slight volume in these figures. The interplay of dark blue against light blue, dark red against light red, and dark yellow against light yellow resembles the complex point and counterpoint rhythm of a vigorous jazz composition, used here to commemorate the workers whose various manual tasks combine to construct the buildings in which we live and work.

Another approach to harmonizing colors is to use colors together that vary in hue independently of any of the above schemes but that are nonetheless similar in value. Bruno Paul's poster (**9.10**) juxtaposes a low saturation blue-green, red, and yellow of nearly the same value—approximately value 6 on the Munsell system—making them appear to belong together. To bring striking contrast into this muted scheme he adds a slightly darker brown (a yellow 5) and fully dark black accents on the storks and the typography. For variations on this basic equal-value theme, one could include colors of slightly higher or lower value. Rigid symmetry would require balancing additions of higher value with some of lower value, but few works of art are so rigidly patterned.

Rather than using hues that balance each other at intervals around a color wheel, or values that line up horizontally across a color map such as the one in Figure 9.5, artists may choose to balance lights against darks. J. M. W. Turner (1775–1851) was an artist who worked primarily in this way, analyzing color combinations in terms of the harmony of value contrasts or, as he put it, "the compelling power of colors used as shade to light, that wrought the whole to harmony."[4] A useful guideline for artists is that it is impossible to get a good light unless it is offset against a dark, and vice versa. If the artist were working so formally as to strive for absolute balance of values, there would still be no need for equal amounts of darks and lights, for lights expand and appear to take up more room than darks. In Turner's *Light and Colour* (**9.11**), wherever the artist wants a light to appear more dramatically luminous, he juxtaposes it to a dark area. The whole painting is like a swirling tunnel, with light appearing through the darkness, an abstract representation of the welcome appearance of light as a storm clears.

Another means of creating harmony among colors was suggested by Chevreul. He described it as:

> the harmony of a dominant coloured light, produced by the simultaneous view of various colours assorted according to the law of contrast, but one of them predominating, as would result from the view of these colours through a slightly coloured glass.[5]

▶ **9.9 Jacob Lawrence, *Builders*, 1980**
Gouache on paper, 34¼ × 25⅜ ins (86.9 × 64.5 cm).
SAFECO Insurance Company, Seattle.
Here values of red, yellow, and blue are used as a triad; any other colors equidistant from each other on a color wheel form a triad, but its character will differ depending on the hues chosen.

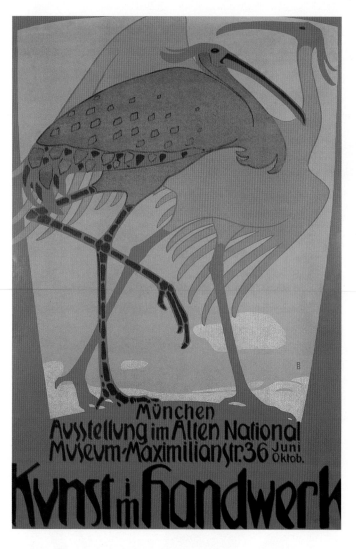

▲ **9.10 Bruno Paul, *Exhibition in the Old National Museum, Munich: Arts and Crafts*, 1901**
Poster. State Museum, Munich.
Colors of equal value may seem to belong together; variations in value within the same composition avoid monotony.

In accordance with this, Mauro & Mauro's promotional piece for Champion International (**9.12**) uses varied hues of very low saturation and high value, all blended by having a single dominant color in common. The die-cut papers all appear to be seen through a film of the same cream color that surrounds them.

Theorist Rudolf Arnheim looked for dynamic relationships among pigment hues: "similarities and differences, mutual completion, concord and discord." From his efforts he came to the following conclusions: 1) The three primaries—red, blue, and yellow—are pure hues and therefore not related to each other except that they add up to a complementary triad. 2) The three secondaries—purple, orange, and green—each consist of equal parts of two of the primaries and therefore act as a "bridge" between them. 3) The six tertiaries contain unequal parts of two primaries (such as a red-purple, which has more red than blue in it—as can easily be seen in the color wheel in Figure 2.9). "Being thus unbalanced," he stated, "the tertiaries are highly dynamic, prone to interact with other colors and, for this reason, particularly inviting for pictorial composition."[6] However, artists work with an enormous palette of potential colors rather than the twelve spectral hues of the color wheel, and can push them this way and that depending on how they choose to use them.

Black and white are typically considered "neutral" and therefore are not often mentioned in theories of harmonious color relationships. However, some artists use them as prominent hues in their own right. Daniel Buren used black and white as strong contrasting colors in his installation *Topical Arguments* (**9.13**) in an old warehouse that has been turned into a museum for contemporary art. He multiplied the effects of the relationships of the black and white stripes to the yellow-lit walls, and the shapes of arches within arches, by reflecting them from an enormous slanting mirror, some 14,000 square feet in extent.

Naive, folk, or "outsider" artists often use color intuitively, without reference to any established system of color harmony. Bessie Harvey's *Tribal Spirits* (**9.14**) employs extremely raw colors, in no seeming order, but juxtaposes hues and combines them with black in such a way that they have a more spiritual quality than we would usually associate with bright reds, blues, golds, and yellows. The spirits she experiences in the wood come to life with a glowing energy from the way she uses the paint, as if dynamic light patterns were emanating from their hair. The spots of white draw everything together and further add to the sensation of pulsating light. She is using color choices very confidently in her own personal way.

▲ **9.11 J. M. W. Turner,** *Light and Colour (Goethe's Theory: The Morning After the Deluge, Moses Writing the Book of Genesis),* **exhibited 1843**
Oil on canvas, octagonal, 30½ ins (77.4 cm). Tate Gallery, London.
Turner was fascinated by the juxtaposition of light and shade, the principle upon which many of his compositions are based.

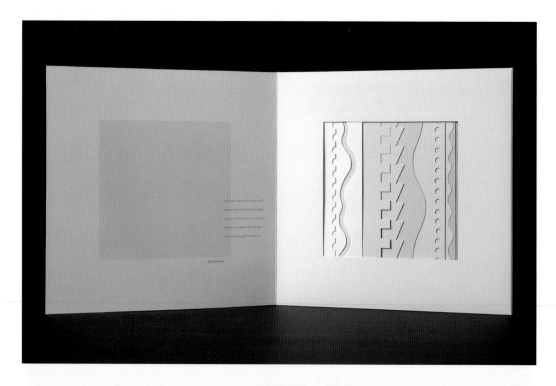

◄ 9.12 Mauro & Mauro, Design for Champion International, Stamford, Connecticut
Promotional piece with layered die-cutting.
One of many possible color harmonies suggested by Chevreul was the impression of a "dominant coloured light" influencing all hues in a work

◄ 9.13 Daniel Buren, *Topical Arguments (Arguments Topiques)*, May 1991
Installation, black-and-white stripes 3½ ins (9 cm) wide, mirror 14,000 square feet (1,300 sq. m).
Contemporary Art Museum (CPAC), Bordeaux, France.
Whereas white and black are often given a supporting or background role in artworks, here they are treated as significant colors in themselves.

▲ 9.14 Bessie Harvey, *Tribal Spirits*, 1988
Mixed media, 45 × 26 × 20 ins (114.3 × 66 × 50.8 cm).
Dallas Museum of Art, Texas.
Spots of white give a unifying framework to this seemingly uninhibited use of color.

Color Interactions

Whether or not colors are combined according to established color schemes, one should always be aware of the optical effects that adjacent colors have on each other. Particularly in two-dimensional work, every color used will be affected by what is next to it. Colors are never seen in isolation.

Consider the perceptive observations of Henri Matisse, who often juxtaposed areas of flat-painted colors, as in *Red Interior, Still-life on a Blue Table* (**9.15**):

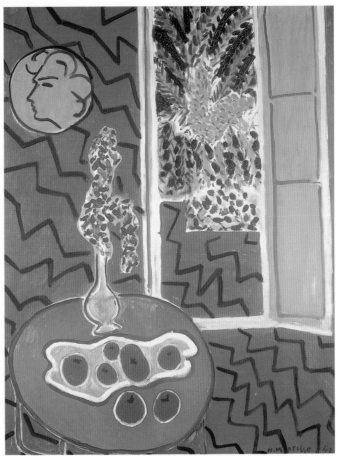

▲ 9.15 Henri Matisse, *Red Interior, Still-life on a Blue Table*, 1947
Oil on canvas, 45¼ × 35 ins (115 × 89 cm).
Kunstsammlung Nordrhein-Westfalen, Düsseldorf, Germany.
To prevent adjacent colors from diminishing each other's perceived brilliance, Matisse has in places separated them by borders of black, white, or gold.

If upon a white canvas I jot down some sensations of blue, of green, of red—every new brush stroke diminishes the importance of the preceding ones. Suppose I set out to paint an interior: I have before me a cupboard; it gives me a sensation of bright red—and I put down a red which satisfies me; immediately a relation is established between this red and the white of the canvas. If I put a green near the red, if I paint in a yellow floor, there must still be between this green, this yellow, and the white of the canvas a relation that will be satisfactory to me. But these tones mutually weaken one another. It is necessary, therefore, that the various elements that I use be so balanced that they do not destroy one another. … My choice of colors does not rest on any scientific theory; it is based on observation, on feeling, on the very nature of each experience.[7]

Beyond this world of perceptible color interactions lie mysterious optical color phenomena that transcend the physical properties of a work of art. Optical color interactions are most apparent to those who know to look for them. Other people may not "see" them because there is no model of reality confirming their existence; they allow their brains to override their visual receptors. Some interactions happen very quickly; others take some time to develop.

One of the optical phenomena noticed by Goethe and Chevreul is what Chevreul called **successive contrast**. That is, as we noted in Chapter 3, if one stares at a color for some time and then looks away, one "sees" its complement as a colored glow. Back in Figure 3.4, after looking at the red turtle, you probably saw a green turtle when you shifted your gaze to the white space next to it. Goethe explained this phenomenon as an innate striving for completeness:

When the eye sees a color it is immediately excited, and it is its nature, spontaneously and of necessity, at once to produce another, which with the original color comprehends the whole chromatic scale. A single color excites, by a specific sensation, the tendency to universality.

To experience this completeness, to satisfy itself, the eye seeks for a colorless space next to every hue in order to produce the complemental hue upon it.[8]

◀ **9.16 Jasper Johns, *Flags*, 1965**
Oil on canvas, 6 × 4 ft (1.82 × 1.22 m). Collection of the artist.
Stare at the dot in the upper flag for perhaps a minute and then quickly transfer your gaze to the dot below to see the effect of successive contrast.

▲ **9.17** Look at the border between red and blue for a while and note the optical effects. Compare them with those occurring when the two hues are separated by broadening bands of white and black.

▲ **9.18 Mary Franks, *Ikon*, 2000.** Etching.
At the edges where two lines meet, what happens? Do all the edges of the central figure work in the same way?

▲ **9.19** A middle mixture will look like two different colors when presented against its parent colors.

▲ **9.20** Two physically different colors can be made to appear nearly identical by careful choice of colored grounds.

If, however, there is no white space next to an intense color sensation, the color we perceive when we shift our gaze is a combination of the complement of the original and the color of the space itself. Jasper Johns worked intentionally with this principle to create *Flags* (**9.16**). If you stare at the dot in the middle of the upper flag for 60 seconds and then shift your gaze to the dot in the center of the rectangle below, you may perceive the red and white stripes and white stars on blue background of the United States flag. This is a complex optical mixture and takes a while to develop.

Johns's *Flags* series is one of the few artistic efforts tha purposefully use the phenomenon of successive contrast However, the effect does occur when we look for a long time at any color. When working with a large area of red, fo example, it may appear to shift toward green or gray; if one does not rest one's eyes by glancing away, one will lose the ability to see the red as another person just looking at it would Visual fatigue can change our perception of any color.

A phenomenon that is used consciously in some art works is what Chevreul called **simultaneous contrast**. In this case, complementary colors—or any strongly contrast ing colors—that are adjacent will intensify each other along the edge where they meet. If you stare at the center of Figure **9.17** for some time, you will begin to see a brighter glow o each color just inside the edge where they meet. Compare this effect with the interactions of these colors when separated by widening bands of black (to the left) and white (to the right). Do the colors intensify each other as much when separated by white as by black? How does widening the intermediate line alter the effect? At what point?

Simultaneous contrast, first commented upon by Leonardo (see Chapter 6), has often been used by painters and graphic designers. Just as to get a good light, you need to place it next to a dark, it is a similar rule of thumb that to get an intense hue it helps to place it next to its complementary. In her *Ikor* (**9.18**) Mary Franks has surrounded Mary's traditional blue robe with a red-orange field, bringing out by simultaneous contrast a glowing quality in the yellow area next to the robe It is not just the depiction of a halo; it actually has a luminous appearance. Josef Albers observed that strongly contrasting hues of high saturation and equal value—even if not precisely complementary—will vibrate optically along the edge where they meet, creating a sensation of transparent, glowing light that enforces the boundary line and the shapes it divides.

Albers also systematically studied the possibilities o making one color look like two different colors, pushing it in opposite directions according to the background color it i seen against. This is an optical illusion of particular usefulness in applications such as graphic designs with limited palettes. In Figure **9.19**, the same blue-green has been placed on green and blue. But because the eye automatically compares these strips with what surrounds them, it sees the strip on the right as bluish in comparison with the green and on the left, greenish in comparison with the blue. In a sense, each ground subtracts its own energy from what lies upon it. This effect is most readily created with a third color that is a **middle mixture** between the other two; the three bars below demonstrate that the color used as the strip is actually a blue-green, a mixture of blue and green. Proportions and distances are also critical; if the two strips were very close, they could more readily be compared with each other than with the grounds and one would see that they were the same.

Less useful but equally fascinating is the ability to deceive the eye into thinking it is seeing fewer colors than have actually been applied. Using the same principle that a ground will subtract its hue from anything applied to it, a blue-purple has been placed on a blue and a red-purple on a red in Figure **9.20**, creating the illusion that the small squares are nearly identical. When compared with each other below, removed from the grounds, they are readily seen as two different hues.

Notice something else in Figure 9.20: The small square almost seems to merge with its ground on the right, whereas it pops out boldly on the left. The greater the difference between colors—in hue, saturation, and/or value—the

▲ **9.21 Josef Albers,** *Equivocal*
From *Homage to the Square: Ten Works by Josef Albers.* Silkscreened print, 11 × 11 ins (27.9 × 27.9 cm). Estate of Arthur Hoener.

◄ **9.22 Dorazio,** *Construction Eurasia,* **1964**
Oil on canvas, 5 ft 6 ins × 8 ft (1.7 × 2.4 m).
Private collection.
Follow the illusionary overlappings of any of these ribbons to discern the nuances of multiple transparency effects.

greater the apparent spatial distance between them, especially if the edges between them are hard rather than soft.
An optical glow caused by the eye's reaction to the contrast
in hues begins to surround the small square on the left,
further lifting it away from the red ground.

Albers devised a single framework for working with these
interactions: a square within a square within a square, set off-
center so that the relative proportions of the colored areas
are varying rather than uniform. This great *Homage to the
Square* series opened up so many possibilities that experimenting with the effects of precise color combinations
occupied Albers for almost 30 years. Albers stated:

> *In my work*
> *I am content to compete*
> *with myself*
> *and to search with simple palette*
> *and with simple color*
> *for manifold instrumentation*
> *So I dare further variants.*[9]

▲ **9.23 Michael James,
*Rhythm/Color: Morris
Men*, 1986**
Machine-pieced cotton
and silk, machine quilted,
8 ft 4 ins × 8 ft 4 ins
(2.54 × 2.54 m).
Within a general framework of
transparency effects,
Michael James contradicts
the effects of see-through
mixtures in many of the color
"intersections" in this quilt.

◄ **9.24 The Bezold Effect**
Changing a single color in this
composition brings out
certain shapes and hides
other ones. The artist has also
rotated the second version
180 degrees, further disguising
the underlying similarity
between the two.

Albers found that in the case of a true middle mixture in hue and value, such as the rust color between the red and the olive in *Equivocal* (**9.21**), the parent colors would seem to leap across to reappear along the far edges of the middle color. Next to the red on the right-hand side, there is an olive-green glow, created by the subtraction of red from the rust. Part-way across the rust band the effect begins to reverse, creating a red glow along the edge that abuts the rust, which is darkest where it can be compared with the white ground. These optical variations create a fluted effect, as though the bands were rounded in or out in space.

Another type of interactive use of color is found in **transparency effects**, in which one color appears like a film lying over another. To make this appear visually sound, one must mix pigments that convincingly give the appearance of visual mixtures of the colors in question. Moreover, the one that is to appear on top must dominate the blend; otherwise it will not make spatial sense. Dorazio's *Construction Eurasia* (**9.22**) presents a complex series of transparencies with, in many places, up to three ribbons overlapping each other on top of a white ground. If the colors are modified accurately, each ribbon's spatial relationship to the others should be discernible.

Often artists play with the suggestion of transparency effects without making them fully logical. Michael James's quilt, *Rhythm/Color* (**9.23**), provokes us to try to follow the effects of overlaid colors, which in this case are not at all transparent in actuality. Rather, they are pieces of opaque fabric pieced together side by side. James has created the fascinating impression of striped bands crossing each other, causing transparent color mixtures in some areas and overlapping non-mixtures in others, with surprises at every turn.

Wilhelm von Bezold, a nineteenth-century rug designer, discovered another optical interaction, which now carries his name: the **Bezold Effect**. He found that he could change the entire appearance of his rugs by changing or adding only one color. Usually this is done by substituting a different color for the one that occupies the most area. In Figure **9.24** the change in the dominant hue from red to blue dramatically alters the whole. Not only do the colors change; different shapes are also brought out in one version and hidden in the other. It is also possible in some cases to alter the whole by changing a color that does not occupy the largest area, especially if it is used in a striking way.

If colors of equal value or very similar hue are juxtaposed, the boundaries between them will vanish. It will be difficult

▲ **9.25 Edouard Vuillard,** *Breakfast***, 1892**
Oil on canvas, 12 × 10½ ins (30.4 × 26.6 cm).
Paul Rosenberg and Co., New York.
Colors of equal value tend to merge with each other optically along their edges, so that the boundary between them vanishes.

to determine where one stops and the other begins. The effect of **vanishing boundaries** is fairly easy to produce with colors of either very low or very high value. In painting the woman's blouse in *Breakfast* (**9.25**), Edouard Vuillard has juxtaposed reds and blues of such high value that one merges quietly into the other, even though at medium value and high saturation these are highly contrasting hues. Elsewhere, such as in the black projection across the woman's lap, the rungs of her chair, and the area of the floor beneath, colors of similar hue but slightly differing value also tend to merge where they are juxtaposed. With highly saturated middle values, colors must be really close in hue to lose the edge between them.

The color theorist Ogden Rood devoted a whole chapter of his *Modern Chromatics* to the subject of "The Small Interval and Gradation," stressing the importance of vanishing boundaries in our perceptions of the world around us:

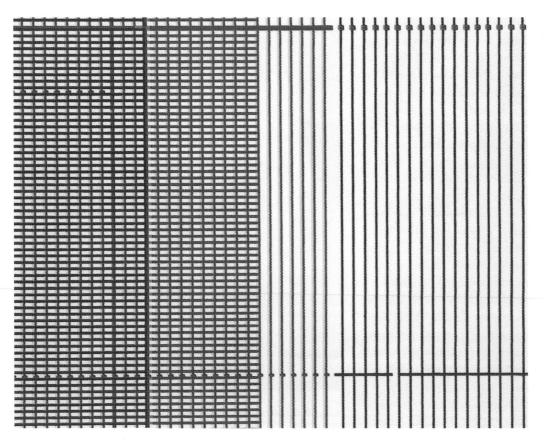

◀ **9.26** Phantom colors are those that tint surrounding neutral colors with their own hue. This effect is most obvious in the "yellow band" of this computer drawing, but it also occurs to a certain extent in the other bands.

One of the most important characteristics of color in nature is the endless, almost infinite gradations which always accompany it. It is impossible to escape from the delicate changes which the color of all natural objects undergoes, owing to the way the light strikes them…. Even if the surface employed be white and flat, still some portions of it are sure to be more highly illuminated than others, and hence to appear a little more yellowish or grayish; and, besides this source of change, it is receiving colored light from all colored objects near it, and reflecting it variously from its different portions. If a painter represents a sheet of paper in a picture by a uniform white or gray patch, it will seem quite wrong, and cannot be made to look right till it is covered by delicate gradations of light and shade and color.[10]

The last three kinds of optical color interactions concern what happens in the spaces between colors. One of these is the phenomenon of **phantom colors**. In some cases, colors spread beyond their physical boundaries to tint larger neutral areas in their own hue. In Figure **9.26**, the ground is a uniform white, but the thin yellow lines alongside the green- and red-dotted lines in the center spread to cast their

influence over the white in the central panel. Where red and green lines cross the verticals in the next panel to the left, the effect changes to ephemeral red and green flashes of color on the white, or an overall brown sensation. And to the far left, the white may have a blue cast. These phantom colors appear most readily when the lines have a slightly jagged edge, rather than a perfectly straight one, perhaps setting up an excited pattern in the eye. What do you see on the white to the far right, where only blue lines have been applied?

As we have discussed, the persistence of our vision allows us to perceive mosaics of tiny dots in a few primaries on a television screen, or in four-color process printing, as areas of optically mixed colors. The nineteenth-century experimentation with application of colors, which can be seen in the work of Delacroix (10.13) and later evolved into Impressionism and Postimpressionism, had as one of its objectives the intensification of painted colors. The Postimpressionists Paul Signac and Georges Seurat tried to achieve this goal by using a palette of pure spectral colors (Seurat used 11 hues spread evenly around the color wheel,

◀ **9.27A Georges Seurat,**
Les Poseuses, **1888**
Oil on canvas, 6 ft 7 ins × 8 ft ¾
in (2 × 2.45 m).
Barnes Foundation.
In some areas, Seurat
juxtaposed dots of pure hues,
mixing them optically rather
than blending them on the
palette.

▼ **9.27B**
In this detail of 9.27A, *Les
Poseuses*, do the dots
create optical mixtures or has
Seurat mixed the perceived
colors on his palette?

plus white for tinting) and applying them in small
unblended bits, in the attempt to coax the eye to blend them
optically. A detail of the technique is shown in Figure
9.27B. In theory, it would avoid the darkening of physical
subtractive mixing and approach the additive effect of light
mixing, with optical mixtures of high saturation. This technique was known as **Divisionism** or, when the white
ground was allowed to show through and assist the blending,
Pointillism. Signac claimed these results:

> *By the elimination of all muddy mixtures, by the exclusive use of the*
> *optical mixture of pure colors, by a methodical divisionism and a*
> *strict observation of the scientific theory of colors, the neoimpressionist*
> *insures a maximum of luminosity, of color intensity, and of*
> *harmony—a result that has never yet been obtained.*[11]

Divisionist painters actually attempted two different kinds of
effects. By juxtaposing dots of analogous colors, they hoped
to create luminous admixtures in spectral hues; by juxtaposing complementaries, they sought luminous gray mixtures.
In Seurat's *Les Poseuses* (**9.27A**), red and blue dots across the

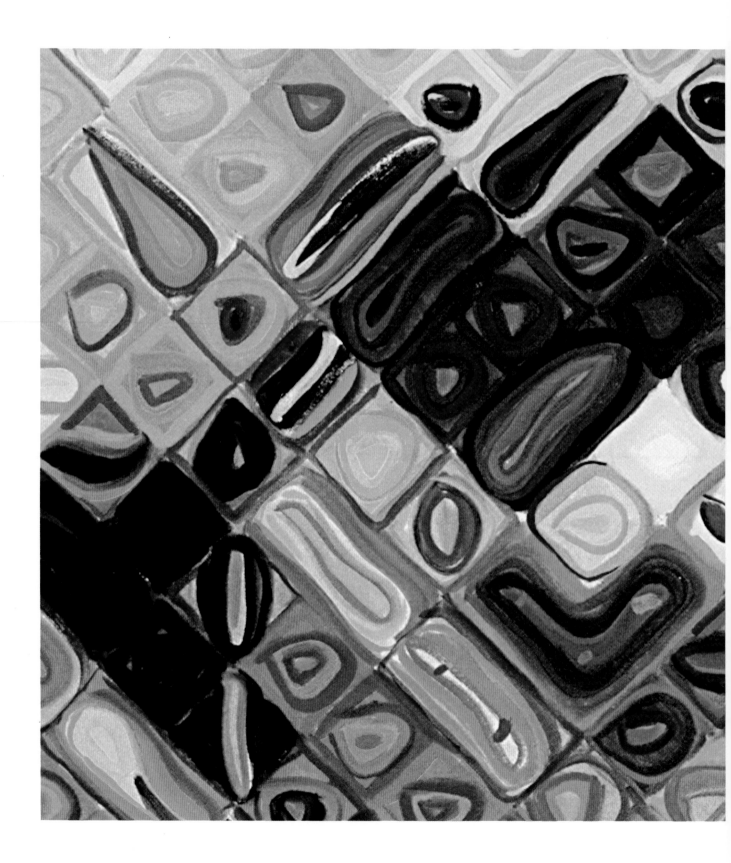

women's contours generate grayish shadows, while in the grass of Seurat's famous painting reproduced on the left of the painting—*A Sunday Afternoon on the Island of La Grande Jatte*—blues, greens, and yellows are used together to stimulate the eye to mix bright greens. In fact, these experiments were not entirely successful. Chevreul had warned that interweaving of the fine threads of complementary colors would create dull optical mixtures, unlike the brilliant additive effect of mixing colored lights.

Such efforts have continued in the work of contemporary artist Chuck Close, who has carried Pointillism to an extreme in his large paintings and prints. In his screenprint *Self Portrait* (**9.28A**), the grid size of his points of color is huge compared with the Postimpressionist's dots, some being several inches across. They are filled with colors of maximum saturation so they will all hold up when working together. Obviously this image has been reduced greatly from the true size of the print, which is nearly five feet tall, so you are unable to get the full impact of this work. Part of the power of Close's work deals with the effect this scale has on the eye, how our vision tries to hold on to the image as we come in closer and closer. The further reduced image in Figure **9.28B** is still not quite small enough for our eye to completely blend the tones, but it represents how far away we would have to be to lose most of the hand-painted grids.

John Roy, on the other hand, became fascinated by the potential interface between science and art. He used a computer to convert photographs into triangular grids of dots, which he then enlarged to one-quarter-inch diameter, and colored in the red, blue, and green phosphors of additive light mixers, like those in computer monitors. These dots are so large that they are clearly visible in the original. But once

◄ ▲ 9.28A and B Chuck Close, *Self Portrait*, 1997
Oil on canvas, 8 ft 6 ins × 7 ft (259.1 × 213.4 cm). Museum of Modern Art, New York.
Chuck Close's signature style is still painted by hand, where he gets results that differ from computer-generated work. The detail on the left is shown at actual size. Viewing Chuck Close's larger-than-life portrait from a far distance, as shown above, pulls the resolutions together.

◄ 9.29 John Roy, *Untitled*, 1999
Computer-plotted Pointillist painting.
Using a triangular grid filled with ¼-inch (6-mm) red, green, and blue dots, John Roy created what he called "purely perceptual colors." He explains: "In this kind of painting, illusionary colors (are) produced by a kind of color mixture that occurs across larger regions of the painting space, which is perceptually disengaged from the physicality of the pigments used to produce them."[12]

▲ **9.30 Arthur Hoener, *Synergistic Color Painting*, 1978**
Acrylic on canvas, 32 × 32 ins (81 × 81 cm).
Estate of the artist.
In Hoener's synergistic color mixtures, a white, gray, or other pale ground is the stage for optical mixtures which become additively lighter than the colors used to mix them.

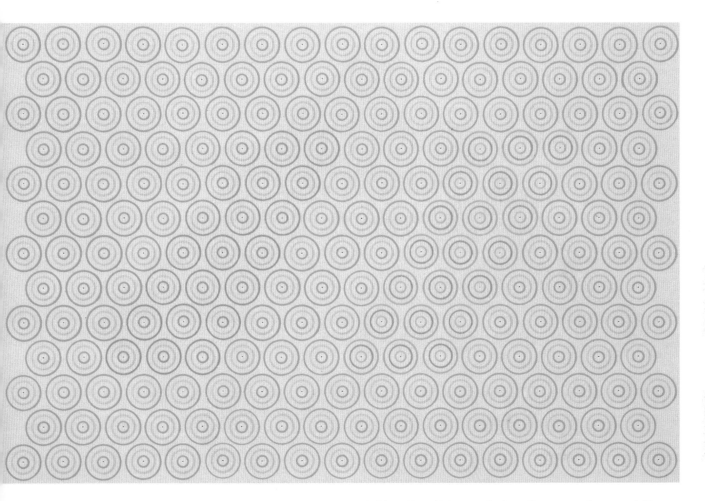

▲ **9.31 Arthur Hoener, Color diagram of synergistic color mixing**

viewers back away far enough—or the image is sufficiently reduced in size—they are able to perceive the image in an approximation of its original colors, mixed optically by the eye from the additive primaries. The yellow you "see" in Roy's autumn landscape shown in Figure **9.29**, for instance, does not actually exist in the painting—it is mixed in your brain as a purely perceptual color.

Extraordinarily successful optical mixtures were created by a twentieth-century artist, Arthur Hoener. Distressed that physicists could perform magic with color, which he felt was really the province of the artist, Hoener experimented with precise colors and proportions until he was able to create convincing optical mixtures, such as the reds, blue, and yellow we see in his *Synergistic Color Painting* (**9.30**). Figure **9.31** reveals his technique at close-hand, showing the mixing hues he was using, all of them high value and none of them a traditional pigment primary. Hoener called his approach

synergistic color mixing because each color seen is the result of the cooperative effect of two colors. He explained:

The thing that is important in order to get the synergistic color to work is to understand the relationship of color to its ground color. A dark color on a white ground will look almost black; it's hard to see the color quality of it. With a medium-value color on a white background you can see the hue of that color and you might even get a simultaneous contrast effect, which would be the opposite of that color developing in between the lines. As the color becomes lighter, the eye does not overreact to what it's looking at and allows you to see the energy of the color.

When physicists talk about color, they always talk about it in terms of energy. Most of the time when artists work with color, they deal

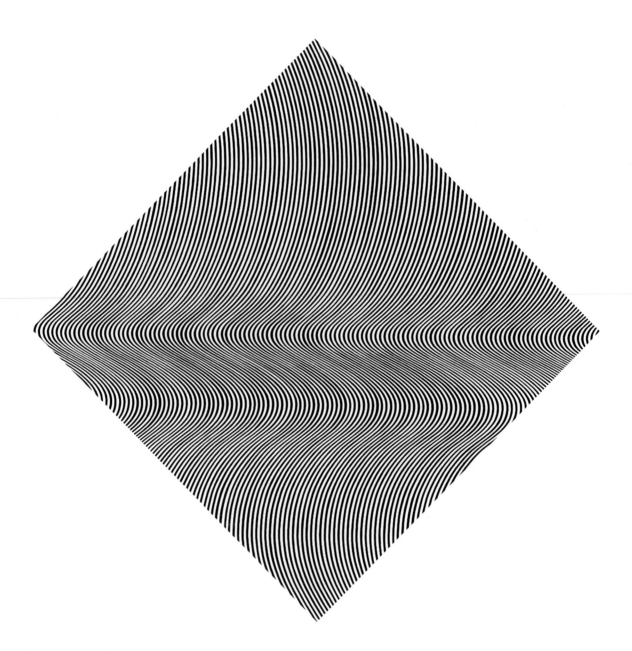

with the overreaction of the eye to the color: an after-image, vibrating colors, contrasting colors, enhancement of green by putting a red next to it, and so forth. Synergistic color is really taking advantage of the fact that the energy of the color is available to be mixed with other colors. Using that principle of how color relates to its background, it is possible to mix almost any color. The color sensation is then highly satisfying, because you, the viewer, are supplying it. But for the artist to create this effect, both the precise hues and the proportions in relationship to the ground are very, very touchy.[13]

▲ **9.32 Bridget Riley, *Crest*, 1964**
Emulsion on board, 5 ft 5 ½ ins × 5 ft 5 ½ ins (1.66 × 1.66 cm).
Mayor Rowan Gallery, London.
Stare at this "black-and-white" work for a while to see what illusory chromatic hues begin to appear.

Hoener said he had to number the jars of paint he used because once he began laying them down together, there was no way he could recognize them. In fact, the mixtures work so well that he intentionally threw them off just slightly so that viewers can see the lines of the mixing hues themselves. Otherwise people simply think they are seeing yellow, failing to recognize that the yellow is a magic combination of thalo green and orange-pink, for instance. Like all color interaction effects, this optical mixing works best if we relax the defensive grid that makes us label things rigidly according to what we "know" we are seeing, and prevents us from recognizing the extraordinarily varied realities of color.

When this defensive grid is truly relaxed, it is even possible to see chromatic hues in a black-and-white work. Bridget Riley is highly successful at this, using linear motion, precise spacing, and the contrast between black and white in her work *Crest* (**9.32**) to coax us to see phantom colors in the white areas. Even the black lines change to unexpected brilliant hues if you look at the work long enough. Just what colors you will perceive and how long it takes them to develop will depend upon your visual flexibility (how willing you are to allow what you see to change), the lighting you are viewing the work in, and how long your eyes can remain out of focus. Goethe observed long ago that looking at the edge between a light and a dark area with a magnifying glass, thus pulling it out of focus, will cause one to see a spectrum of hues. The lens of the glass is curved just like the human eye. It may be that when the eye is thrown slightly out of focus—in *Crest* by being cast off by the repeated wavy lines—this same spectral effect occurs. Since we will perceive more of the world around us if we are carefully attentive, appreciating optical colors requires that we first abandon our attempts to control what we see and then carefully observe the optical realities of our perceptions.

10 Color in Fine Art

● ● ● ●

We treated color like sticks of dynamite,
exploding them to produce light.

MAURICE VLAMINCK

OVER time and across cultures there have been many different ways of using color in the fine arts. To a certain extent, these have been governed by technology. The earliest peoples had a palette limited to the pigments that were common in local earth, chiefly the red and yellow ochers of iron and the black of manganese. The most primitive of cave paintings are monochromatic drawings, but some—such as those in the caves at Lascaux, France, dated around 15,000 to 10,000 B.C.—incorporated washes to suggest three-dimensional form within the drawn out-

lines (8.1). These were polychromatic, involving more than one color for subtle shading.

The White Lady (**10.1**) of Brandberg Mountain in Namibia, Africa, first recorded in 1918 by a surveyor in the German Colonial Army, Reinhard Maack, is the best known of the Brandberg rock paintings, in part due to Maack's misidentification of the figure. Archeologists now feel this particular painting depicts a young male priest, or shaman, decorated with white body paint.[1] Unlike the cave paintings of Lascaux, all of Brandberg's paintings and etched figures are

◀ **10.1** *The White Lady*, **Brandberg Mountain Bushman painting**
Brandberg Mountain in western Namibia, Africa, shelters a storehouse of ancient rock art along its walls, believed to have been made by the San Bushmen hunter-gatherers 2,000 to 5,000 years ago.

in the open, or under overhangs with only slight protection from the strong desert sun. The fact that their colors are still visible after thousands of years of exposure to weather is a testament to the permanence of the earth colors used.

Non-Western Traditions

Surviving small-scale, technologically simple societies tend to use natural dyes, paints, and found objects for color in the ritual pieces we now regard as works of art. Within the limitations of what is at hand, they use color with great sophistication. Using only green, red, white, and black pigments set against the natural colors of wood, the Northwest American Coast headdress maker has created a bright, lively composition through complementary contrast (**10.2**).

As synthetic, chemically based colors become available to developing cultures, they readily adopt them for their brilliance. The introduction of glass beads to the Plains Indians of the United States supplanted earlier work in dyed porcupine quills with such masterpieces as Mrs. Minnie Sky Arrow's

▲ 10.2 Raven and ermine headdress from the Oowekeeno at River Inlet
Cedar wood and bark, eagle feather, wool, steel, and iron, length 32¼ ins (82 cm). Courtesy of the U'mista Cultural Society, Alert Bay, British Columbia, Canada.
Complementary colors add to the fresh appeal of this traditional mask.

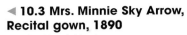

◄ 10.3 Mrs. Minnie Sky Arrow, Recital gown, 1890
Beaded buckskin dress.
Smithsonian Institution, Washington, D.C.
Among the traditional Plains Indians, the introduction of glass beads allowed intense color harmonies, worked out in precise geometric designs.

seven-pound fully beaded buckskin piano recital dress (**10.3**). In rural India, some women now use brilliantly pigmented manufactured powders for their *rangoli*—designs painted on the earth or floor to welcome guests. The difference in saturation is evident in the *rangoli* pattern being created in Figure **10.4**. Some areas of the designs are created with powder made by rubbing *geru*, a soft stone that yields a red-brown dust, whereas the rest of the pattern is created with bright modern manufactured pigmented powders. Yellow was traditionally created with turmeric powder, which like the *geru* is considerably less saturated than the synthetic powders of the same hues. Saturated or not, the hues celebrate auspicious aspects of life, such as white for purity, red for fertility, yellow for good fortune, and green for the abundance of plant life.

Being limited to what they could find or trade for in colored materials has not restricted color awareness in non-industrial societies. The vocabulary of the Maoris in New Zealand, for example, includes 40 color words used to distinguish between different kinds of clouds and over a hundred words for what Westerners call "red." In the evolution of languages, the first color terms seem to have referred to a distinction between light and dark; names of hues came later. In some languages, when talking about the surface appearance of an object, people use words that include references to texture and value; hue does not belong to a separate category of observations.

Often color use in works of art is determined by philosophical principles. Colors often carry symbolic meanings as we have seen. Moreover, many peoples have strong ideas about which colors "should" be used. Chan (Zen) Buddhist and Daoist influences in China led some painters to shun bright colors in favor of the subtle inks used in calligraphy, considered the highest of the arts. Li Cheng's *A Solitary Temple Amid Clearing Peaks* (**10.5**), where washes of very unsaturated color are used to create forms, reveals a highly restrained interpolation of local colors.

The principles of classical Japanese painting place restrictions on adjacent colors. Using a color wheel of five primaries (yellow, blue, black, white, and red), the masters of this tradition say that no color should be juxtaposed with either of its parents, for to do so would detract from both colors. This observation is in alignment with principles of color interaction discussed in Chapter 9. The Persian miniature tradition in painting depicts an idealized world without shadows. This tradition was carried to India and adapted to devotional painting of beloved Hindu deities, as beautifully illustrated by the gouache of Lord Krishna and his consort Radha (**10.6**). In the tiny idealized space, colors serve a spiritual purpose, with bright yellow emphasizing the pure light emanating from the figures, and paradisal jewel-like hues surrounding them. This is a world of pure beauty, seen through the eyes of love.

▲ 10.5 Li Cheng, *A Solitary Temple Amid Clearing Peaks*, Northern Song dynasty (c. A.D. 950)

Ink and slight color on silk hanging scroll, 44 × 22 ins (11.8 × 55.9 cm). The Nelson-Atkins Museum of Art, Kansas City, Missouri. Purchase: Nelson Trust. 47–71.

An austere aesthetic led Chinese landscape painters to avoid bright hues, even though they were available.

Historical Western Approaches

The expansion of the limited prehistoric palette within Western art has been plotted on the C.I.E. diagram by Stephen Rees Jones (**10.7**). He has taken four representative periods in the history of Western art to show the gradual outward expansion of hues available: prehistory, Egyptian antiquity, Early Renaissance (A.D. 1500), and the nineteenth century. From the diagram you can see that up to 1900, artists were not able to capture a full range of spectral hues with existing dyes and pigments. Today the frontiers of color have been pushed outward by petrochemical dyes and computer graphics, and there are literally millions of colors in use. As more pigments and improved media have become available, ways of using color have changed as well. In the following sections, we explore some distinctively different approaches to color in the evolution of Western art.

The Western tradition in painting is thought to have begun with the ancient Egyptians. Archeologists have found their paint-boxes of stone or marble, up to 3,500 years old, with eight to fourteen wells for different colors. These apparently included terracotta red, light and medium yellow ochers, turquoise-blue, green, black, and white, all used to fill in flat drawn shapes. In the fifth century B.C., certain Greek wall painters who applied tempera to wood, stone, plaster, and terracotta began to use a little shading to suggest three-dimensional form in space. Remarks by ancient historians—particularly Pliny—have led us to believe that these painters limited themselves to a bold four-color palette: red, yellow, white, and black. However, recent research reveals that blue was also used, often for shadow effects rather than for dominant colors of objects.

Until the thirteenth century, tempera was often applied to dry walls of plaster, with a brilliant white gesso ground added to hold the paint and give it a luminous quality. The **fresco** technique, developed to a high art during the Renaissance, involved applying water-mixed pigments directly to wet plaster. Only those pigments that were water-soluble and resistant to the lime of the plaster could be used in this way—chiefly the subtle earth colors of ochers, umbers, chalk, charcoal, and pink and green clays. More brilliant mineral pigments, such as those used for blues, had to be added in tempera (which included a binder such as egg or glue) *a secco*, that is, after the plaster was dry. Those painted *al buon fresco* (true fresco) were more durable but tended to

▲ **10.6** *Hindu Deities Krishna and Radha in a Grove,*
c. 1780
Gouache on paper, 4⅞ × 6¾ ins (12.3 × 17.2 cm).
Courtesy of the Trustees of the Victoria and Albert Museum, London.
Crown copyright.

have a pale transparent quality, as in Giotto's *Lamentation*
(**10.8**). Giotto (c. 1267–1337) was notable for his emphasis
on modeling of figures by use of highlights and shading,
creating the illusion of three-dimensional form on a two-
dimensional surface by mimicking the way light acts in the
natural world. Because colors could not be blended on the
fresco but instead had to be applied stroke by stroke, gradations in tone were built up in side-by-side value sequences
and then blended by hatching with a brush. Note that
Giotto uses not only shades and tints of the same hue for

▶ **10.7 After Rees Jones, The history of the artist's
palette in terms of chromaticity**
The newest colors available to artists have extended the range
of saturation possible, though the purity of the spectral hues,
shown around the outside of the C.I.E. diagram, still eludes us.

▲ **10.8 Giotto, *Lamentation*, c. 1304–13**
Fresco, 91 × 67½ ins (230 × 202 cm).
Scrovegni Chapel, Padua, Italy.
Giotto's shading technique involved use of darker and lighter
values of the same hues or, in some areas, shadows of
complementary hues.

highlights and shadows in most of his figures, but also
shadows of complementary colors, especially in the garment
worn by the disciple to the far right.

Approximately two centuries later, Michelangelo
(1475–1564) was commissioned to fresco the ceiling of the
Sistine Chapel in the Vatican. Controversy rages among art
historians about the colors he actually used, for the work has
been restored from very subtle, dark hues (**10.9A**) to colors
of great freshness and brilliance (**10.9B**). Those in favor
of the restoration point out that the somber colors long
associated with Michelangelo were actually the result of dust
accumulation, smoke from lighting and heating devices, and
dark overpaintings and darkened glue added by previous
restorers. Removing this accumulation with special chemicals reveals very vivid colors. However, some critics prefer
the frescoes in their darker, less saturated state, perhaps
following nineteenth-century preferences for the unifying
dark, golden glow associated with Venetian oil paintings (for
a while, even museums treated paintings with dark varnish
that grew darker over time).

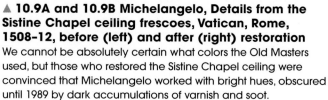

▲ **10.9A and 10.9B Michelangelo, Details from the Sistine Chapel ceiling frescoes, Vatican, Rome, 1508–12, before (left) and after (right) restoration**
We cannot be absolutely certain what colors the Old Masters used, but those who restored the Sistine Chapel ceiling were convinced that Michelangelo worked with bright hues, obscured until 1989 by dark accumulations of varnish and soot.

A new surface brilliance in hues appeared with the introduction of oil as a medium for pigments. Initially difficult to work with because of its slow drying time, oil was adopted by painters in the Netherlands once drying catalysts had been invented in the late fourteenth century. The first great master of the medium was Jan van Eyck (c. 1390–1441), who fully exploited the greater saturation, transparency, and opacity possible when oil rather than tempera was used to carry the pigments. The many layers he used included a white ground which glowed through the upper layers of oils, an underdrawing, and then layers of paint from light to opaque darker values or more saturated colors and transparent glazes. The optical effects of this layering created varia-

tions and vividness in hues that far transcended the limited palette of the time. One of Van Eyck's early fifteenth-century palettes consisted simply of brown verdaccio (a dull pigment used for shading), red madder (a bright hue from the root of the madder plant), ultramarine (genuine lapis lazuli), yellow ocher, terre-verte (green earth), orpiment (yellow), sinopia (iron oxide red), and peach black. Van Eyck's great *Arnolfini Marriage*, or *Giovanni Arnolfini and His Bride* (**10.10**), illustrates that skillful use of these pigments in oils allowed very subtle and continual gradations of tone. But Van Eyck still maintained the old tradition of precise color boundaries between figures, based on the original drawing, no matter how distant they were.

▶ **10.10 Jan van Eyck, *The Arnolfini Marriage (Giovanni Arnolfini and His Bride)*, 1434**
Oil on panel, 33 × 22½ ins (84 × 57 cm).
National Gallery, London.
Van Eyck was a great master of using glazes to increase the brightness of hues in the limited palette of early oil paints.

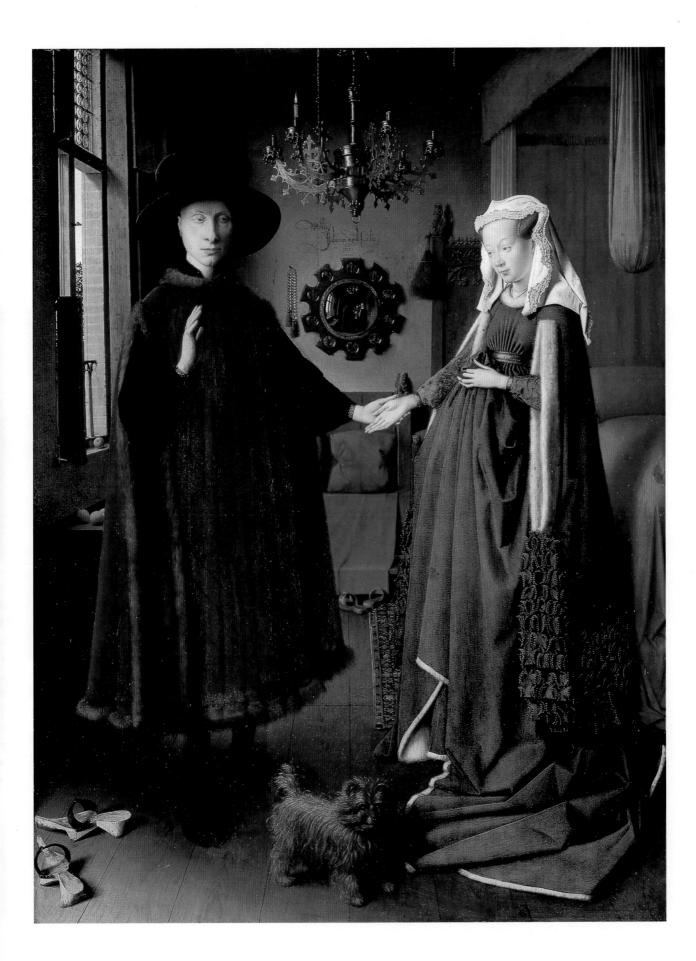

Color began to break loose from the rigid outlines of drawing in the sixteenth-century work of the Venetian artist Titian (c. 1490–1576), who is considered one of the greatest colorists of all times. Cleaning of some of his works reveals that they were originally far brighter in hue than the golden glow they have acquired through aging of the oil and accumulations of varnish. Venice was a major port and Titian had access to rare and expensive imported pigments. Even more

▼ **10.11 Titian, *Venus and the Lute Player*, c. 1565–70**
Oil on canvas, 65 × 82½ ins (165.1 × 209.6 cm).
Metropolitan Museum of Art, New York. Munsey Fund, 1936 (36.29).
Titian was famous in his time as a great colorist who painted directly with colors rather than filling in drawings.

▶ **10.12 Jan Vermeer, *The Lacemaker*, c. 1669–70**
Oil on canvas on wood, 9¾ × 8¼ ins (25 × 21 cm).
Musée du Louvre, Paris.

significant is his direct use of paint as a drawing medium. Rather than beginning with an underdrawing and then filling it in, according to sixteenth-century art historian Giorgio Vasari, Titian painted "broadly with tints crude or soft as the life demanded, without doing any drawing, holding it as certain that to paint with colors only, without the study of drawing on paper, was the true and best method of working, and the true design."[2] X-ray analysis suggests that Titian reworked many sections, composing with areas of contrasting colors as he went along. If the dancing figures in the distance in Titian's *Venus and the Lute Player* (**10.11**) are compared with the brilliantly realized miniatures in the mirror of *The Arnolfini Marriage*, the difference in use of colors becomes obvious. Titian suggested form with dynamic slashes of color, although he worked in a far more controlled way to create the luminous, softly modeled nude Venus. He maintained the time-consuming practice of glazing for these transparent effects and spoke of using up to 30 or 40 glazes.

In the seventeenth century, Jan Vermeer painted a small corpus of exquisite works in which subjects are informally posed, but depicted with very careful compositional use of color. In Vermeer's *The Lacemaker* (**10.12**), a single splash of brilliant red yarn spills over from its confines as a bold counterpoint to the high yellow and the subtleties of the rest of the composition. Note that Vermeer also works very carefully with complementary hue changes for shadows and added pearl-like flecks of high value to give a precious excitement to the image. There seem to be two light sources—one from the rear, casting a purple shadow on the wall beyond the woman, and one from the front right, throwing a strong light onto the left side of her face and gown. However, the effects of the lighting are subtly manipulated to balance one color against another in the composition, rather than to portray precise visual realism.

By the nineteenth century, color had become one of the major focuses of certain artists. One was Eugène Delacroix (1798–1863), who observed color effects in nature very carefully and sought to recreate natural lighting by a sort of additive optical mixing on the canvas. He juxtaposed unmixed bright pigments, often in complementary colors, coaxing the eye to mix them when the work is seen from a distance. This **broken color**, such as the many interwoven hues in the garments of the horsemen in *The Combat of the Giaour and Hassan* (**10.13**), is quite different from earlier works, where, for example, a red form would be painted entirely in shades and tints of red. Like his contemporary Goethe, Delacroix observed complex optical phenomena such as color shadows. From a seacoast studio he saw:

> *the shadows of people passing in the sun on the sands of the port: the sand here is violet in reality, but it is gilded by the sun: the shadows of these persons are so violet that the ground about them becomes yellow.*

And on a person reclining in the sun against a fountain, he saw:

> *dull orange in the carnations, the strongest violets for the cast shadows, and golden reflections in the shadows which were relieved against the ground. The orange and violet tints dominated alternately, or mingled. The golden tone had green in it. Flesh only shows its true color in the open air, and above all in the sun.*[3]

With Claude Monet and his fellow French Impressionists, attempts to capture the color effects of light took precedence over depiction of forms. Monet's pioneering effort in this direction, *Impression—Sunrise* (**10.14**), is a patchwork of colors arrayed as if they were just striking the eye, without being interpreted as forms by the brain. Monet counseled a young artist:

> *When you go out to paint, try to forget what object you have before you—a tree, a house, a field, or whatever. Merely think, here is a little square of blue, here an oblong of pink, here a streak of yellow, and paint it just as it looks to you, the exact color and shape, until it gives you your own naive impression of the scene before you.*[4]

The nineteenth-century development of portable tubes for premixed permanent pigments in all hues had made it feasible for artists to paint outside, directly from nature, as opposed to tediously grinding and mixing each color in the studio and trying to use layers and juxtapositions to create brilliant hues that were not available in earth pigments. Monet mixed these tube colors with lead white to give them a pastel light-struck quality and then positioned them unblended on the canvas. As we saw in Chapter 3, Monet did not paint in local colors—the hues stereotypically associated with objects as seen under average lighting from close by, such as green for tree leaves. Instead, he attempted to record the evanescent realities of light as its vibrations were reflected off the material world.

Of the Postimpressionists, Seurat continued the experimentation with optical mixing of unblended dabs of color (9.27), though with a far more controlled technique than Monet, for whom speed was of vital importance in capturing a fleeting impression. Paul Gauguin (1848–1903) took color in another direction, juxtaposing broad masses of contrasting colors which intensify each other, as in *The Day of the God* (**10.15**), rather than breaking local color into small pieces that blend optically to a gray. Gauguin said:

> *A meter of green is greener than a centimeter if you wish to express greenness. ... How does that tree look to you? Green? All right, then use green, the greenest on your palette. And that shadow, a little bluish? Don't be afraid. Paint it as blue as you can.*[5]

Gauguin used colors not only to emphasize nature but also to reflect the mysteries of inner responses to life, "feeling expressed before thought."[6]

▲ **10.14 Claude Monet,** *Impression—Sunrise,* **1872**
Oil on canvas, 19½ × 25½ ins (49.5 × 64.8 cm).
Musée Marmottan, Paris.
This is the painting from which the Impressionist movement got its name. It is an attempt to capture ephemeral light sensations rather than solidly defined forms.

Twentieth-Century Western Approaches

In the twentieth century, some artists have continued the tradition of representing local colors in their works, while others have carried the nonrepresentational color trend to its extreme. A particular escape from the local color of objects occurred with the Fauves ("wild beasts," as their critics called them). Influenced by non-Western arts, they used intense colors joyously in whatever way they chose rather than trying to imitate nature. André Derain's *Turning Road, l'Estaque* (**10.16**) plays lines and masses of highly saturated color against each other. "The problem," he wrote of his intentions for this painting, "is to group forms in light."[7]

In *Improvisation 28* (**10.17**) Vassily Kandinsky used color as a key to the expressive in art, equating each different hue as having the ability to affect us in many ways. He wrote about his color theories in his book *Concerning the Spiritual in Art* (1912), in which he stated:

> *In general, therefore, color is a means of exerting a direct influence upon the soul. Color is the keyboard. The eye is the hammer. The soul is the piano with its many strings. The artist is the hand that purposefully sets the soul vibrating by means of this or that key.*[8]

Kandinsky felt that eliminating the forms of the natural world in his artwork allowed him to better express the realm

▲ **10.15 Paul Gauguin, *The Day of the God (Mahana No Atua)*, 1894**
Oil on canvas, 27⅝ × 35⅝ ins (69.5 × 90.4 cm).
Art Institute of Chicago.
Gauguin was one of the first Western artists to use colors expressively, selectively intensifying certain color tones seen in the outside world for the sake of design and expressiveness.

of the subconscious, using the pureness of color to show us pure emotions.

In the works of Sonia and Robert Delaunay, color became a playful design tool entirely divorced from form. Through explorations in the crafts, Sonia Delaunay transcended the traditional boundaries of painting and entered a world of pure color. In her *Tango-Magic-City* (**10.18**), non-figurative color shapes seem to be in constant rhythmic motion, with many things happening simultaneously, as they do in life. They stem purely from the active imagination of the artist, the liberated child within.

Another of the many new approaches to painting evolving early in the twentieth century was the **collage**. In these relatively two-dimensional works, **found objects** are glued to a flat surface in such a way that one looks from one to the next to assess their interrelationship.

Artists working in collage or low-relief constructions with found objects are forever on the lookout for interesting and beautiful shapes and colors in objects around them.

▲ **10.16 André Derain, *The Turning Road, l'Estaque*, 1906**
Oil on canvas, 4 ft 3 ins × 6 ft 4¾ ins (1.3 × 1.95 m).
The Museum of Fine Arts, Houston; The John A. and Audrey Jones
Beck Collection.
**The Fauves—"wild beasts"—moved even farther from local colors,
substituting exuberant, highly saturated hues for the duller tones
of real life.**

Some become very appreciative of subtleties of color that
would be difficult to paint—the beauty of rust, for example,
the patina of long handling, or the faded hues of something
that has often been rained on. They collect discards that have
caught their eye—leaves, unusual stamps, bits of printed
matter—the innate beauty or interesting design of which
they can expose through placement and contrast.

Although modern art often tended toward non-figurative work, representational art continued to evolve, and with
it, the usage of color. Many artists worked independently,
with a great variety of idiosyncratic approaches. Pierre
Bonnard attempted to paint the subtleties of light as it played
across surfaces. He was one of a group of painters who called
themselves "Nabis" ("prophets"), for they experimented
with new ways of using color and composition in order to
bring forth certain emotional responses as well as to explore
visual patterns. In Bonnard's *Nude in a Bathtub* series (such as
Figure **10.19**), paint of various hues is dabbed on in such a
way that the model's body is almost lost as a distinct form.
Her skin becomes an evanescent, iridescent surface which
merges with the water. Bonnard wrote:

> *The object is not to paint life. The object is to make painting. The
> main subject is the surface, which has its color, its laws, over and
> above the objects.*[9]

By mid-century, the so-called New York School had established two particular directions in use of color. One was

◀ **10.17 Vassily Kandinsky, *Improvisation 28 (Second Version)*, 1912**
Oil on canvas, approximately 44 × 63¾ ins (111.7 × 161.9 cm). Solomon R. Guggenheim Museum, Gift, Solomon R. Guggenheim.
The Russian-born Kandinsky was known for the power of his colorful nonrepresentational works. He felt it was necessary to "express mystery in terms of mystery."[10]

Abstract Expressionism, exemplified here by Franz Kline's *Scudera* (**10.20**). The direct use of oils—and increasingly, acrylics—without underpainting or underdrawing had with this group become an end in itself. The free, expressive gesture of the artist, traced through the trail of color it left on the canvas, became the focal point of the painting. Some of these artists, including Kline, used white and black as colors in themselves, of equal importance to the chromatic hues. In works such as *Scudera*, colors interlock on the same plane rather than existing in figure-to-ground relationships where one would appear to lie in front of the other in space.

Helen Frankenthaler even erased the spatial distinction between color and the canvas on which it sits by staining unprimed canvases with thinned acrylic paints. Acrylics—industrial pigments in synthetic resin—were becoming available in clear, highly saturated, sometimes even fluorescent or metallic hues that did not yellow with age as oils tend

◀ **10.18 Sonia Delaunay, *Tango-Magic-City*, 1913**
Oil on canvas, 21¾ × 18⅛ ins (55.4 × 46 cm). Collection Kunsthalle, Bielefeld, Germany.
Delaunay's paintings reflect a total divorce of color from form, allowing it free play as a plastic element of design.

◀ **10.19 Pierre Bonnard, *Nude in a Bathtub*, 1937**
Oil on canvas, 48 × 59½ ins (122 × 151 cm). Musée National d'Art Moderne, Paris.

to do. Frankenthaler's *Nature Abhors a Vacuum* (**10.21**) revels in the interplay of these radiant hues floating in a boundless space, the whiteness of which accentuates their brilliance. Acrylics dry so quickly that they are difficult to blend; pouring or mopping these thinned paints onto the canvas one at a time produces transparent overlapping rather than blended color sensations. This is not to say, however, that Frankenthaler did not mix her colors. She experimented freely with mixtures, explaining:

> *It occurred to me that something ugly or muddy could be a color as well as something clear and bright and a namable, beautiful known color. ... I will buy a quantity of paint but I hate it when it dries up and I haven't used it. If I have a pot of leftover green and a pot of leftover pink I will very often mix it just because I want to use it up. If it doesn't work—well, that's a loss.... For every [painting] that I show there are many, many in shreds in garbage cans.*[11]

Frankenthaler's abstract organic color areas are somewhere between Abstract Expressionism and what is often called **Color-Field painting**. This label is used for works which consist of large colored fields rather than the color trails of paint gestures. Mark Rothko's *Blue, Orange, Red* (**10.23**) almost hides the hand of the painter but it is not laid down in solid, uniform masses of color. Rather, it is built up of

transparent layers of oils which give the impression of glowing light.

Compare the subtle variety in coloration of Rothko's painting with another development—the **Hard-Edged painting** typified here by the work of Ellsworth Kelly. His *Blue, Green, Red* (**10.22**) is exactly what it says it is. There is no attempt to develop subtleties of color or texture in the color field; each area is painted uniformly in unmodulated color, as if to industrial standards. One is confronted by the sheer facts of the three colors. This absolutely nonobjective approach leaves the viewer to explore the only points of drama in the painting: the hard edges where the colors meet. If you stare at the edge shared by the red and green you may begin to see some simultaneous interaction effects. Just inside the green border a luminous glow of even more highly saturated green develops; the red on the other side of the boundary similarly becomes even redder, as each hue optically "subtracts" any trace of itself from the other. The

▶ **10.20 Franz Kline, *Scudera*, 1961**
Oil on canvas, 9 ft × 6 ft 6 ins (2.7 × 1.9 m). Courtesy of Philip Samuels Fine Art.
In the work of some Abstract Expressionists, black and white maintain their status as true colors.

◄ **10.21 Helen Frankenthaler, *Nature Abhors a Vacuum*, 1973**
Acrylic on canvas, 8 ft 7½ ins × 9 ft 4½ ins (2.63 × 2.86 m). Private collection.
In Frankenthaler's radiant stained canvases, flowing colors and background merge in an endless space.

▲ **10.22 Ellsworth Kelly, *Blue, Green, Red*, 1964**
Oil on canvas, 6 ft 1 in × 8 ft 4 ins (1.8 × 2.5 m).
Whitney Museum of American Art, New York.
Follow the hard edges between hues to be aware of their interactive visual effects.

same thing begins to happen along the edge shared by the blue and red if you stare at it long enough.

Taken to an extreme, this kind of optical interaction becomes Op Art. As we have seen, painters such as Josef Albers (9.21) and Richard Anuszkiewicz (3.12) give the viewer more color sensations than they have physically created. Their color combinations confuse our perceptual apparatus, and somewhere in the passage from eye to brain illusory colors begin to appear. Another figure in this movement—Bridget Riley—is highly successful at making us perceive chromatic colors where only black and white actually exist (see Figure 9.32).

Charles Csuri began experimenting with the computer in the 1960s, laboriously feeding stacks of punch cards into a

▶ **10.23 Mark Rothko, *Blue, Orange, Red*, 1961**
Oil on canvas, 7 ft 6¼ ins × 6 ft 9¼ ins (2.3 × 2.07 m).
Hirshhorn Museum and Sculpture Garden, Smithsonian Institution, Washington, D.C. Gift of Joseph M. Hirshhorn Foundation, 1966.

▲ **10.24 Charles Csuri, *Wondrous Spring*, 1992**
Computer illustration.
Charles Csuri was a pioneer in the field of computer-generated art, and as such could easily be referred to as an "Old Master" in the short history of computer art.[12]

main frame and translating images into mathematical formulas. In those early years, computers were still very much the stronghold of engineers and mathematicians. They were unwieldy and time-consuming to use as an art tool because of the nature of programming. Csuri was confident of the possibilities the computer had to offer the art world, however, and kept exploring, learning, and experimenting. As the technology became more user-friendly, and microprocessors became readily available, more artists woke up to the new challenges. Software programs eliminated the need for programming, although Csuri still maintained that programming offered a deeper control of images than was provided by software programs. He continued to be fascinated with the computer's ability to show transparency with its light-generated colors, as in *Wondrous Spring* (**10.24**). He explained:

▶ **10.25 Alan J. Kegler, *The Surveyors*, 1993**
Computer image.
Confronted with the availability of more color choices than the human eye can even distinguish, early computer artists often chose the brightest of colors. Mature use of the computer as an art medium now means that less saturated colors and an intentionally muted palette may instead be employed.

▲ **10.26 Bill Viola, *Stations* (detail), 1994**
Video/sound installation with five granite slabs, five projections and
five projection screens. The Museum of Modern Art, New York.
Gift to the Bohen Foundation in honor of Richard F. Oldenburg.

*Just because the computer can do perspective and beautiful shadows
and shininess, or make things look like glass, you still need to have
an esthetic sensibility; you need a sense of culture and history. Even
though we have all this marvelous technology, the problems for the
artist are still the same. You can very easily be seduced by some
special effect, but that in and of itself doesn't do it. You have to have
some way of communicating what you feel as a human being.*[13]

Today many of the approaches to color developed in the past
are still in use, but new ones are also continually evolving. In
computer art, a vast range of luminous colors, some of them
never before available to artists, is now readily mixed and
viewed on the screen.

With the potential for creating millions of colors—more
colors than the eye can even distinguish—computer artists
now have the opposite challenge of that faced by the earliest
artists, who had to make the most of a limited palette of earth
pigments. The challenge in computer art is to make effective
color choices in the midst of so many possibilities. There is
also the challenge of capturing the attention of contemporary viewers who spend many hours a day being visually
assaulted by extremely rapid image changes on television,
and who have a world of color imagery competing for their
attention on the Internet.

Amidst the visual noise of our times, a quiet or sober
voice may draw attention by its very subtlety. After an
initial period of gay abandon in choosing and juxtaposing
highly saturated colors, many computer artists are now
intentionally limiting or subduing their palettes to suit the
"painterly" aesthetics of what many people would catego-
rize as fine art, as in Figure **10.25**, which advertised the work
of the Center for Creative Imaging in Maine.

Nevertheless, the luminous brilliance and variety in
colors available to computer artists, especially to those using
television screens or colored films rather than printing inks
for their final production, has initiated a new aesthetic which
will be judged by different standards of taste from those of
the older media, such as oil and watercolor paintings.

The extent of the new possibilities has not yet been fully
explored. As computer artist David Em says:

*How physically and spiritually removed sitting in front of a computer
terminal is from the experience of a prehistoric cave painter making a*

*red handprint on a cave wall. Perhaps, if the prehistoric painter were
presented with Velázquez's paint box and brushes it would take him
a little while to grasp what had been delivered into his hands. And
perhaps it will take us a little while to appreciate that the computer,
which has so suddenly appeared in our midst, is likewise a wonderful
and mysterious gift.*[14]

Modern technologies are also being brought into play to
create installation pieces that surround the viewer with
unique color environments and even virtual realities. Bill
Viola uses video projections and sound to immerse viewers
in dynamic imagery that is manipulated to blur the boundary between real and unreal. His *Stations* (**10.26**), installed in
the Museum of Modern Art in New York, does so with five

granite slabs, video projections, and projection screens. This
installation work itself refers to the "crisis of representation
and identity" created by the new technologies.

A parallel art universe continues to travel in tandem with
the newest technological discoveries, as evidenced in Wolf
Kahn's *Lilac and Green* (**10.27**), where he uses the colors of
the New York school of Abstract Expressionism to showcase

◀ **10.28 Judy Pfaff,
Tsubo, 2004**
Mixed media of bamboo,
paper, ink, wood, gauze,
and formica,
h: 103.2 × w: 162.2 × d: 6 ins
(262.1 × 412 × 15.2 cm).
Bellas Artes Gallery.
In this work, Judy Pfaff uses a
muted color range, creating
additional colors by hanging
the transparent material as
an overlay. When a large
proportion of a work is neutral
in color, any saturated color
gains in visual importance.

his very personal landscape format. The unique hands-on immediacy of chalk to paper, or paints to canvas or clay, evokes its own particular force on the viewer, and holds for the artist a continual fascination indigenous to the media.

Artist Judy Pfaff, who is well known for the large installation works she has produced since the 1970s (her *cirque CIRQUE*, 1995, used 250 x 210 x 40 feet at the Pennsylvania Convention Center in Philadelphia), has created a wall assemblage in *Tsubo* (**10.28**) that is measured in inches rather than feet but it is still assembled in the gallery in the same manner as her larger, site-specific works. The muted neutral colors in this work are a departure from Pfaff's earlier works, which were often filled with strong, saturated hues. *Tsubo* means "a courtyard garden" in Japanese, and part of this work references floor plans of an ancient

house and courtyards in Kyoto. Having spent the last few years renovating her own Victorian house, those influences are apparent here as well. They blend with the Japanese influences in this work, thus combining her interest in East and West.[15]

There is still a great appreciation for the other end of the nontechnological spectrum, too: folk art, multicultural art, and outsider art. Serious attention is being paid to works created outside the mainstream of the Western aesthetic tradition, and thus uninfluenced by academic ideas of appropriate color choices, as in Bessie Harvey's sculpture shown in Figure 9.14.

Each new development requires flexibility and imagination in our aesthetics if we are to explore fully its particular contribution to our work with colors.

11 Color in Applied Design

● ● ● ●

The dynamic structure of color and light delights my eye, disturbs my lazy thoughts,
lends wings to the rhythm of my heart and to the quick breath of my wishes.

HEINZ MACK

IN applied design, as in the fine arts, color use has broken away from its traditional restrictions. There are, however, certain commercial and practical limitations on color choices. Many applied design disciplines—from giftwrap to product design—are affected by shifting tastes in color. Psychological associations with certain colors may also play an important role. Colors have compositional and spatial effects, already examined in previous chapters, that influence their commercial use.

Beyond these general considerations, each discipline has its own practical and aesthetic factors influencing color use. For instance, the increasing use of Internet websites for conveying information and selling products has brought great creativity to the medium of computer graphics, featuring eye-catching color imagery animated through time.

Color Trends

In applied design fields, color choices are strongly influenced by the demands of the marketplace. To a certain extent, trends in public color preferences are manipulated by the commercial industries; change is orchestrated for the sake of increased sales. Trends in color palettes are usually led by the fashion industry, with home fashion colors often following sometime later. As Ed. [sic] Newman of the American Textile Manufacturers Institute puts it:

The word "fashion" is synonymous with the word "change."
Fashion begins with fabric. Fabrics begin with color. Each season,
color must make a new statement for fashion to continue its natural
evolution. Our eyes need refreshment. … We may have disliked the
way we looked in last season's clothes, but this season offers the
opportunity to wear new colors, groom differently and appear as a
new person. And if we are still unsatisfied, three months later there's
a new season.[1]

When buying ready-to-wear clothing, consumers seem to be initially drawn to the two inches of color they can see in a garment sandwiched amongst others on a rack. Only if they like the color will they take it off the rack and consider its other features. Color is therefore so important that most industrial countries have color councils who gather and feed information about changing consumer preferences to manufacturers. The International Color Marketing Group of the Color Association of the United States, for example, supplies its color forecasts to members in the textile, apparel, interior design, paint, building products, automobile, and communications industries two years ahead of each selling season. Each season's palette takes into account aesthetic judgments about suggested color combinations. It considers the practicalities of translating the predictions into technically feasible dyeing and printing processes. Fanciful names are given to these trendsetting colors, such as "Wallstreet Green," "Tahitian Sunset," "Mountain Mauve," and "Barbarossa Brown." To help communicate the precise meanings of these names, color swatches and a color matching service are provided. Nevertheless, designers in certain industries—such as office furniture—maintain that they avoid specifying

▲ **11.1 Kazuo Kawasaki, *Wheelchair***
Lightweight titanium frame, aluminum honeycomb wheels.
Courtesy eX-Design, Inc., Japan.

the fact that blue leads in consumer preference tests in the United States, observed:

> *It comes as no surprise that Americans overwhelmingly chose the color that best evokes a soothing, calming tranquillity in a frantically fast, often insecure world. It may seem a stretch to equate color and design directions with our state of mind and body, but these trends have always reflected society's concerns and interests, and surviving stress is a key issue in today's world.*[2]

However, color preferences differ within different social groups within the same culture. Eiseman notes:

> *A preference for red is directly linked to the most secure within a society, with the most economically stable segment, or achievers, such as high-powered active women who are unafraid to take risks.*[3]

Another general observation is that for every action there will be a reaction. Brilliant colors that glorified the limits of modern dyeing technology peaked in the late 1970s, followed by a reactionary preference for more subdued tones and a certain discretion in color combinations. Then in the 1980s came the excitement of vibrant color choices in computer graphics, followed by more subtle aesthetics in some computer art but even wilder choices in other computer works.

Aside from these ups and downs in public preferences, it appears that the public has become accustomed to a high degree of color use in the designed environment. The day when cars came in only one color (black) and when a "color" telephone meant one in white or ivory are unlikely to return. Designer colors now run to salmon and lavender office chairs, pink portable radios, tables of brilliant primary colors, and airplanes painted orange. Consumers have long since become accustomed to color in their kitchens as well as their living rooms. Many magazines and newspapers use color extensively, old black-and-white movies are being tinted for modern audiences, wheelchairs are now offered in vivid colors (**11.1**), and even staid universities are advertising themselves through multicolored websites.

Eduardo Arroyo's Lasesarre football stadium in Barakaldo, Spain (**11.2**), incorporates color in a surprising way. Its seats in various bright hues give the impression that it is filled with fans even when it is empty. The seats themselves are like energetic sports fans, creating a visual noise and a youthful exuberance within the surrounding tones of steel, plastic, and glass.

these "custom" colors because of color matching and production scheduling problems.

Although color trends quickly change, certain generalizations have been formulated about color preferences. They are thought to revolve around the state of the economy. During recessions, those who can afford them surround themselves with luxurious fabrics, such as velvets and chiffons in rich colors, as an uplifting antidote to the mood of the times. In times of abundance, the balance in industrial countries tends to shift toward "naive" fabrics and colors. During the affluent 1960s, for instance, the all-white look and faded denim prevailed.

Affluence inevitably brings tension, so for decades, there has been an overall preference for blue in industrial societies. Leatrice Eiseman of the Pantone Color Institute, speaking of

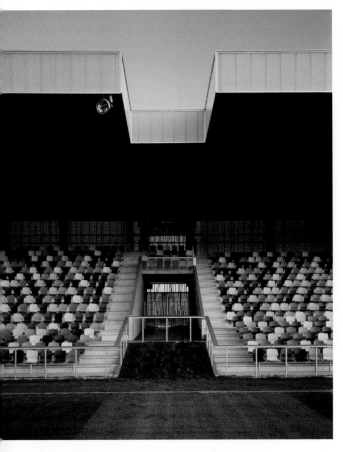

▲ 11.2 Eduardo Arroyo, Lasesarre Stadium, Barakaldo, Spain
Tucked between the warehouses and train depots of industrial Barakaldo, the angular steel exterior of Lasesarre stadium blends well with its surroundings, but viewed from the inside, the stadium comes alive with color.

Color Psychology

In addition to color trends, designers must be aware of innate psychological reactions to colors. As we found in Chapter 4, it is difficult to generalize about the way that colors affect us. But it is clear that warm colors tend to stimulate, whereas cool colors have a calming influence. Such information should be used thoughtfully. Research into the effect of colors in store interiors suggests that while red is alluringly striking and works well in drawing people into a good selling environment, warm colors, on the whole, may make people feel somewhat tense. Their effectiveness in promoting purchases inside stores could depend on whether the items are inexpensive, for quick impulse-buying, or whether they are costly purchases that require deliberation. If the latter, then cooler colors might encourage staying long enough to make a relaxed decision. The same principles are applied in restaurant interiors. Designer Kevin Grady explains, "Yellow [and] orange are intentionally used at fast food restaurants because they're seen both as hungry colors and jarring colors, so that you get people in, give them their food, and get them out."[4]

In packaging, the first goal is to catch the eye. Research indicates that consumers scan each package on a supermarket shelf for only 0.03 seconds. Thus the packaging must attract the customer to buy it, and the color should also help to convey an image of the contents. Considerable market research has been done about the effects of colors on buying habits, but most of it is closely guarded by the companies, who use it to get ahead of their competition. Yellow, orange, and red are often effectively used to stimulate and draw attention; purple is frequently associated with luxury products; blue suggests cleanliness, quietness, or financial stability; green and brown evoke an impression of nature and are often used in packaging to suggest environmental "friendliness." Gold, silver, and black effectively promise sophistication and high-quality merchandise. Gray is favored for conservative audiences, promising practicality and soberness.

Do you think the Audi ad in Figure **11.3** targets the right market for Audi's newest auto? Computer-aided design elements allow the repetition of the words "Vorsprung Durch Technik" to promote the image of their new A6 in tones of black and gray. The highest gray tones suggest silver or platinum, which further attaches the car to its high-priced market niche. As Dr. Russell Ferstandig, a psychiatrist and marketing consultant, explains, "Color serves as a cue. It's a condensed message that has all sorts of meanings."[5]

In commercial use of color, there are conventions about which colors to avoid as well as which ones to use to create certain effects. Black is rarely used in food products, because in the West it is associated with death; on cigarette packaging, people could associate it with lung cancer. Red may remind people of debt. Pink is linked with femininity and is therefore avoided in "masculine" products, and also in products for contemporary businesswomen. Too much yellow is thought to be disturbing, and too much purple overwhelming. Since white has a close association with purity, bottled

◀ **11.3 *The New Audi A6 Vorsprung Durch Technik*, Audi advertisement for *Wallpaper** magazine, July/August 2004**
Some current color trends showcase autos in muted tones of gray and black, in an attempt to speak to conservative, wealthy buyers.

beverage companies capitalize on this by using either white or slightly tinted but transparent bottling designs. "Clear says purity, and clear says refreshment," explains Jeffrey B. Hirsch, a marketing consultant, referring to "Clearly Canadian" flavored water, one of the first to start the trend.

Combinations of warm and cool hues can be used symbolically to convey mixed messages. A package of laundry detergent printed in blue and red suggests a more aggressive cleaning action than blue alone.

Designers of logos attempt to use colors as well as line and shape to establish corporate identity. Reds—which seem to suggest a certain assertiveness and activity—are still the going favorites. However, new entries in this field include bright yellows, oranges, and purples. Banks, on the other hand, are said to prefer reds, blues, and violets. In all graphic arts, the designer's ideas are restricted by the client's requirements.

Limiting the palette of available colors can be a highly effective way of getting the viewer's attention, especially in today's computer-savvy viewing market, as the 30-second television advertising piece *Artists Against Piracy* clearly shows (**11.4**). Software that allows sound waves and graphics to be linked was used for the entire piece, so that as the guitar music begins, and is played over and over, each time getting

better, a variety of words is created on the screen—practice, dedication, sacrifice, creation—all carrying the © symbol wherever a "c" appears in a word. The musician playing the guitar finally "nails the riff" when the word "musi©" appears. And then the final word of "respect" is created, with the guitarist bursting into an amazing improvisation. The use of the monochromatic color scheme encourages the viewer to pay attention to the content without any other distractions, and it does exactly that.

Graphic Design

Graphic designers are not as bound by color trends as fashion and interior designers. Their mandate is to evolve fresh ideas in exciting and stimulating designs continually, and this includes exploring the whole range of colors and combinations. Nevertheless, graphic design does have its own special considerations. Color may be used for specific practical purposes in business communications, and is thus expected to show practical results. It may be expected to call attention to important information, to help people locate information (as in signboards routing drivers through busy airports to specific terminals), to convey meanings non-

 11.4 Artists Against Piracy, television advertisement, January/February 2005 For this television ad, a nearly monochromatic color palette was chosen to capture the interest of the viewer. Keeping the same background color gave unity to the music and clever graphics of this piece.

verbally (such as "Go" or "Stop!"), to break down information into categories (as in the colored grounds and graphics that are used with increasing sophistication in Internet websites), and to make information more readable.

Another major consideration in graphic design is where and how a design will be printed or displayed. A logo, for example, must be reproduced on a variety of surfaces, including different kinds of papers and perhaps even fabrics, but the customer expects the logo color to remain exactly the same no matter where it is printed. This does not happen automatically; uniformity in color may require many adjustments by the designer. Furthermore, deep blues and greens and hot reds are often difficult to obtain because printing inks are transparent and must be applied in several layers to achieve these colors.

In computer graphics, by contrast, an enormous range of colors is theoretically at the artist's disposal; great discrimination is needed in making choices among them. Designers of Internet web pages have to work within one severe constraint: Their graphics must download quickly, lest the viewer should become impatient and switch to another website. Quick downloading may necessitate a somewhat limited palette, or use of solid colors across broad areas instead of broken colors, or selective compressing of color data, placing speed ahead of picture quality.

For budgetary reasons, graphic designers in print media must often work with a limited palette—perhaps only one or two colors of flat-printed ink on a white or colored ground (if the latter, its hue will show through and alter the transparent inks). This limitation has led to great ingenuity to achieve the appearance of variety. Some common techniques are the use of percentage screens or half-tones for value gradations, overlapping color blends, and **reverses** (in which images or typography appear in the ground color, surrounded by ink, rather than the other way around). Milton Glaser's novel cover (**11.5**) uses black and green ink on white stock, with the green ground printed first, the black printed over it for the typography and the dark areas of the half-tone figure, and a reverse for the title and cook's head and hat. This use of colors accentuates the white, which is responsible for conveying the essentials of the message. For a reverse to be effective, the ink surrounding the ground must be dark enough for the ground color to show up well by contrast.

In the brochure for the Wadsworth Mansion at Long Hill

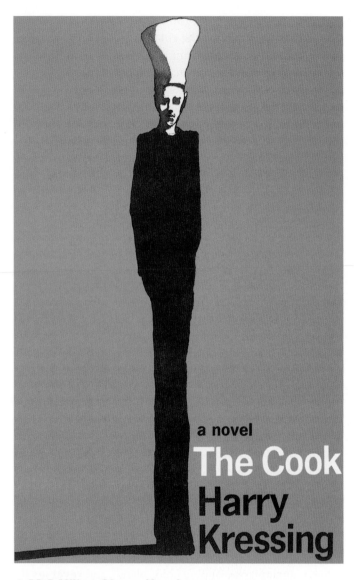

▲ **11.5 Milton Glaser, Novel cover**
Reverses—used for the white areas of this cover—are used to extend the possibilities when a graphic designer is limited to only a few ink colors.

We chose offset printing to produce the piece, with a total of seven plates: four-color process (CMYK) colors, one spot PMS (Pantone Matching System) color in order to best represent the clients "corporate" color, and two clear coatings printed offline—after the other colors are printed and dry—a dull varnish only on the seafoam green PMS color, and a spot aqueous coating only on the four-color photographs to brighten up its four-color process. In some cases, color pigment can be added to varnish in order to add a tint to an image or a solid. In this particular case, however, the varnish and spot aqueous coatings were utilized to give overall protection, to enhance the richness in the saturation of the four-color photographs, and to prolong overall color fastness. These coatings were used to control the finish of the printed sheet as well—adding both visual and tactile contrast between the soft PMS and the slick four-color photographs.

Certainly other design issues were used here to get the end result: spatial effects of the thin white rule around each photograph helped lift them off the page; the logo placements optically "held" the photos on the front and back covers but exaggerated the feeling of the photo being on top of the background; muted tones of the typography created balance within the visual hierarchy. The most important component we had for this job, however, was color. The brochure couldn't have had the same impact in black and white. The interior of the brochure was set up as a virtual photographic tour of the building; the color photos were full page throughout, with only the border of seafoam green and the narrow rule of white framing each one, with historical text limited to two interior pages. Color gave the desired richness of tone, gave an emotional and lyrical quality to the building while keeping it firmly in reality. After all the decisions of the printing process were precisely calibrated, we had a successful brochure package that we were happy to present to the client.[6]

In order to deliver maximum impact at minimal cost to the client, How 2 Design created two postcards that could fit in the press sheet "waste" space. This allowed for the extra pieces to be produced at virtually no additional cost while taking advantage of the full-color setup of the job.

In multicolored, two-dimensional graphic design, colors have strong effects on each other because they exist side by side on the same plane. Vigorous contrasts are optically interesting but may tire the eye; customers may prefer something that does not vibrate when they look at it.

One way of capitalizing on the liveliness of hue contrast without overstimulating the eye, as we saw in Chapter 9, is to use very small amounts of a very bright hue with large

Estate (**11.6**), the City of Middletown wanted to reintroduce to the town the recently purchased and renovated Wadsworth Mansion. The Friends of the Mansion wanted to publicize its readiness to host ceremonial and cultural activities, and they wanted to attract the highest quality clientele. With this in mind, How 2 Design's Principal Noemi Kearns explains:

▲ **11.6 How 2 Design,** *A Distinguished History, An Enchanting Future,* **October 2000**
Brochure for the Wadsworth Mansion at Long Hill Estate, Middletown, Connecticut, United States. Eight pages, 9 × 12 ins (22.8 × 30.4 cm). Includes logo mark, stationery package, brochure, pocket inserts, two postcards, and mailing envelope.
Having a high-quality brochure helped promote the newly renovated Wadsworth Mansion's capabilities to host corporate events, wedding groups, and cultural celebrations of all kinds.

amounts of a darker hue. In the *Wallpaper*✱ magazine advertisement (**11.7**), our interest is captured by the undulating colored lines of varying shades of cyan and magenta that ripple down the black page, a movement that pushes our eyes down to the important words—the name of the magazine, the web address, the phone number. We are repeatedly drawn back to the lines of color, however, because we notice that "35%" is peeking through the linear pattern. Our eyes jump back and forth between the activity of the colors and the straightforward white type, not staying long enough on the bright colors to become optically tired. The large amount of black serves to tone down the colors just enough. The advertisers succeed in getting us to read their information; they bring us into the work by the use of a clever treatment of colored lines, and our interest in the visual movement makes us scan the whole page several times.

Graphic designers also work carefully with the traditional principles of design, such as repetition, variety, rhythm, balance, compositional unity, emphasis, economy, and proportion. Color use is often a key feature of these factors. Consider the brilliant two-page advertisement in Figure

11.8. One would have thought this a very difficult assignment. The product is white, and what is it? A bathtub. How can it be made to appear as something special and desirable? Firstly, the ad occupies the first two pages of *Dwell* magazine, inside the front cover. Then there is the choice of color: a solid, warm, earthy red. The entire left page is a block of this unusual color, broken only by the white words written on it: "Relax the mind. Replenish the spirit." Then we look across to the right page and see a white shape against this same color, with the white already established in our mind and ready to be amplified. The use of light grays behind the red makes it stand out and even makes the red

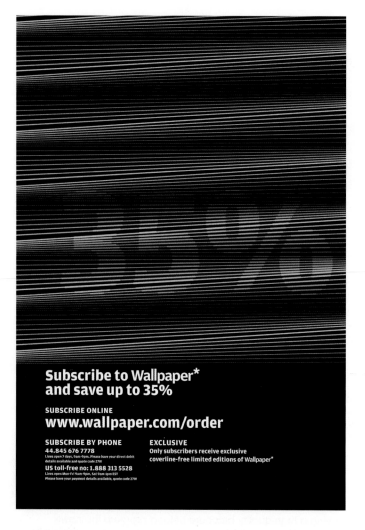

▲ **11.7 Dior advertisement for *Wallpaper** magazine, May 2004**
With very small amounts of a brilliant hue to grab our attention, mixed with a larger area of darker hues to calm our eyes, our interest is held long enough for the advertiser to show us something about the product.

optically darker, helping to balance the two pages. The choice of the inside front cover means that the left page is printed on heavy cover stock. When you turn the page and discover the ad, the weight you feel helps to make the red seem more stable, more solid. In every way, the designer has made the bathtub seem special by its surroundings.

Although the practical considerations of graphic design sometimes seem to place it in a different world from fine arts, many graphic designers nonetheless take clues from fine arts in the use of color. In the laptop computer advertisement shown in Figure **11.9**, the approach to lighting is borrowed from the Old Masters of painting. A strong light source creates dramatic contrasts between light and shadow falling across the forms and balances light and dark areas of the composition, rather as in Vermeer's *The Lacemaker* (10.12). The reference to tradition also serves a psychological purpose, suggesting that a woman does not have to sacrifice her traditional role in the home in order to carry on her career. The advertisement combines the old and the new: With miniaturized computer in her lap, a mother can work while staying home with her sick child, in a warm and cozy atmosphere bathed in sunlight and fresh air blowing in through the open window.

Interior Design

In interior design, in addition to the client's color preferences, suspected psychological effects of colors, color fashions, and aesthetic workability, there are also certain practical considerations for color choices in furnishings, flat surfaces, and lighting. Traditionally, interior designers were taught standard color harmonies (see Chapter 9) and cautioned that: 1) floors should be relatively low in value and saturation so they would hide soil and provide an optically firm base; 2) walls should be rather light and neutral in hue to provide a value gradation from floor to ceiling and to avoid clashes with the colors of paintings and furniture; 3) ceilings should be very light in value to give a sense of spaciousness and reflect lighting well.

These limitations have not inhibited the imagination of contemporary designers, however. They combine any colors they choose, so long as they can make them work. New ease of upkeep in floor finishes has led to widespread use of light-colored flooring. At the same time, dark walls and ceilings are now often used to create a cozy atmosphere. As for acceptable harmonies, consider the striking combination of hot pink and yellow in the Emmanuel Chapel of Corpus Christi Cathedral (**11.10**). Like the gem-colored lights entering Gothic cathedrals through stained-glass windows, these high-keyed, high-value colors create an inspiring color environment. The hue and strength of the lighting is carefully coordinated to harmonize with the altarpiece, rug, wall and ceiling paint, and wooden furniture and framing.

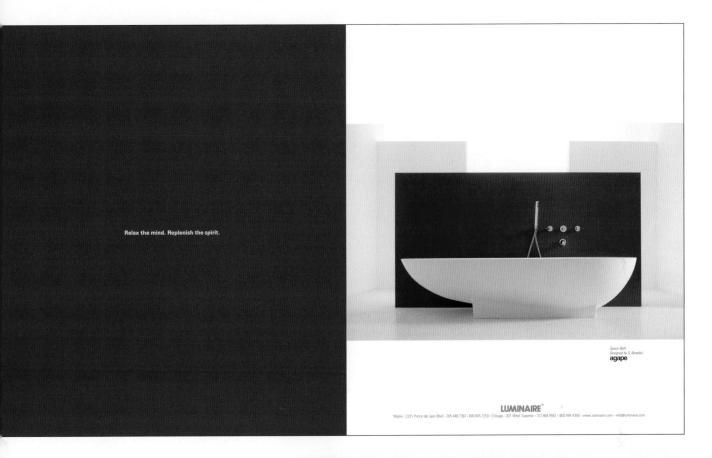

▲ **11.8** Ad for Luminaire spoon bath designed by G. Benedini, *Dwell* magazine, August 2001, two-page spread inside front cover.

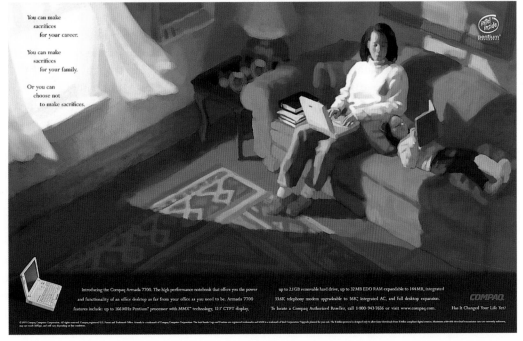

▶ **11.9** *Moments* **campaign, advertisement for Compaq Armada 7700 Computer from** *Wired* **magazine, October 1997** This advertisement borrows lighting techniques from the Old Masters of painting.

▲ **11.10 Emmanuel Chapel, Corpus Christi Cathedral, Corpus Christi, Texas**
Even church interiors may be the subject of contemporary color experimentation.

Color choices for interiors should be made under the lighting in which the materials will be seen. Lighting is equally important in other arts, but only in interior designs is the type of lighting known in advance. A cool fluorescent light will emphasize blue-purple, blue, blue-green, and green but produce disastrous results in the warmer hues; warm fluorescent lights enhance the yellows, oranges, reds, and red-purples but do not show cool colors to best advantage. Incandescent light gives everything a somewhat reddish tint. Full-spectrum fluorescent lighting attempts to simulate sunlight. An alternative is to use both warm and cool fluorescent lights for color balance. In some cases, however, balance is not desired. The General Electric Company suggests use of cool white fluorescent lights alone for banks, to create a sedate mood that implies stability of the institution, and warm fluorescents for displays of baked goods, upon which a bluish tint would be highly unappetizing.

Seen in large amounts, colors seem far more saturated than they do on small paint chips or fabric swatches. If one wants a quiet, subdued effect, it is often wise to choose colors from samples that are more toned down than the final result one envisions. The standard measurement tool for color selections and relationships in interior design is the Munsell Color Atlas. It consists of 1,500 detachable samples, in both glossy and matte finishes. Better still, large swatches of fabric or painted areas should be sampled in the area in question, with all colors to be used together present.

Early in the twentieth century, Western interior designers were told that bright colors should be reserved for small accents, with large areas reserved for subdued tones. In contrast to the earlier insistence on quiet color schemes for interiors, many contemporary designers are using large areas of bright colors for certain applications, as in Rufino Tamayo's living room (9.8) and the Emmanuel Chapel (11.10). Strong colors can be invigorating, and some human environments are thought to benefit from their use. As we saw in Chapter 4, bright colors encourage activity and mental alertness, and are therefore increasingly used in interiors of schools and offices, as well as in fast-food places. Again, just as with quieter color

◄ **11.11 Ndebele house, South Africa**
The strong sunlight of equatorial environments tends to wash out colors visually at midday, so brilliant colors that would seem garish in cloudier climates may be used in clothing and architecture.

harmonies, bright colors should be seen in samples large enough to judge the final effect, with particular attention to interactions between colors. Seen against backgrounds of a different hue from the white or gray ground of color samples, they may appear quite different. Often a range of potential colors is painted on a wall before final choices are made. Allowance should also be made for the fact that colors affect our sense of space. Highly saturated and warm colors make things look larger and closer; bright red walls or furniture would therefore have the overall effect of making a room itself appear smaller, for they would intrude optically into the space more than pale blue walls or furniture.

Architecture

The lighting across the outsides of buildings changes continually. Exterior colors are therefore dynamic, and their appearance depends partly on the local climate and relationships to the sun. Under a bright tropical sun, bright colors tend to wash out visually, especially at midday, so very strong colors may be used without an overwhelming effect. The brilliantly contrasting synthetic pigments used by Ndebele

women of South Africa to decorate architectural details, such as the house entrance in Figure **11.11**, are powerful enough to retain their excitement even under the naturally brilliant lighting conditions.

In areas further from the equator with less direct, and also less frequent, sunlight—such as often overcast parts of Europe—colors appear more brilliant. Hues of walls and roofs will also affect absorption of solar energy. Hot climates often necessitate white walls and roofs to reflect heat away from the interior; darker walls and roofs will help warm a building in a cold climate. Even darker values may give a cooling visual impression if they are from the cooler range of hues, such as the blues used in the magnificent tilework of Muslim mosques. To the desert nomads living in a hot sand-colored environment, the cool blues and greens were a refreshing foretaste of a heavenly paradise. Lustrous finishes were created by applying and firing metal oxides on the surface of initially glazed and fired tiles. This effect reflected highlights which visually raised the value of the hues to near-white (**11.12**).

In addition to the geographical and climatic considerations unique to architecture, aesthetic concerns also come into play. Throughout time and space, there have been two

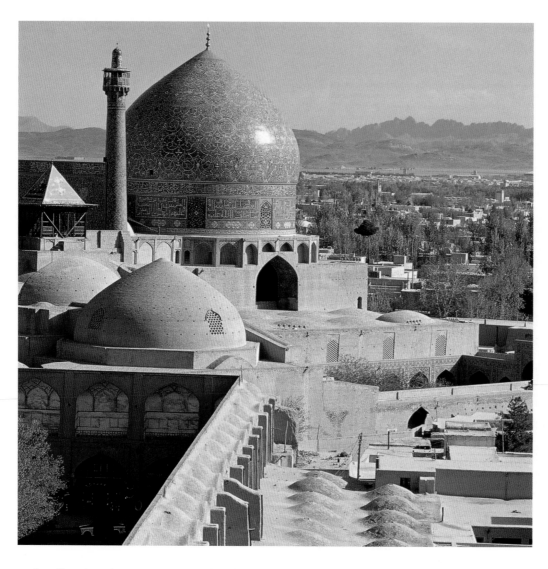

◄ **11.12 The Masjid-i-Shah mosque at Isfah, Iran, Safavid period (1612)**
Cool colors are a welcome visual oasis in hot desert environments. Lustrous finishes on tiles gleam near-white when reflecting the brilliant sunlight.

major directions in exteriors: use of the colors of nature or of the materials themselves, or use of applied colors. The latter has been common throughout history. The exteriors of great public buildings of ancient South and Central America, Greece, Egypt, the Middle East, and the Far East were often richly colored with applied paints and tiles. The conservative, no-color approach to exteriors entered Western history with the Protestant Reformation, when ostentatiousness was declared vulgar and inappropriate for spirituality. This sparse aesthetic culminated in twentieth-century International Style architecture, which celebrates the integrity of unadorned modern building materials—raw concrete, glass, and steel.

Frank Lloyd Wright led the way to a different set of conventions in architecture. He denounced vivid chromatic hues as the province of "interior desecrators" and honored the earthy colors of nature, in an attempt to make buildings blend with the land. He worked with the warm colors of wood and local rock, and eschewed paint, using only a sand-finish coating or a terracotta red—the color of clay—when necessary. His famous Arizona home, Taliesin West (**11.13**), is a monument to his "Organic Architecture."

A very different reaction to the International Style is manifested in the eccentricities of what is called "Postmodern" architecture. No one style predominates, but versions range from the romantic to the playful, and often involve explorations back into the world of applied exterior color. The Pompidou Center for modern arts, designed by Renzo Piano and Richard Rogers (**11.14**), strikes a brilliant contrast to the sober hues of historic Paris, flaunting its exposed air-conditioning, electrical, water, and elevator equipment, color-coded in blue, yellow, green, and red respectively. These colors, which mimic those used for industrial safety classifications, are intended to make the machinery of the building easily recognized and fun to see. Whereas ancient temples featured painted statues of the gods, in this building the gods of the machine age are given top billing.

In the currently popular "Deconstructionist" architecture of Frank Gehry, such as the Guggenheim Museum in Bilbao (**11.15**), there is a return to unadorned industrial materials.

▲ **11.13 Frank Lloyd Wright, Taliesin West, Arizona**
Wright, the apostle of "Organic Architecture," worked with the
colors of the earth.

But here the titanium cladding is treated very sensually,
swathing dynamic curvaceous forms, so that it continually
changes in color as we look across the sculptural surface.
Before this famous museum was built, Bilbao was known
primarily for its bad weather, but now even its cloudy
climate has been turned into an asset, for in that dim light,
the subtle nuances of color changes reflected across the
silvery metal surfaces can be fully appreciated.

Landscape Design

Landscape designers have the entire color palette of the
natural world at their fingertips. Green might be the pre-
dominant natural color in many areas of the world, but the
infinite shades of green and the textural variety of leaves

allows unlimited creativity even if a designer is restricted to
using only that one hue. Designers don't usually stay within
such limited restrictions, but they do have to work within
certain boundaries, including the local climate, short flowering periods of perennials, eventual size of specimens,
availability of certain species to a given area, client preferences, budgetary issues, and the physicality of the site itself.
And they have to be willing to give the trump card to
mother nature, who always has the final word. Even long-
established gardens continue to offer color surprises to
those who tend them. Weather conditions might adversely
affect one species in a particular season, infestations of
insects may take a toll on a plant, or a flowering perennial
might sow seeds everywhere but where the original plant
was intended to grow. Color variations ebb and flow
throughout the seasons, as various plants come into bloom.
Elements pertaining to plant color are taken into account
by designers in the planning stages and, along with a familiarity with the plants themselves, the understanding of color
principles is one of the most necessary tools a landscape

◄ **11.14 Renzo Piano and Richard Rogers, Pompidou Center, Paris (detail), 1971–8**
Industrial color-coding provides a brilliant exterior color scheme for the controversial—and highly popular—Pompidou Center

◄ **11.15 Frank Gehry, Guggenheim Museum, Bilbao, Spain, 1997**
Guggenheim Foundation.

◄ **11.16 Jack Lenor Larsen's "Red Garden"**
At his home on Long Island Jack Lenor Larsen uses a monochromatic color scheme and clever use of false perspective to showcase a stoneware urn by Toshiko Takaezu.

designer can have, perhaps even more essential than pen and paper, for it is this color knowledge that needs to be present at the beginning of a good design, as well as tapped into for the life of a garden.

Color plays as important a role in designs used for public spaces, such as parks and cityscapes, as it does for the residential owner. Even rooftop gardens in the inner city utilize landscape design elements. Highly saturated and warm colors in a variety of flowering species will make a garden space seem smaller, while cooler, less saturated colors will seem to expand a space. It is possible to make a small garden appear larger by putting the brightest colors closest to the point of entry, and the less saturated hues in the background, thereby creating an illusion of distance.

Japanese temple gardens put the principles of color theory to good use, often using large areas of the neutral colors of sand or rocks to suggest great space. A point of interest is usually created by the addition of at least one splash of color from a flowering plant, set into the design in a calculated way, creating an exclamation of color within the visual serenity.

Ecological issues are a part of landscape designing too, and therefore affect color in planning designs. In the dry alpine areas of Colorado, a type of gardening known as "xeriscaping" has become popular, a term coined locally in which water conservation is a primary focus. In xeriscaping, there is a preference for indigenous plants, which are already well acclimatized to low water needs, and in higher elevation areas in Colorado, plants that do not mind the occasional frost in July are also incorporated. Xeriscaping uses drip-irrigation systems rather than sprinklers, so precious water only goes to the roots of the plants. It is inspiring to see the results of these efforts, and to know that color can still be incorporated into gardens in a variety of ways, even under the somewhat restrictive conditions of high altitude, low water availability, and the occasional frost in summer.

World-renowned weaver and textile designer Jack Lenor Larsen, when speaking about the subtle color interactions of light and shadow on gray foliage of dune plants near his home in East Hampton, Long Island, states:

This quiet beauty would not be noticed at the edge of an exuberant flower border; there, instead, the grasses would seem to be just waiting to be pulled out or whacked off. The lesson is clear: just as a great actress doesn't throw away her lines when drums are rolling, if a place is designated for such ethereal reticence, clear the stage for it.[7]

In Larsen's "Red Garden," one among many gardens he has created at his LongHouse property (**11.16**), he seems to have cleared the stage quite cleverly. A stoneware urn by Toshiko Takaezu is presented at the end of a brightly enticing path flanked by cedar posts painted the same red as the torii gates of Shinto shrines. Red flowering azaleas are planted between the posts and these are offset by purple plums and red barberries near the tree line to give a continuing shade of red in all seasons. However, the avenue has a false perspective, because the posts are not the same height (something we would discover only when walking the path). They diminish in height as well as in size as they go back toward the urn, giving the illusion of a deeper depth to the walkway as well as making the urn appear bigger than it really is. The space has been controlled effectively like a stage set. With the use of color and design, our eyes are led back to the focal point of the urn every time we look at it in spite of the contrast of the colors between the earth-colored stoneware and the wild reds. Larsen feels that the garden is a "master instructor" of color in all seasons of the year. After studying the subtle color combinations of the winter landscape, when he tries to replicate these color combinations in his weaving, he states "the elusiveness of success only heightens my awe of nature as a designer."[8]

Crafts

The world of fine art owes a deep debt of gratitude to the world of craft. As those two classifications begin to shift in either direction, as the definition of each continues to evolve, we might be closer to a more historical interpretation of both, where the crafting of an object was done at the hands of a skilled and creative artisan.

Although we still think of crafts as involving a handmade, functional object, even this definition can be questioned, as installation artists sometimes take functional objects but render them dysfunctional in the process of creating new statements. In the case of computer-generated artwork, the areas of fine art are blurred as the machine takes over some or

▲ **11.17 Nam-Son Choi,** *Snowflowers* **necklace, 2004**
White seed beads and white freshwater pearls.
Following a heavy snowstorm, Nam-Son Choi was inspired to create her monochromatic version of the beauty of snow on trees, which she aptly named *Snowflowers*.

all of the direct "hand" of the artist. The digital camera, with its use of computer printers, has altered the course of dark room work in photography. Woodworkers create unique pieces by using very sophisticated power tools. Somewhere between the concept and the hands, art is still in full swing.

As far as color is concerned, however, classifications and categories are a moot point, since color has been part of the human creative experience from the beginning of time, or certainly since the first functional object was refashioned using conscious decisions which we now consider aesthetic ones. You might say that the field of crafts is a mother-lode, a vein of colorful creativity linking us back to the artistic part of our ancient human roots. As human beings, we were artisans and craftspeople long before we were fine artists. For that very reason, a discussion of color in crafts is our choice for the final section of this book.

Specific crafts can go in and out of "fashion," but certainly a rise in interest in a specific one can generate a better avail bility of resources. A recent surge in the craft of knitting has created markets for yarn manufacturers unlike anything seen for decades, which is a great boon to all fiber artists, whose choices of yarn types, fiber combinations, and colors were on the wane until this recent surge of interest created a new market. When yarn colors were limited or even as yarn stores closed, knitters and other fiber artists often spent more time with the ongoing crafts of spinning and dyeing, and created their own fiber combinations and colors. Rug hookers have long dyed their own woolens in order to obtain all the precise hues needed for their rugs, as have handweavers and basket makers to supply their colored fiber needs. The popularity of quilting has kept 100 percent cotton materials available in a wide range of colors and prints in spite of other declines in the home-sewing industry. Handcrafts of all kinds can benefit when the market economy is favorable, but they seem to continue independently too, as long as there are creative people with a desire to create. The Internet has helped to bond a global craft awareness, as blogs crop up to share ideas and to support the learning process. To anyone familiar with the craft scene of 40 years ago, when few books were available to teach young people some of the old forgotten skills, it is an amazing revolution that the Internet is fueling.

With infinite color variations available throughout a limitless selection of crafts, we have chosen these final images: one in white, one in black. Black and white have always been part of the color scene, in spite of the semantic question "Are black and white really colors?" One need only to check back to Figures 2.6 and 2.7 to confirm their importance in the integrity of chromatic hues, where white is created from the combination of the light primaries of red, green, and blue, and black is created from the combination of the pigment primaries of red, yellow, and blue. We feel that white and black are "mother-lode colors," workhorses amid the brighter hues that are absolutely essential to the value scale of all colors, neutral in character but strong enough to be fitting representatives for the closing section of this book.

For her *Snowflowers* necklace (**11.17**), Nam-Son Choi was inspired by her impressions of heavy snow on the trees after a storm. Her combination of white seed beads and the slightly off-white freshwater pearls creates a dense, fractalized snowscape that manages to startle us simultaneously with its complexity and simplicity. The necklace can reflect the light of its surroundings, adding subtly to its dimensional quality. It has unity of form and content, a purity of vision

▲ **11.18 Joshua Salesin, *Honeycomb* wood vessel, part of the *Mandala Cup* series, 2004**
Hand-turned and hand-finished African Blackwood, 1¾ × 2½ ins (4.4 × 6.3 cm).
The circular designs on this tiny cup resemble those of a mandala, a symbol of the universe of the Buddhist tradition. The choice of African Blackwood gives a refined tonality to the design, especially when a light shines on or through it.

uncomplicated by any color other than a blizzard of white.

Joshua Salesin created a diminutive vessel (**11.18**) using an antique ornamental rose engine lathe, a machine used by master craftsmen like Fabergé, but now quite rare and hard to find. He chose African Blackwood, known for its strength and elegant color, as a perfect material for the intricacies of his designs. The wood is a rich, deep black, and in the cutaway areas of the bowl, thinner areas are created by the design that tend to glow with hints of color as the light shines through them. It adds to the mystery of this piece— a tiny cup, the repetitive mathematical pattern incised precisely within its concavity, with a hint of color being continually released from within the density of black.

Color in the hands of master craftspeople of all disciplines offers us a universe of visual stimuli. New technical discoveries in the science of color continue to expand our options, while the attempt to control it still remains one of the most challenging and essential endeavors within the world of art.

Color Problems

THESE problems are based on the core course of Josef Albers, with many additions from the color courses taught by Paul Zelanski and John Fawcett at the University of Connecticut. The problems are abstract experiments with principles of color usage that can be applied to any media. We prefer to have students use silk-screened papers (including grays, which may have to be purchased separately) for their initial work with color. Cut papers are simple to manipulate and then affix with rubber cement, and they pique interest in colors that most beginning students would never mix with paints. Paint mixing problems are introduced later in the course, along with instruction in application of paints, modeling, blending, and use of a ruling pen. After some work with acrylic paints, problems can be solved either with paints or with papers—or with any other media, including fibers, photography, video, computer graphics, pastels, and collage with found materials. For an approach to the problems in the order they appear in the text, relevant chapter numbers are given in brackets.

1 Ideal color

[2]: From the silk-screened papers, select a group of colors from the same family. From these, choose the one you think most representative of the hue, such as the reddest red. Present it within its family to express this idea visually.

2 Make three colors look like four

[2, 3, 9]: Select two different colors to be used as ground colors and place them side by side. Then choose a third color that will, when placed in small quantities upon each ground, look different in each instance, producing the effect of having four colors. A value change is relatively easy, espe-

cially if the third color is a middle mixture of the first two. If you can create a good value change, then try another one in which a hue change is created (as in Figure 9.19).

3 Make three colors look like two

[2, 3, 9]: Select two different colors to be used as ground colors and place them side by side. Then choose a third color that will, when placed in small quantities upon each of the ground colors, appear to be the same color as the ground opposite the one on which it is placed. This difficult effect is most easily created when working with very high or low values.

4 Make four colors look like three

[2, 3, 9]: Select papers in two different colors to be used as ground colors and place them side by side. Then select two other colors that, when placed in small quantities upon each of the ground colors, will appear to be the same color (as in Figure 9.20).

5 Make one gray act as both black and white

[3]: Cut many different grays out of magazine pictures and paste them on a board so that they will evenly graduate from white at the top to black at the bottom. Then select a middle gray from the silk-screened paper and glue a thin strip of it over the graduated grays. The result will be that at the top the middle gray will appear black, whereas at the bottom it will appear as white (compare with Figure 3.11).

6 Monochromatic free study

[2]: Do a free study with silk-screened or found papers using values and saturations of only one hue.

7 Light and shadow

[2, 3]: Select four different colors of paper; then select a second set of four colors that relate to the first set in hue, but that are all equally darker or lighter. By placement of these colors, suggest that light is falling on one section, raising the value of all the colors equally.

8 A third vibrating color

[2, 3, 9]: Select two different colors that will vibrate when placed next to each other and that will produce a third color glow along the edge where they are joined.

9 After-images

[3, 9]: Using rather saturated colors: (1) Use a large flat shape to create an after-image in its complementary (see Figure 3.3). (2) Use a series of smaller shapes (circles work well) to create a complementary glow at the edges of these shapes, with an after-image in the same color as the original (see Figure 3.4).

10 Losing edges

[2, 5]: Select two colors that are close to each other in the Munsell Color Tree (Figure 2.15) so that when they are juxtaposed, the edge between them will tend to disappear. How far apart can they be in the color solid and still lose the edge?

11 Spatial effects with values

[2, 5]: The stronger the value contrast between adjoining edges, the greater the apparent spatial distance between. The closer they are in value, the closer they will appear spatially. Select a ground color and place upon it a series of colors that range in value contrast with this ground, from extreme to very slight. By ordering the series of colors, create a logical spatial regression.

12 Spatial effects with hues

[2, 3, 5]: Repeat #11 but using hue rather than value contrasts, holding value constant.

13 Free study in the plastic effects of color

[2, 3, 5]: Make a free study in colors using discoveries from problems 11 and 12.

14 Psychological distances

[5]: Create three distinct illusions of distance by use of principles in #11 and #12: close view (using hard edges and strong contrast with the ground), middle distant view (soft colors and soft edges), and far view (edges being lost through lack of contrast with the ground). Use essentially the same design and palette and place all three on the same board.

15 Four seasons

[4, 5]: Select four colors and, by varying the amounts used of each, create four designs with distinctively different color "climates."

16 Color atmosphere free studies

[4]: (1) Create a color atmosphere that will relate to an obvious sensory experience, such as cold, hot, wet, etc. (2) Do the same thing for a human emotion. See if the class recognizes it.

17 Relativity of hot and cold

[4]: Select two colors that are of different "temperature," one hotter than the other. In approximately five equal steps, cool both hues until the originally hotter hue is demonstrably cooler than the original version of the cooler hue.

18 Free study

[4]: Create a free study using papers you have so far avoided because you didn't like the colors. By manipulating color combinations and proportions, make the result aesthetically pleasing.

19 Vertical stripes

[5]: Cut stripes of identical width and place them from top to bottom of a groundsheet in such a way that they develop different groups and spatial effects.

20 Paint mixing introduction

[8]: Cover a small square—no more than 8 x 8 inches—with a series of similar shapes or similar strokes. Each should be a different color that you have mixed by blending tube colors.

21 Weber-Fechner Law

[8]: Using layers of clear colored acetate or layers of glazes, create stair-steps or sequences of value steps in one hue that graphically demonstrate the difference between arithmetical progression in mixing (adding one unit each time) and geometric progression (1, 2, 4, 8, etc.), which produces optically equal steps in value.

22 Value scale

[2, 8]: Use the Weber-Fechner principle and your eye to mix ten equal steps from black to white.

23 Value chart

[2, 6, 8]: Using the 12-hue Liquitex® Color Map (Figure 8.9) or a 10-hue Munsell chart of value changes, mix and paint all hues in the full range of values, from 1 to 9. All rows should be painted horizontally. Rather than painting all values of a single hue at once, paint value 5 in all hues, then value 6, and so on.

24 Neutralizing complementaries

[2, 6, 8]: Mix any two complementary hues as if moving in equal steps through the Munsell tree from one side to the other, passing through neutral gray at the center. If steps are visually equal, there will be more of them for certain hues, such as red, than for their complement. A bit of white can be mixed in to keep the value from decreasing.

25 Magazine image I

[8]: Select a black-and-white picture from a magazine and paint a section that is approximately 25 percent of the total area in local hues that so closely match the values of the original that the line between black-and-white and colored areas tends to disappear.

26 Magazine image II

[8]: Do the reverse of #25, starting with a colored magazine image and painting at least 25 percent of it in gray values that match the values of the original.

27 Color story

Create a sequence of designs as a fold-out book on an accordion-pleated series of stiff papers. Colored papers or paints should be used nonobjectively to tell a visual story with a beginning, middle, and end.

28 Optical mixtures

[6, 9]: Select three different colors to be used as ground colors and place them side by side. Then select the color that, when placed as thin vertical stripes upon the ground colors, will act like three different colors and produce different optical mixtures on each. The colors can be displayed separately below.

29 Stationary optical mixture

[9]: Using black and white in approximately equal amounts, create a design that evokes optical color illusions (see Figure 9.32).

30 Color schemes

[9]: With the whole class using black-and-white xeroxes of a single painting (preferably one done in flat color areas), each student can be assigned a different kind of color scheme (monochromatic, analogous, etc.) in which to paint the work. Compare the effects.

31 Interpenetration of colors

[9]: Select two colors and then a third that, when placed between the original two, will transmit a color sensation of the opposite color upon the edges of the middle color, thus creating a rounded or modeled effect upon the central band of color (see Figure 9.21).

32 Optical transparencies I

[8, 9]: Select two opaque colors, plus a third that appears to be the result of one's being transparent and overlying the other. Place them in a simple design that convincingly demonstrates this transparency illusion.

33 Optical transparencies II

[5, 8, 9]: First choose one colored paper to use as a shape and a second to be used as a groundsheet. Then create three designs starting from these colors and adding three additional colors that give the illusion that the shape is (a) a transparent material overlapping the ground sheet, (b) a color being overlapped by a transparent groundsheet, (c) a mixture so evenly divided between the color of the shape and that of the ground that its spatial position is totally ambiguous.

34 Painted transparencies

[8, 9]: Using mixed colors, repeat #32 with paints.

35 Overlapping of light

[7, 9]: Select colors that will produce the effect of a ribbon of light being overlapped by itself. When an overlap occurs, the color of that overlap will be lighter than the original single section of light. Build up these overlaps to the point where five overlaps will occur.

36 Overlapping of a transparent colored ribbon

[9]: Same as #35, but in this subtractive case, overlaps will become darker (see Figure 9.22).

37 Bezold Effect

[9]: Create two designs that are exactly the same except that one of the five colors used in the first is different in the second. By this change, make the second look entirely different from the first (see Figure 9.24).

Suggested Free Studies:

a

Work with the subtleties of the outer limits of value, doing a study only in whites or near-blacks.

b

Do a free study incorporating both papers or paints and pressed leaves or flowers. Use the found materials as areas of color; their original identity should not be obvious.

c

Do a free study in variations on a single hue with one unexpected accent of another hue.

d

Using any colors or style, do a self-portrait in cut or torn papers.

e

Working from careful observation, do an image of a local landscape in cut or torn papers. This can be done in two different seasons for comparison of the changes.

f

Use a Fauvist approach to color for the same landscape.

g

Use two-color media in the same image in such a way that they cooperate rather than fight with each other.

Glossary

Where a definition includes a term that is itself defined elsewhere in the Glossary, that word is printed in italics.

additive colors Colors made by lights which, when mixed, become lighter in *value*.

after-image The illusion of color and shape produced in the visual apparatus after staring at a strong color for some time. A positive after-image is the same color as the original; a negative after-image is its *complement*. See *successive contrast*.

analogous hues Those lying next to each other on a *color wheel*.

aniline dyes A family of colorants synthesized from coal-tar, including reds, black, greens, and blue-reds.

atmospheric perspective The tendency of forms seen at a great distance through a hazy atmosphere to blur toward uniformity in *hue* and *value*, with no sharp distinctions between colors or edges. In many atmospheres, everything will take on a blue cast.

azo dyes A large family of colorfast, highly saturated, synthetic colorants developed from petroleum.

Bezold Effect The possibility of changing a design considerably by simply changing one of its colors; discovered by rugmaker Wilhelm von Bezold in the nineteenth century.

broken color Layers of different colors applied to a painting so that they show through each other as opposed to being physically blended on the canvas or mixed on the palette.

chiaroscuro The use of light and shadow effects in a painting.

chromatic hue Any color other than black, grays, and white.

chromaticity In lights, a measure of the combination of *hue* and *saturation* in a color.

Chromaticity Diagram The plotting of *hue* and *saturation* coordinates on a two-dimensional grid.

chrominance In television, a signal indicating both *hue* and *saturation*.

chromotherapy The use of colored lights for healing purposes.

CMYK Notation for the four subtractive primary inks used in the printing process—cyan, magenta, yellow, and black.

coherent light Theoretically, light in which the waves are all of the same length and in unchanging relationship to each other, as approximated by a laser beam.

collage A two-dimensional work of art in which *found objects* are glued to a flat surface.

color constancy A visual phenomenon where we see the color of an object in one light and continue to associate that color with the object even though the color continues to change with the lighting conditions throughout the day.

Color-Field painting A style originating from the mid-twentieth-century New York School featuring large, nonobjective areas of color.

colorimeter A computerized instrument that measures the amount of power in each *wavelength* in a light source. See *spectrophotometer*.

color management In computerized processes, attempting to hold colors the same no matter in what medium they are displayed or printed.

color negative process In color print photography, the activation of *dyes* in the film to release colors that are *complementary* to those in the original scene. A positive print in the original colors is then created from this negative.

color positive (reversal) process In the creation of color transparencies, a series of steps which culminates in the release of magenta, cyan, and yellow *dyes* in the film's three layers. These mix to form the colors of the original when the developed film is seen in the light.

color separation In printing, colored images are broken down into screens of certain *primaries* (in a *four-color process*, they are magenta, cyan, yellow, and black) which when superimposed and printed will yield an approximation of the original colors.

color wheel A circular, two-dimensional model showing color relationships, originating from Sir Isaac Newton's bending of the straight array of *spectral hues* into a circle.

complementary hues Colors that lie opposite each other on a *color wheel*. When placed side by side they will intensify each other visually; when mixed as *pigments* they will dull each other.

cones Special cells in the *retina* at the back of the eye which enable us to distinguish *hues* in daylight.

continuous tone In printing, referring to any image with a range of gradually changing *values*.

critical color matching The precise mixing of *pigments* or ink *dyes* to match a given sample.

direct dyeing Coloring of materials by immersion in water with water-soluble *dyes*.

dispersed dye A material colorant that is not water-soluble but can be applied in a soap solution.

dithering Juxtaposition of dots of different colors in computer printing to produce optical color mixtures.

Divisionism The juxtaposition of tiny dots of unmixed paints, giving an overall effect of color when mixed optically by the viewer's eye from a distance, usually associated with the Postimpressionists. See *Pointillism*.

dominant wavelength In light mixtures, another term for *hue*.

double complementary A color combination in which *hues* adjacent to each other on the *color wheel* are used with their respective *complementaries*. See *split complementary*.

dpi Dots per inch, the dot formations within a printer, deriving from *ppi*.

dye Coloring material dissolved in a liquid solvent.

dye sublimation Computer printing technology similar to *thermal wax transfer*, but with variations in the amount of heat applied to produce varying colors.

expressionistic color Colors chosen for their emotional impact rather than their fidelity to "standard" colors perceived in the external world.

flat (match) color In printing, the use of solid areas of unbroken color, often specified by a numerical system such as PMS (Pantone Matching System). See *four-color process*.

found object An object presented as a work of art or forming part of one, which was not initially intended for artistic purposes.

four-color process In printing, a technique for reproducing colored images by separating them into the *primaries* magenta, cyan, yellow, and black and printing each color from a separate plate. See *color separation*.

fresco A wall painting in which *pigments* are ground in water and stroked onto fresh plaster; when the plaster dries, the pigments form part of the surface itself.

giclée printing Computerized printing in which *CMYK* separations can be overlaid in advance to view the final effect, and in which colors are sprayed onto the paper as tiny drops of varying size for an effect approximating a *continuous tone* photograph.

glaze In oil painting, a transparent film of color painted over another layer of color. In ceramics, a glass-like coating of silicates that melts and fuses to the clay when it is fired.

Hard-Edged painting A painting with precise boundaries between nonobjective colored areas, characteristic of some mid-twentieth-century work.

hologram A two-dimensional image that appears three-dimensional, created from waves of light or other energy forms which develop interference patterns when deflected off a three-dimensional object.

HSB *Hue*, *saturation*, and brightness—the variables in color specified in television technologies.

hue The color quality identified by color names, such as "red" and "blue." This is determined by the color's *wavelength*.

inkjet printing Computer-based technology in which ink is sent through nozzles by heat or pressure.

integral tripack The common format for today's photographic film, in which three thin layers of gelatin containing chemicals that are sensitive to blue, green, or red lights are sandwiched together.

iodopsins Light-sensitive *pigments* in the *cones* of the eyes, thought to be somehow involved in our ability to distinguish *hues*.

lakes *Pigments* that are made from *dyes*.

limited palette The use of relatively few colors in a work of art.

local color The color sensation received from a nearby object under average lighting conditions.

luminance The degree of lightness or darkness in light mixtures, corresponding to *value* in *pigments*.

metamerism An aspect of our vision that allows us to perceive matching colors under certain lighting conditions, when shown two color samples which have different spectral wavelengths. This complex visual phenomenon makes color reproduction possible.

middle mixture In Josef Albers's color interaction experiments, a color that results from mixing equal parts of two other colors and is then shown between these two "parents."

monochromatic Referring to a color combination based on variations in *value* and *saturation* of a single *hue*, perhaps with the addition of some *neutral* colors.

mordant In fabric dyeing, a fixative.

nanometer One billionth of a meter, used in measuring *wavelengths* of light.

neutral A black, white, or gray—one of the nonchromatic *hues*.

open palette The use of a wide range of colors in a work of art.

Opponent Theory A model that accounts for color vision by means of hypothetical pairs of receptors responding to opposing colors; if they respond to one, its opposite is inhibited.

phantom colors Colors that spread beyond their physical boundaries causing illusory color sensations on adjacent *neutral* surfaces.

phase change/solid ink printing Computer-based technology in which colorants are solid wax, liquefied only long enough for application to paper.

phosphors On the back of a television screen, tiny dots of blue, green, and red fluorescing powder, which radiate light when struck by an electron signal.

pigment Powdered coloring material used to give *hues* to paints and inks.

pixel In computer graphics, one of many tiny points on the computer screen determined by intersections of *x* and *y* axes.

Pointillism A technique in painting whereby dots of pure *hues* are placed close together on a white ground to coax the viewer's eye to mix them optically. (*Divisionism* is a similar technique, but without the white ground showing.)

polychromatic Multicolored.

posterization In photography, a developing process in which continuous tone images are converted into flat areas of any colors.

ppi Pixels per inch, the pixels (**pic**ture

element) of a computer, which become dot formations, or *dpi* (dots per inch), within the printer.

primary colors Those *hues* from which all others can theoretically be mixed; in *refracted colors*, red, green, and blue; in *reflected colors*, red, yellow, and blue.

principal hues Albert Munsell's term for the five *pigment primaries* used in his color model (green, blue, purple, red, and yellow).

profiling The act of profiling sets up a record of how a computer, printer, or scanner is behaving. Calibration features are built into many computers. These enable the computer's behavior to be kept in line with the color profile that has been set up.

purity In *video*, another word for *saturation*.

reactive dye A colorant that bonds chemically with the fiber.

reflected color Color seen when light is reflected from a *pigmented* surface.

refracted color Color resulting from passing light through a prism, breaking it down into its constituent *wavelengths*.

retina The inner surface of the back of the eye, where *rods* and *cones* respond to qualities of light.

reverse In graphic design, designation of shapes or letters that will not be printed with ink but remain the color of the paper, as a negative of the positive image provided.

RGB Red, green, blue—the additive *primary colors* of light mixtures, used in color television and color computer monitors.

rhodopsin Visual purple, a light-sensitive *pigment* in the *rods* of the retina.

rods Light-sensitive cells in the eye that operate in dim light to distinguish *values*.

saturation The relative purity of a color, also called intensity.

screen In printing, a dot pattern used to create the impression of a certain *value*.

secondary colors *Hues* made by mixing two *primary colors*.

sfumato Softly graded tones in an oil painting, giving a hazy atmospheric effect, highly developed in the work of Leonardo da Vinci.

shading In Ostwald's model, the color change that results when one adds black and decreases the percentage of the original *hue*.

shadow mask In common television sets, a metal grid with tiny holes lying opposite triads of *phosphors*, used to focus electron beams directly on the phosphors.

simultaneous contrast In general, the optical effect of adjacent colors on each other; more specifically, the tendency of *complementary* colors to intensify each other when placed side by side.

solarization A special photographic development effect in which development includes brief exposure to low-intensity colored lights, thus reversing colors.

spectral hues Those colors seen in a rainbow, or in the spectrum created when white light passes through a prism.

Spectral Sensitivity Curve A graphic representation of the degree of brightness perceived by the human eye in lights of different *wavelengths*.

spectrophotometer A machine used to measure properties of energy in each part of the spectrum in a sample of light or a *pigmented* surface. See *colorimeter*.

split complementary A color combination whereby a *hue* is used with the hues lying to either side of its direct *complementary*. See *double complementary*.

subtractive color mixing Combination of *pigments*, which results in darkened mixtures.

successive contrast The color phenomenon observed when differently colored areas are viewed one after another, as in looking at a white area after staring at a red one. If the initial image is highly saturated, its *complement* may seem to appear in the second area. See *after-image*.

synergistic color mixing Allowing the energies of certain *hues* to combine optically on a *neutral* ground color.

synesthesia The ability to gather sense perceptions from perceptual systems not usually associated with them, such as hearing colors.

tertiary colors The colors created by mixing a *primary* and an adjacent *secondary*.

thermal wax transfer A computer-based printing technology in which small dots of cyan, magenta, yellow, and black ink are fused by heat to paper.

tinting In Ostwald's model of color relationship, the effect of adding white and decreasing the percentage of the original *hue*.

toning In Ostwald's system, the effect of adding both black and white and decreasing the percentage of the original *hue*.

transparency effect A painted effect when one film of color is lying over another color.

triadic color scheme The use of three colors equally spaced from each other on a *color wheel*.

triadic color system An early-twentieth-century rule that there should be equal proportions of "sunlight" and "shadow" *hues* in a painting.

Trichromatic Theory The idea that there are basically three kinds of cones in the human eye: red-sensitive, green-sensitive, and blue-sensitive.

value The degree of lightness or darkness in a color.

vat dye A colorant that does not give the desired *hue* in a fiber until a second influence has been added, such as exposure to sunlight or an acid solution.

video Electronic light signals recorded from images and then displayed on a television monitor.

virtual reality Computer-generated illusionary experience of three-dimensional environments.

visible spectrum The range of *wavelengths* seen by the human eye.

wavelength The distance from crest to crest in a wave of energy.

Weber–Fechner Law The observation that to mix visually equal steps in *value*, one must mix geometrically increasing proportions of black or white.

Notes

Preface

1   In conversation with Stephen Alcorn, artist and teacher, May 4, 2005. Stephen's website is www.alcorngallery.com

Chapter 3

1   Edwin H. Land, "The Retinex Theory of Color Vision," *Scientific American*, December 1977, p. 108

2   Claude Monet, conversation with W. G. C. Byvanck, quoted in Robert Gordon and Andrew Forge, *Monet*, New York: Harry N. Abrams, Inc., 1983, p. 163

3   Scriabin, quoted in Kenneth Peacock, "Synesthetic Perception: Alexander Scriabin's Color Hearing," *Music Perception*, Summer 1985 (vol. 2, no. 4), p. 483

4   Scriabin, quoted in Corrine Dunklee Heline, *Healing and Regeneration Through Color*, Santa Barbara, California: J. F. Rowny Press, 1944, p. 21

5   Wassily Kandinsky, *Concerning the Spiritual in Art*, New York: Dover Publications, Inc., 1977; London: Constable & Co Ltd, 1977, p. 25 (originally published in 1914 as *The Art of Spiritual Harmony*)

6   Carol Steen in Susan Hornik, "For Some, Pain Is Orange," *Smithsonian*, February 2001, p.50

Chapter 4

1   Chris, quoted in Harry Wohlfarth and Catharine Sam, "The Effects of Color Psychodynamic Environment Modification upon Psycho-physiological and Behavioral Reactions of Severely Handicapped Children," *International Journal of Biosocial Research*, 1982 (vol. 3, no. 1), p. 31

2   Adapted from Suzy Chiazzari, *The Complete Book of Color*, Shaftesbury, Dorset/Boston: Element Books, 1998, p. 21

3   Faber Birren, "Color as a Force," *Coronet*, January 1937, p. 192

4   George Chaplin, personal communication

Chapter 5

1   Paul Claudel, as quoted in Jean-Louis Ferrier, director, English translation by Walter D. Glanze and Lisa Davidson, *Art of the Twentieth Century*, Paris: Editions du Chêne/Hachette Livre

2   Gene Davis, interview with Walter Hopps, in *Gene Davis*, Donald Wall, ed., New York: Praeger Publishers, 1975, pp. 117–18

3   Leonardo da Vinci, *The Notebooks of Leonardo da Vinci*, Pamela Taylor, ed., New York: The New American Library, Inc., 1970; London: Cape Ltd, 1977, p. 36

4   Gene Davis, op. cit., pp. 119–20

Chapter 6

1   Aristotle, *De Coloribus*, quoted in Faber Birren, *History of Color in Painting*, New York; London: Van Nostrand Reinhold Company, Inc., 1965, p. 16

2   Leonardo da Vinci, op. cit., p. 38; and in Faber Birren, op. cit., p. 79

3   Ibid.

4   Sir Isaac Newton. *Opticks*, 4th edition, 1730. Reprinted by McGraw-Hill Book Co., New York, 1931, pp. 156–7

5   Johann Wolfgang von Goethe, *Theory of Colors*, trans. Charles Lock Eastlake, Cambridge, Mass.: The MIT Press, 1970, pp. 34–5

6   Johannes Itten, *The Elements of Color*. English ed., New York: Van Nostrand Reinhold Company, Inc., 1970, p. 66 (originally published in 1961 as *Kunst der Farbe*)

7   M. E. Chevreul, *The Principles of Harmony and Contrast of Colors*, 1839, quoted in Faber Birren, *Principles of Color*, New York; London: Van Nostrand Reinhold Company, Inc., 1973, p. 163

8   Ogden N. Rood, *Modern Chromatics*, 1879. Facsimile edition, New York: Van Nostrand Reinhold Company, Inc., 1973, p. 163

9   Ibid., p. 219

10   Roland Rood, *The Scrip*, April 1906, quoted in Rood, op. cit., p. 28

11   Faber Birren, *The World of Color*, 1939, 1948

12   Paul Klee, quoted in *Color*, London: Marshall Editions Ltd., 1980, p. 95

Chapter 7

1   MP3 is the acronym for musicPeg, a compressor of digital sound much like the jpeg compressor of images, and it was the third version that became universal in the marketplace. There are many MP3 players now, one of the earliest being the iPod

2   Douglas Kirkland, quoted in Lynda Weinman, "Celebrity Makeovers in Photoshop," *Step-by-Step Graphics*, 1993 (vol. 9, no. 4), p. 36

3   Ursula Freer, quoted in Harald Johnson, *Mastering Digital Printing*, 2nd edition, Boston: Thomson Course Technology PTR, 2005, p. 25

4   Personal statement by the artist, March 2005

5   Ron Lambert, personal communication, July 2001

6   www.lynda.com/hex.html
7   Herbert W. Franke, "Computer Graphics/Computer Film Metamorphoses," in Igildo G. Biesele, *Experiment Design*, Zurich: ABC Verlag, 1986, p. 54
8   Liz Slagus and Katie McGraw, in *The Upgrade Documents*, from www.treasurecrumbs.com
9   Dan Flavin quoted in "How Does this Artist's Statement Influence How You View His Work?" in *Sculpture*, December 2004 (vol. 23, no. 10), p. 9
10 Char Davies, "Landscape, Earth, Body, Being, Space and Time in the Immersive Virtual Environment: Osmose and Ephemere," in Judy Malloy, ed., *Women in New Media*, Boston: MIT Press, 1998
11 David Joselit, "Planet Paik," *Art in America*, June 2000, p. 78

Chapter 8
1   Quote taken from essay "Splash of Color: Glass by Dale Chihuly Holds Its Own in a Room" on the website www.chihuly.com/essays/stmt_splashofcolor.html
2   Harald Johnson, *Mastering Digital Printing*, 2nd edition, Boston: Thomson Course Technology PTR, 2005, pp. 32–3
3   Jan Good, personal communication, December 11, 2001
4   Johnson, op. cit., p. 176
5   Ibid., p. 237
6   Keith Edwards, designer at How 2 Design, personal communication, March 2005
7   Frank Noelker, personal communication, May 24, 2001

Chapter 9
1   Deborah Muirhead, personal communication, November 1993
2   Goethe, op. cit., p. 319
3   Rufino Tamayo, in Roger Toll, "An Artist's Mexico," *House and Garden*, November 1985, p. 150
4   J. M. W. Turner, Lecture V, 181, in John Gage, *Color in Turner*, New York: Praeger Publishers, 1969, p. 208
5   M. E. Chevreul, *The Laws of Contrast of Color*, trans. John Spanton, London: Routledge, Warner, and Routledge, 1859, p. 48
6   Rudolf Arnheim, "Progress in Color Composition," *Leonardo*, vol. 20, no. 2, p. 166

7   Henri Matisse, *Notes of a Painter*, in R. Goldwater and M. Treves, *Artists on Art*, Pantheon Books, 1945, pp. 411–412
8   Goethe, op. cit., p. 317
9   Josef Albers, in *Albers: Josef Albers at the Metropolitan Museum of Art*, undated, unpaginated exhibition catalog
10 Rood, op. cit., p. 231
11 Paul Signac, "The Color Contribution of Delacroix, the Impressionists, and the Neoimpressionists," Paris, 1899. Quoted in *Artists on Art*, Robert Goldwater and Marco Treves, eds., third edition, New York: Pantheon Books, Inc. (originally published 1945): J. Murray Ltd, 1976, p. 378
12 John Roy, from catalog for Springfield Museum of Fine Arts solo exhibit, 1999
13 Arthur Hoener, personal communication, November 1987

Chapter 10
1   National Museum of Namibia website, http://www.natmus.cul.na/events/rockart/early.html
2   Cited in Birren, *History of Color in Painting*, p. 238
3   Ibid., p. 83
4   Claude Monet, 1889 letter to a young American artist, in Hugh Honour and John Fleming, *The Visual Arts: A History*, fourth edition, New York: Prentice Hall, Inc., 1995, p. 660
5   Paul Gauguin, in Helen Gardner, *Art Through the Ages*, seventh edition, New York: Harcourt Brace Jovanovich, Inc., 1976, p. 788
6   Paul Gauguin, 1885 letter quoted in Rene Huyghe, *Gauguin*, New York: Crown Publishers, Inc., 1959, p. 39
7   André Derain, quoted by Helen Dudar, "In turn-of-the-century Paris, an explosion of brash new art," *Smithsonian*, October 1990, p. 65
8   Hugh Honour and John Fleming, *The Visual Arts, A History*, 4th edition, Englewood Cliffs, NJ: Prentice Hall, 1995, p. 728
9   Pierre Bonnard in Jean-Louis Ferrier, director, *Art of the Twentieth Century*, op. cit., p. 447
10 Will Grohmann, *Kandinsky, Life and Work*, New York: Harry N. Abrahams, Inc., n.d., p. 9

11 Helen Frankenthaler, in Barbara Rose. *Frankenthaler*, New York: Harry N. Abrams, Inc., 1970, pp. 61–2
12 Paul Trachtman, "Charles Csuri Is an 'Old Master' in a New Medium," *Smithsonian*, February 1995 (vol. 25, issue 11).
13 Ibid., p. 56
14 David Em, *The Art of David Em*, by O. David Ross and David Em, New York: Harry N. Abrams, Inc.
15 Paraphrased material from website http:/bellasartesgallery.com/pfaff_bio.html

Chapter 11
1   Ed. Newman, "Color in Textiles," *American Fashion and Fabric Magazine*, September/October 1986, p. 53
2   Leatrice Eiseman, "Results of the Roper/Pantone Consumer Color Preference Study," www.pantone.com/allaboutcolor, 2001
3   Ibid.
4   Kevin Grady, in Jennifer Mattson, "Color Therapy: How Color Works in Design," *Desktop Publishers*, June 1997, p. 64
5   Dr. Russell Ferstandig, quoted in Trish Hall, "The Quest for Colors That Make Lips Smack," *New York Times*, November 4, 1992, p. C1
6   Noemi Kearns, Principal of How 2 Design, personal communication, March 2005
7   Jack Lenor Larson, *A Weaver's Memoir*, New York: Harry N. Abrams, Inc., 1998, p. 107
8   Ibid., p. 109

Index